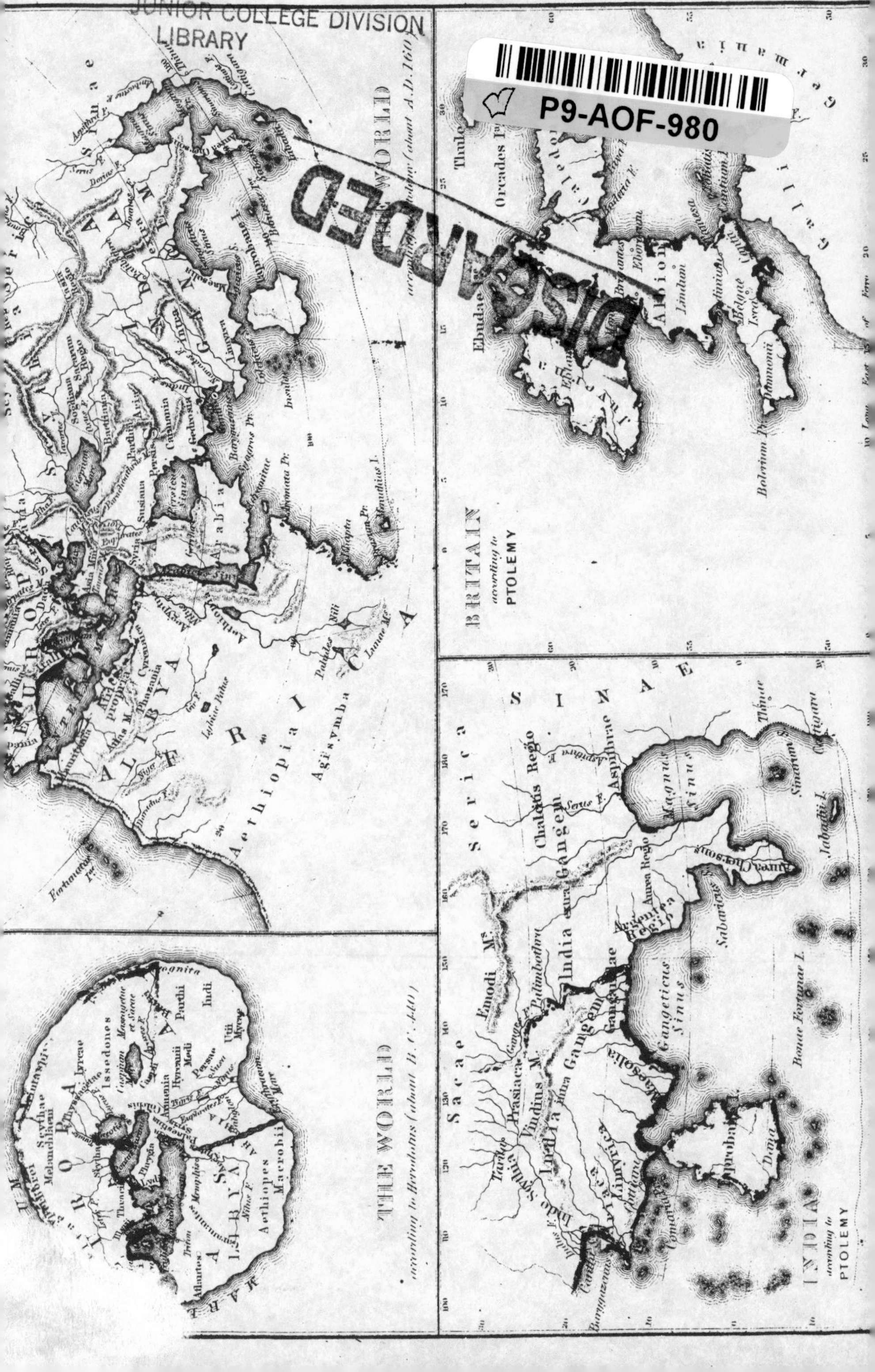
THE WORLD
according to Ptolemy (about A.D. 160)
BRITAIN
according to
PTOLEMY
THE WORLD
according to Herodotus (about B.C. 440)
INDIA
according to
PTOLEMY

A Guide To Writing History

WRITER'S DIGEST, CINCINNATI, OHIO 45242

John Adams and the American Revolution, copyright 1949, 1950 by Catherine Drinker Bowen and *Yankee From Olmpus: Justice Holmes and His Family,* copyright 1943, 1944, both by permission of Little Brown and Company in association with The Atlantic Monthly Press. *T.R.,* copyright 1970 by Noel B. Gerson, and *Those Who Love,* copyright 1965 by Irving Stone, both by permission of Doubleday and Company, Inc.

Library of Congress Cataloging in Publication Data

Marston, Doris
A guide to writing history.

1. Historiography.   2. Fiction — Technique.
I. Title.
D13.M313   808′.066′9   75-33732
ISBN 0-911654-34-8

Library of Congress Catalog Card Number 75-33732
International Standard Book Number 0-911654-34-8

Copyright 1976, Writer's Digest

Writer's Digest
Div., F&W Publishing Corporation
9933 Alliance Rd.
Cincinnati OH 45242

p. 21

To
David Oakes Woodbury
Inspiring Teacher
Faithful Friend

ACKNOWLEDGEMENTS

While I have been working on this book, information, help and encouragement have been given to me by many people. Among them are Jean Longland, librarian of the Hispanic Society of America in New York City; Dr. Louis M. Starr of Columbia University; Rose Denise Allen of Cape Neddick, Maine, whose editing of the original manuscript was of inestimable help; the librarians at York, Portsmouth and the University of New Hampshire; my students and members of the York Writers Club, who have served as audience and critics; and, most of all my husband, Philip A. Marston, who has accepted late dinners and benevolent neglect with patience.

D. R. M.

End-paper, front:
Various views of the world from Homer (900 B.C.) to Ptolemy (160 A.D.) from *An Atlas of Classical Geography* constructed by William Hughes and edited by George Long. Sheldon and Company, New York, 1856.

End-paper, Back:
Map of the United States from *Maps Showing Explorers' Routes, Trails & Early Roads in the United States,* an annotated list. Washington DC, Library of Congress, 1962.

DESIGN: Direct Communications

CONTENTS

Encyclopedias. Reference books. Juveniles. Newspaper and magazine sources. Types of libraries: state, private, college, genealogy, special, outside U.S. Other research sources: historical societies, professional organizations, public relations offices, government. Additional aids: vocabulary sources, manuscript collections, weather resources, microfilm sources.

5 *The Historian As Explorer*

Visiting actual historical sites. Maps and charts. Museums of history, art, marine lore, special occupations. Historic houses and buildings. Living history at national parks and monuments. Towns and landmarks. Cemeteries and churches and their records. Historic trails, rivers and canals. Forts and battlefield sites. Lighthouses. Restoration villages. Resources listed in the *Directory of Historical Societies and Agencies*. Pageants, dramas, musicals. Commercial developments.

6 *Exploring Through Personal Involvement*

Personal experiments and experiences. The Environmental Living Program. Seminars and classes. Meeting people. Interviews to secure information. Using the mail. Getting books through inter-library loan.

7 *The Interview: Oral History*

How and where the oral history interview techniques began. Importance of oral history as fewer and fewer people write letters, keep journals. Interviewing technique. Doing your own research first. Autobiographical and topical interviews. Fallibility of recall. Perpetuating myths. Testing the accuracy of statements. The rights to taped material. Tapes vs. transcriptions. Oral history collections included in the *National Union Catalog of Manuscript Collections*, Oral History Association. Books based entirely on oral history.

Americana in history publications, antiques magazines, some women's publications, Sunday newspapers, regional magazines. *Anniversary tie-ins* with local personages or businesses, and national specialized subjects. *Archaeology* in both national publications and regionals where "digs" are in progress. *The arts* — especially the architecture of historical buildings, famous paintings, regional arts and crafts. *Biographical articles* in both general interest and special subject magazines. *Essays* in the literary magazines. *Foreign history* and American ties with countries abroad. *Personal experiences* in travel and retirement magazines. *Photo essays* on historical subjects. *Social concerns* in educational, religious, Black magazines. *Topical tie-ins* as newspaper features, magazine articles. *Writing a column* or series of articles. Newspaper syndicates. Fillers.

12 *Historical Poetry And Short Fiction* *101*

Three hundred years of history, tragedy and comedy in *American Folk Poetry*. Magazines using historical poetry today. Six basic rules for writing short historical fiction. Magazines using short historical fiction: general interest, literary, men's and regional publications. Some rules for using history in fiction.

13 *Illustrating Your Work* *105*

Paintings and photographs in collections. Advertisements, calendars, posters, playbills, silhouettes, cartoons, caricatures. Sources: books, where library's card catalogue shows "Illus."; magazines where *Reader's Guide* entry shows "Por." for portraits, or "Ill." for illustrations. Government sources. Cities and towns. State archives. Museums. Historic buildings. Libraries. Industry and business. Special interest groups. Stock photo agencies. Private firms and collectors. Commercial artists. Films and slides. Researching and writing the pictorial history book: Step-by-step suggestions for researching the market for the idea, outlining the book, locating illustrations. Querying the editor. Published examples, and how they came about.

much material for a book? How some published books came into being. Finding a publisher. Helpful techniques: transitions, flashbacks. Using footnotes. Quoting and securing permissions. Payments of fees. Titles: how to create a catchy one. Indexing.

Past in relation to present. Relevancy. Heroes to learn from. Racism, sexism in textbooks. Controversy over children's books — their goals and effects. True-to-life-as-it-was vs. contemporary minority attitudes. The challenge of writing for young people. Vocabulary lists — who uses them. Language suitability and *today's* books for young people. Selecting the subject. Know your reader's interests by age level; their preferences in subject matter. Markets for articles and short stories. Poetry, puzzles and quizzes on history in juvenile magazines. The juvenile book market. Series books for specific grade levels by publishers.

Research sources. How to write freelance publicity. Newspaper features. Different leads: news story vs. features. Radio and television publicity. Special tips on writing to be heard. Historical booklets. Selling the idea to the local chamber of commerce. Advertising sales to support. How to figure advertising page costs. Estimates from printers. Family history and genealogy. Regional history. Commercially published examples. Regional and local freelance markets. Town and regional books: four examples of ways they get published. Additional audiovisual opportunities. Writing mini-books for resale: at historic houses, villages, museums, historic sites. Commemorative booklets. How much to charge for writing. Publishing your own mini-book. Examining the potential market. Some specific examples of costs on published booklets. Profits and losses on same. Procedure to follow. Planning publicity and selling.

INTRODUCTION

The idea for this book came out of the frustration of my students who were interested in writing historical material, but who became bogged down in the intricacies of professional research. Too many reference books are written in technical language which amateur researchers have to struggle to understand. Simplifying the methods of research which I learned while working for my master's degree in history at the University of New Hampshire, I have used information shared with my students and then expanded it to cover many types of historical writing. The result is intended to show beginners how to write history and advanced researchers how to make the most of research tools.

Not a book on writing technique, it does review some of the important tools of the writer. Here the student will learn how to find ideas, organize research material, make the most of his knowledge and experience, and adapt his work for the proper market.

At Boston University I studied "American Lit" with Prof. Everett Getchell, a dedicated man with an impish sense of humor. He taught me how to take notes, how to prepare a bibliography and how to correlate notes into an acceptable thesis. Years later, when I realized my debt to him, I wrote and thanked him.

What I remember most were the field trips to literary landmarks around Boston, where we saw Louisa May Alcott, Henry Thoreau, Ralph Waldo Emerson, Nathaniel Hawthorne and countless other giants of the past as real people who lived on in the hearts and minds of future generations. When I visited the homes of those who lived near "the rude bridge that arched the flood" in Concord, Massachusetts, history came alive for me and I've never been the same since that day.

But I didn't know it was *history*. Today young people visit historic shrines and learn the past through first hand experience, but they don't think of this as history, either. It is reassuring to us to see an increasing number of educators scheduling time for this method of exploration and encouraging a livelier teaching of history.

Most teachers could be helped to make history of greater impact to their students if they had the aid of inspiring historical material and more imaginative textbooks. Publishers are aware of this need and are beginning to offer more attractive textbooks than ever before. They are looking for historical writers who can combine scholarship with a lively writing ability.

In this book I share some of the skills I have learned during an apprenticeship of more than forty years, as teenage reporter, city newspaper correspondent and reporter, student writer, public relations and advertising agent, freelance writer, editor and teacher — much of the time while rearing a family and assuming responsibility in community affairs.

Some of my strong feelings about the high calling of authorship are expressed here, stressing the responsibilities of a writer toward his reader and toward himself, not only in the learning of his craft but in his search for personal fulfillment.

I could not expect that all of you who read this book will learn as much as I have while writing it. I shall be satisfied to know that a few of you absorb its practical information and encouragement and learn to write about our precious American heritage with confidence and joy.

Doris Ricker Marston

Cape Neddick, Maine
June 1975

XIV

CHAPTER ONE

WRITING HISTORY FOR TODAY'S READERS

Even the past second has become history. Those who are thinking of writing in this field have the whole world and the past ages from which to choose. The reason so many find the study of history dull is that many teachers and historians become so involved with their facts and wars and dates that they forget the most important fact of all.

History is made by people. By men and women whose courage and imagination changed the course of a war or the human condition.

It is also the story of rebellion and revolution against government, the "Establishment," or a smug society; of ruthless men and nations greedy for power, position and wealth; of exploitation and tyranny; of the downtrodden and persecuted; of bastards as well as of heroes.

When you write history, you stress not only events, either good or bad or both, but touch the lives of many people. When you write biography, you tell the story of one person and other people's effect on him. A writer needs to remember that people of the past were very much like himself, and try to bring them so vividly to life that his reader will identify with the hero or heroine.

You might find it more intriguing to tell about a rascal rather than a paragon. Seen in perspective and with newly uncovered data, a man eulogized in his time might now be considered a villain, or a blackguard of the past might now be vindicated.

When you write about the past, make it the story of humanity. Those living in the times of Homer and Chaucer learned the history of their people through ballads and the telling of tales. Folklore and legends of mighty deeds related by their elders have been the heritage of children around the world for hundreds of years. It was the human, personal flavor which has kept so many sagas and folk songs alive.

Religious fervor filled the folk tales of the medieval period and continued to influence literature, including historical writings, through the seventeenth century. Emphasis was given to the premise that forces from without were responsible for mankind's woes and good fortune, and directly responsible for the events happening in the world.

Then came the Enlightenment of the eighteenth century, the beginning of the understanding of the science of philosophy, with its logical conception of natural law working in the universe in an orderly, continuous manner.

With the coming of the nineteenth century, nationalist ideals began to receive recognition. Literature became livelier, finding a willing advocate in historians such as Francis Parkman. By the end of the century the writing of American history became a profession rather than the avocation of teachers like Jared Sparks. Unlike Sparks — who saw nothing illogical in improving the grammar of George Washington's letters — writers now recognized history as a discipline and consequently gave particular attention to accuracy of detail. Some of the writing, while gaining in verity, lost its spontaneity and interest.

Men began to study the development of such ideas as the influence of geographical and numerous other forces on the actions of people, the effect on a nation of the state of its economy, and soon came the growing thought of history as more than the story of politics. This broadening ideology brought to the new historians (Turner, Robinson, Beard and Becker among others) the realization that proper history was the life of a people in all its aspects.

Man cannot separate himself from his society, environment, government, economics. Therefore, twentieth-century historians welcome the aid of students in the disciplines of the social sciences, plus information from auxiliary fields like genealogy and heraldry, and from literature, art, religion, archeology and all the humanities. The wide world and everything in it can be used by the historian to gain understanding of the activities and motivations of mankind.

In this day of instant communication through television and radio, newspapers and other periodicals, historical writing is emerging from the dullness of the past to become a living social science for thousands of Americans.

Speaking as a private citizen, rather than in an official capacity, Dr. Robert L. Hilliard, chief of the FCC's Educational Broadcasting Branch, noted that by the time a child enters kindergarten he has already spent more hours in front of the television learning about the world, than he will spend in a classroom earning a bachelor's and a master's degree; so today's writer of history in print form has a greater challenge than ever before to gain the reader's attention and interest.

People who did not understand or appreciate history in their school days (and this includes me) are joining historical societies in unprecedented numbers and finding satisfaction in the study of the past in their own town and state. There were 2,050 historical societies in the United States in 1961, 3,300 in 1969, and nearly 5,000 in 1974.

Families, traveling in increasing numbers, include in their itinerary visits to museums of art, social science and technology and go to places like Old Sturbridge Village in Massachusetts, Dodge City in Kansas, Greenfield Village in Michigan and Old Tucson in Arizona. So easily can young folks and their parents learn the facts of "living history."

Scholarly works on history are being supplemented by "popular" textbooks, historical novels and entertaining biographies. Everyone who reads a newspaper or a magazine or watches television or listens to radio is exposed to history in the making.

Yet most of us fail to relate the lessons of the past to the present.

History is the richness of the records of the past, whether they are buildings or books, family journals or state papers, tintypes or tapes. There will never be an end to the treasures to be discovered by those who care. Somewhere, stolen from Montpelier, Henry Knox's homestead in Thomaston, Maine, are the tiny slippers which Lucy Knox once wore. In attics and musty boxes and cubbyholes all over the world — and in caves like those where the Dead Sea Scrolls were found — are artifacts and manuscripts which would bring us additional knowledge.

In every age, historians influence the thinking of a people. With their special "corner" on the young mind reached through studies at school and college, they have a particular responsibility to give of their best in accuracy, unbiased interpretation and inspiration.

Naturally, ideology has changed through the years, just as family life has changed from its original agriculturally-based unity to the concept of individual enterprise, fostered by the Industrial Revolution. I doubt, however, if the Horatio Alger brand of optimism will ever wholly die, even when weighed against the pessimistic views held by so many people in a time of economic slump.

There are always dangers that a historian will ride his own hobby horse so hard he will forget that there are other ideas to be considered with equal attention. An example of this is the bias shown in some books written by members of opposing political parties. You must scrutinize your own work to be sure that you are making every effort to avoid prejudice.

WRITING HISTORY FOR TODAY'S READERS

Writing history is a literary art, but with proper background and preparation, even the beginner can have some success in getting his work published. There are more than five hundred newspapers, magazines, journals, bulletins, university quarterlies and children's periodicals which publish historical material on a local, regional, national or international basis.

How does one become a writer of history? If you feel that your education is limited, don't be discouraged. Learning is as near as your public library, college or adult evening class. If you are at a distance from a public library, the mails will bring you books from your state library for one-way book-rate postage. The cost is mere pennies. And university extension and other home study courses are available at your own mailbox if a campus or school is inaccessible to you.

But reading is only a beginning. The historian Arnold Toynbee stresses the importance of travel in the life of a historian; he believes that travel ought to have precedence for one who writes or teaches history. You will understand people better if you see their environment at first-hand. From your own travel, you know that what is described in a travel brochure or a book becomes familiar only when you see it for yourself.

During this exploratory period of your adventure into the writing of history, your chief concern should be a study of your own temperament. It is likely that if you have set yourself one of the educational goals just mentioned, you have a more than casual interest in history. A "casual" approach to the writing of history is dangerous, for the most important criterion in the writing of history is accuracy.

A writer cannot write accurately unless he is willing to dig for the facts. Historical writing cannot be based upon clippings and quotations, but involves dedicated research, a weighing of evidence based on primary (original) and secondary sources, and a considered interpretation of what you learn.

A beginner will obviously not start with an involved subject, nor be ready to write professorial dissertations.

If you love accuracy for its own sake and have pride in good workmanship, you will do extra research just to make sure your details are factual. If you don't *know,* never guess. You can develop a sense of logic which will lighten the perplexities of research, and bless you with a patient tenacity.

You can write historical material without a love for order, but it will be harder and take longer to do the work. I'll have some suggestions about ways to take notes and how to keep your facts together in future chapters. Here I want to speak of the importance of keeping track of every bit of reading you do. Even experienced writers slip up and spend needless hectic hours looking for the source of an idea or quotation.

From your very first reading, keep a list of the books you study, where you found them and the library call number. For the bibliography I like to use a small looseleaf notebook, with a page for each book, because it is easy to carry and the pages can be quickly put in alphabetical order by author, or whatever method you choose.

This may seem a lot of work; but if you don't take this fifteen minutes, you may spend two hours looking for your notes or trying to remember in which book you have read a needed fact.

Imagination is an important characteristic to develop as an aid in every kind of writing. It seems especially helpful in historical work, since with imagination you can become more resourceful. Every detective must have imagination — and a historian is a literary detective, seeking out new facts, new sources, new secrets, looking for ways to use old facts in a new way, thinking how a bit of information might have been indexed or filed.

This is the greatest fun and satisfaction for many historians! The search is rewarding in itself, but beyond that, even the experienced researcher thrills every time he finds an unexpected fact or a new idea. To me, the most exciting time of all comes through serendipity — while I am looking for one certain fact and suddenly I find another fact or another idea which brings into focus a completely different train of thought.

While I was working on my master's thesis — a biography of Sally Wood (1759-1855) Maine's first woman novelist — I read or skimmed many books looking for information about life in Portland during the time she lived there. One day I was more or less browsing along the shelves in the Brick Store Museum, Kennebunk, Maine, when I came across a little book of Portland history. Scanning its contents, I was suddenly electrified to come across a reference to "Madam Wood's school for young ladies," in an essay of reminiscence. This was the only reference I ever found to the fact that Sally had taught a "dame's school" when she lived in Portland.

While you become acquainted with historians of past and present, you will be choosing your favorites and adding them to your bibliography. You will be writing the stories to be found in your community and state, selecting a field of history about which you can write with assurance, and perhaps developing that field of knowledge in detail enough to write fiction or to write for children.

You can learn to move the emotions of men or inspire the minds of children. You can learn to think reflectively, to ask *why* and to find the answers in past events and their relevancy to the present.

One fact is certain: once you start on the pathway to the study and writing of history, you will never be the same again. Your mind will be enriched, your understanding of people more tolerant and more compassionate. Your waking hours will be filled with an awareness of adventure, and heightened by everlasting curiosity. A historian cannot be a lazy man. The study and writing of history will become a way of life, a rewarding way for those who woo it.

CHAPTER TWO

HOW TO FIND THE RIGHT IDEAS

A newcomer to our town was bubbling over with enthusiasm. "There are so many glorious scenes to paint, I'll never get them all," she told me. Several years later I met her in the supermarket and asked her how her painting was going. She shrugged her shoulders. "Everything seems so commonplace," she said. Yet she hadn't painted even a quarter of the beautiful scenery which had enthralled her just a few years before.

The writer must remember that the gold in his own backyard is there for the digging. How many times we walk or drive the same road not seeing the scene which the newcomer raves about. Every road in every village and city is filled with historical material waiting to be discovered. Material familiar to you is unknown to others, and many of these persons would be interested in it.

Your viewpoint is unique, unlike that of anyone else, because no one else in the world is quite like you.

To start on the road to a discovery of the historical treasures awaiting you, write down a list of your own interests and activities, your hobbies, things you would like to know more about if you had the time to explore them. What do you see when you look around your neighborhood? What do you know? What do you wish you knew? Write as long a list as you can, starting with an 8-1/2 x 11 page.

What you write about will determine the scope of your involvement with life and people, show a little of how and what you think, and help you to develop self-awareness and greater alertness to the world around you. Your interests will be a guidepost in your search for ideas for any form of writing.

Your views and your ability as a writer and researcher will determine whether you present your material as short story or novel, article or nonfiction book, as poetry or drama.

WHERE DO WE FIND IDEAS?

1. *In your own experience* and interests and knowledge. This would include travel. The *Christian Science Monitor* Travel Page editor accepted my article "Lafayette Slept Here: So Did We," a personal account of the night my husband and I occupied the same room in the Peyton Randolph House, Williamsburg, Virginia, where Lafayette had slept two centuries before. The article included both travel information and our reaction to the historical impact of the place.

Your particular interests — oceanography, Indians, travel, pirates, golf, for example — may find a home in some of the "special interest" and regional magazines.

To learn first-hand about a subject, you will welcome new experiences. Francis Parkman, admired historian of the nineteenth century, believed that experience was an essential element and set out to see for himself how life was lived along the Oregon Trail. In no other way could he have written so eloquently about it.

2. *Something you see* that intrigues you. Cleo Stephens found a tiny feather on a beach; later saw in a museum a feathered cloak worn only by royalty; and from this grew her novel, *The Royal Feather,* with the plot based on the discovery of the lost burial place of Hawaii's King Kamehameha.

Intrigued by the mystery and glamour of sea monsters, James B. Sweeney spent countless hours researching *A Pictorial History of Sea Monsters and Other Dangerous Marine Life.*

3. Conversations with *elderly citizens* of your community will give you material for tales of yesteryear — and recording these would be of public service, too.

Children, as well as adults, are interested in tales of "the olden days" — sailing ships, horsecars, pioneering.

4. Start collecting such lists as "Fifty Years Ago," found in local newspapers. *Start a Calendar notebook,* with month dividers, and there make note of anniversaries. centennials, and so forth of towns, countries, business firms, historic sites, and so on.

5. Make note also of annual *Holidays and special events* (like the

Ides of March, Flag Day, Easter), the birthdays of venerable people in your town and state (check birth announcements in early newspapers and in town and city yearbooks if they printed vital statistics), and of anniversaries of people not well-known who you think should be.

A helpful publication in this area is *Chase's Calendar of Annual Events,* published annually in November by Apple Tree Press, Box 1102, Flint, Michigan 48501. (Price: $5.00)

To be salable with editors this work should be done a year or more ahead of the date you wish to write about.

6. *Watch newspapers and magazines* for information. You will find many new ideas, and an item an inch long may put you on the trail of a great story. Paste these clippings in an idea notebook, one idea to a page. Don't get bogged down with ideas you will never use. Select those which common sense tells you might be worth following up.

"Milestones" in *Time Magazine* is a source for biography and there are hundreds of suggestions in biographical dictionaries.

Start a file of folders marked "Special Days" or "Historic Sites in our State" or "Places People Would Like to Know More About," and gather material on your own special interests, adding to these as you read your daily and Sunday newspapers and magazines. Now and then buy and study Sunday newspapers of another area than your own. Each month buy two or three magazines unknown to you, or browse in the periodicals room at your library. Swap magazines with friends.

Reading the writers' magazines will furnish you with numerous leads. There you may read that a university press is looking for book material on regional Indians or a researcher is seeking material on the circus or an editor wants narrative poetry.

7. *Read* — read every type of book, and always with a notebook or file cards nearby. You'll be surprised at the ideas that will come to a writer with a curious mind. I've found many creative ideas while reading the Bible — and not just ideas for the religious field.

8. Speaking of *curiosity!* Make notes of the times you say, or hear someone else say, "I wonder why?" "Where do you suppose that idea came from—" "How did this town get its unusual name—"

"I wonder who made the first doughnut — or flatiron — or dress pattern?" Curiosity is a sparkplug for every writer.

9. Listen to the *questions of children* as well as of adults. "Where did peanut butter come from?" "What toys did children play with when you were a boy, Grandpa?" "Darn the guy who invented overshoes. Do I have to wear 'em?" "Did little kids fight long ago, Daddy — like they are in Ireland now?" You have a gold mine of ideas here, and an opportunity to help children to know more of the many wonderful things and people and events of this world.

10. *Social Concerns.* Emerson said "The use of history is to give value to the present hour." What subjects of historical interest can you explore to prepare an article or story of timely importance?

Catherine Gaskin based the plot of her novel *Fiona* on the uprising of the slaves in the West Indies in the 1830's. Using authentic customs and actual events as background, she wove her fictional plot into a story which has immediacy today.

In view of the issue of morality in the 1970's, what villains, traitors, swindlers, politicians of the past, can find a current counterpart? Did the so-called "muckrakers" of the past perform the same kind of service that modern investigative reporters are giving today?

Why is the story of Henri Charriere, "the greatest rogue of the century," so popular in 1974 books and movies: *Papillon* and *Banco?* These vie with the best adventure stories of past and present.

The problems and triumphs of ethnic and "minority" groups will never be completely recorded, although many books, films, plays about them are now being produced.

Many interpretations are given to the word "revolutionary." The whole area of revolution is of social concern, whether we are dealing with campus rebels or the Gray Panthers of the senior citizenry or the women's movement.

Social concern is important in writing for children. Children exposed to the openness of television and the press are ready at an earlier age to tackle contemporary problems, shown in their relation to the past: poverty, crime, drug addiction, misuse of power.

I believe, however, that writers today have a greater responsibility than ever before to guide youthful readers to an appreciation of ethical values.

11. Take a walk through *your town*. Visit the Chamber of Commerce, pick up publicity booklets for city and state, and ask for information about business firms which might be fifty years old or more. This might make a story for a trade journal. Comparison of the past with present economics, legal affairs, business development, trade, are effective subjects for those who have some background interest in them.

Around town, watch for monuments, signs, boulders marking historic sites. Make a list. Most states, and some towns, publish pamphlets describing historic spots.

12. Visit your town library — and the state library, if possible — and study the material to find ideas about *local and state history*. Talk with your librarian, the historian's best friend. See what has been published — and what still needs to be written — about your town and your state. If no history has been written, could you do the necessary research and write it, perhaps a pamphlet as a starter?

A fascinating example of this category is *The New Eldorado* by Phyllis Flanders Dorset (Macmillan 1970), a "biography" of Colorado.

13. It will be helpful to those who wish to write about their area to join both the local and the state *historical societies.* Doors to archives will open wide if you do. Learn and listen and explore and you will find plenty to write about, and you will receive cooperation in your search for material. Society library personnel will also be generous with assistance to non-members, but usually only members are permitted to have free rein in the files.

After you have had some experience in writing and have learned a great deal about your region, you might have a freelance opportunity to edit a newsletter or write a pamphlet for the society.

14. Much information about the *customs of the past* remains to be told, and you might find it interesting to write about food, fashions, homemaking, families, even when current topics of this type are written by a magazine's staff. *American Heritage* once published an article describing Thomas Jefferson as a gourmet.

15. Many phases of *the growth of industrialism* have not yet been explored. Or you might find it fascinating to write about trends in agriculture (from the hand plow to the time Uncle Sam paid farmers NOT to raise grain and the reasons why) or the making of furniture (think of the craze for wicker furniture just a decade after we were throwing ours in the dump) or comparing antique tools and craftsmanship with present customs.

16. Is *conservation* one of your concerns? Did you know that the Forest Historical Society systematically preserves, researches, writes and publishes the history of man's use of North American forests? Who are the pioneers in conservation, the designers of parks, the crusaders for open spaces and preservation of wild life?

17. *Adventure,* anyone? The range of possibilities in this field is not only limitless, but this is the place to search for ideas for the men's magazines, and for material to interest children. Pirates, Indians, spies, the battle front, are only the most exploited ideas. There is adventure in pioneering, sports, true crime, exploration and in a quieter but no less meaningful way, in the fields of medical and scientific research.

Biography, too, may come within this field. Remember *PT 109* and John F. Kennedy? Under this category comes *Lewis & Clark and the Crossing of North America,* by David Holloway, an alternate of the Book-of-the-Month Club in August, 1974.

The high point need not always be victory or successful accomplishment: Geoffrey Moorhouse tells of his nightmare struggle for survival in the Sahara in *The Fearful Void.* Peter Brent's book. *Captain Scott and the Antarctic Tragedy,* is another example.

18. If the *Arts* are of primary importance to you, a treasure trove of ideas can be found in literature, art, music, sculpture and related areas. Very little has been written in this field for children: the inspiring or often sad stories of dancers, singers, painters, composers. Donald Knox's presentation of Renoir's life, tied in with a Renoir exhibit at the Art Institute of Chicago in 1973, was televised in June 1974. He used paintings, pictures, letters, and musical accents to tell his story.

Shirley Glubok shows us art as history in her popular Macmillan children's series. She tells her readers, through art, the story of America.

Art books for adults are popular and expensive, and take great expertise. They are an important part of our world history.

19. Movie and theatre buffs might like to write about the history of *show business,* which is a part of the nostalgic movement of the decade. There are many older folk who would enjoy being reminded of Pearl White and "The Perils of Pauline" or the silent movies and that honky tonk piano player whose playing made small boys' blood run cold as they watched Indians chase the cowboys across the prairie! What can old-timers in your town remember?

Somehow, people never tire of hearing stories about glamorous figures, and are eager to know more about the Broadway actors who work in summer theatres. Interviews can be arranged through the theatres and the stars' press agents.

20. *Archaeology* is a challenge to the imagination. Both an art and a science, it seems to belong in a niche of its own. Have any "digs" been started in your area? What colleges near you have scheduled excursions to fields being uncovered? Sometimes the curator of a museum or an interested group will look for artifacts at the site of a community's first homestead. And think of the old dumps which attract seekers of bottles and other artifacts!

The Government has several projects going on in various parts of the country. One is that of Pecos National Monument in New Mexico, where a church has been uncovered and restored by the National Park Service. It was a thrilling sight to see the archaeologists in their bright yellow helmets carefully digging into the red, red clay! Here is an opportunity to combine travel and history. Watch the newspapers for information about "digs" nearby.

21. Geology and other *natural sciences* are also of historical importance. The findings of geologists have given us insight into the mysteries of millions of years of the earth's history. Fossils, bones, the similarity of lizards and dinosaurs, the evolution of the sequoias, the preservation of species, are as vital to our knowledge as the opening of King Tut's Tomb.

22. *Records and journals* are wonderful sources for ideas. You may have a Civil War diary or set of letters in your own home; your library and historical society library will probably have many more.

Ideas for short stories, articles and other types of writing may be sparked by such items as diaries, old letters, journals, notebooks, memoirs, coins, medals, account books, ship logs.

My greatest thrill during many years of research experience was holding in my hand, and reading, the worn brown journal kept by Henry Knox — George Washington's captain of artillery in the American Revolution — while he was bringing the guns from Fort Ticonderoga to Boston. On this little book was based my article on Henry Knox, which was published in an issue of *New England Galaxy*. I found this precious journal in the Massachusetts Historical Society in Boston.

Talk about adventure! Probably nothing is more important than such records, which reveal the life of a man for his biographer.

23. *Relics or artifacts* give us a hint of how the people of the past lived. A collection of tools and farming equipment like those at the Farm in Cooperstown, New York, or the exhibit of lighting through the years at Old Sturbridge Village in Massachusetts or the Factory and other buildings at Fort Osage, Missouri, help us to recreate a period and give us ideas for current projects, too.

Tombstones, inscriptions in churches, medals, musical instruments, clothing, furniture, dishes and other household articles (including those old bottles) give a picture of history in the making, and ideas for stories.

24. *Oral History,* the preservation on tape of voices and speeches which have historical import, is now an art. Colleges, state and national archives are commissioning experienced interviewers to talk to a wide variety of people and to record their recollections of both long ago and recent events.

For instance, the National Archives of American Art, a branch of the Smithsonian Institution, is collecting every possible bit of information about art, artists, art dealers, art shows and numerous other offshoots of the field.

Using your tape recorder, you can do your own oral history, interviewing people in a particular phase of history.

25. We may put *ballads, sagas, folk tales* and similar ideas in a separate listing, although they are a part of oral history. Middlebury College, Vermont, has a collection of records which give us the voices of those who remembered from their childhood old sea chanties and folk songs. These, like the works of Virgil, Homer and Chaucer, the sagas of the Vikings, the legends of mythology, have come down to us through oral folk tales. They are a precious legacy of ages which will always hold their own special glamour, and they are always worth retelling.

26. Visiting *museums* may weigh you down with too much to think about — or give you innumerable ideas for stories. Make it a point to know what all museums in your area have to offer. And then try to cover only a portion of any one on a single visit.

When you travel, learn as much as you can about the museums which emphasize the culture of the area. For example, the Cowboy Hall of Fame in Oklahoma City, Oklahoma, is filled with memorabilia of the West. The University of Texas Museum in Canyon, Texas, has a fabulous collection of guns, worth at least a million dollars, and a replica of a pioneer village, like those Loula Grace Erdman portrays so well in her books. All state museums have a diversified collection of regional material.

27. Ideas abound for writing *biography* in article, story, book or ballad — probably the most popular form of historical writing. Finding just the right subject and then writing a compelling portrait is not easy.

Yet there are always the "sleepers," a writer's exciting discovery of an unknown or little known person who captures the imagination and is sure to intrigue a large coterie of readers. Search for such a subject can be absorbing.

The stories of dozens of interesting people can be told to each new generation. The lives of perennials such as Thomas Jefferson or Aaron Burr however, *must* be given a fresh touch, an imaginative approach.

28. Do you speak and read a foreign language well enough to do a *translation* of an important book? An August, 1974 alternate of the Book-of-the-Month Club was *Triestes Tropiques* by Claude

Levi-Strauss, translated by John and Dorsen Weightman. Published in 1955 and revised in 1968, this book was called by reviewers "an enchantment" . . . "a masterpiece of . . . autobiography, travelogue, confession" and widely regarded as a classic. Perhaps you know of interesting material which has never been translated. You must be sure your labors would be worthwhile, your book one which would give you personal satisfaction and be of interest to many readers. A firm expression of interest based on an outline and some sample chapters should be obtained from a publisher before extensive work is completed.

29. Church or Biblical history are only two of the possibilities in the field of *religion and philosophy*.

Willa Cather was amazed to find herself writing history of the Roman Catholic Church. *Death Comes for the Archbishop* is based on the life of Archbishop Lamy, the first bishop of New Mexico, whose story fascinated her while she was visiting there and in Arizona. It didn't occur to her to write about it, for she thought such material belonged to a Catholic writer.

But after she discovered letters and other material associated with Father Lamy, she could not get on with other writing until she told his story.

This is the way that you make ideas that appeal to you into a product which can belong to no other writer, even though the same material is available to everyone.

30. A consistent, methodical source of ideas is available through the facilities of the *U. S. Government*. Lists of publications by subject may be obtained from the U. S. Government Printing Office, Public Documents Department, Washington, D.C. 20402. (Ask to be put on their mailing list for a free subscription to *Selected U.S. Government Publications*.) The National Park Service, for example, has more than fifty brochures.

How many of those who have received the Congressional Medal of Honor are known to the general public? What ideas are hidden in U. S. Naval documents, in the National Archives or the huge, rambling Smithsonian Institution? What information is available in that nearby Air Force Base or historic fortress, at Annapolis or West Point?

SELECTING A SUBJECT

From this wealth of material which I have been suggesting to you, you should select a field of special interest — a period, a country, an event; one phase of a subject, not the whole field; one phase of the arts broken down into a life or a craft.

It might be wise to start with a short article as your first history writing effort. For example, suppose you selected "Gardens of the Past" for a subject. You might decide, after doing some reading, to narrow this to "The Gardens of Monticello." Then you might find so much on herbs and their use in Colonial times that you would change your subject to "The Use of Herbs for Medicinal Purposes." To your surprise, your final subject might be "How Herbs Are Used In Witchcraft."

It's not necessary to select a topic of great moment, for history is made of the stuff of "little things." One incident in a battle is enough to light the fire for a ballad. Anything which has touched the life of man may do for a start. Something through which you can answer why? or how?

Now we have come to the point where you should be able to write down three to five ideas based on your preliminary research of yourself, your interests and this wealth of ideas. Be sure one idea is very easy, and that not more than one is difficult. Now ask yourself questions to see if your selections will make a good story or article. Ask yourself:

1. Do I have an urge to tell others what I am learning?
2. Will people say "So what?" or will they want to listen?
3. Can many readers identify with what I want to say?
4. Are there drama and conflict? (Yes, there should be, even in article writing.)
5. Does my topic offer worthwhile information? entertainment? delight? Any one is valid; all three should be terrific.
6. Have many other writers already worked with my idea? Have I a new point of view or angle which will justify trying it again?
7. Can I find enough information quickly — or is it important enough to justify spending many hours on research? Is it too big or too important a subject for me to handle right now? (Your degree of interest and educational qualifications are measured here, and

must determine your decision.)

8. Is this a subject few know about, though I think they should?

9. Will this stir my continued interest? enthusiasm? emotions? imagination? Have I the talent to pass these along to my readers? Can I learn how?

10. Does it have relevancy to today's world?

STARTING THE SURVEY

Your next step is to visit the library and see whether other writers have discovered these subjects of yours. Look first in the *Reader's Guide to Periodical Literature,* in your library's reference section. Go back at least five years, looking under subject headings. I use a spiralringed notebook with holes, so the sheets can be removed and later placed in a looseleaf notebook or file folder. List subject, title of article, author, magazine, date, volume and page numbers.

Before you go to the periodicals room, also look up your subject in the *Encyclopedia Americana,* and perhaps in the *Britannica.* When I was seeking information about the Sandemanian religion, founded in England, the current Britannica did not have a single reference, but the *older* edition had a satisfying amount of material.

At the end of each article in the encyclopedia is a bibliography for further reference. Take down the names of any books which seem promising. Today in most libraries rather than take copious notes from this and other books you can make a photocopy of material you can use. Obviously, this can be used only for reference, not to be recopied into your manuscript verbatim; but you can quote and give credit to the source, with permission.

By the time you have taken these preliminary steps, you'll know whether these are the topics you wish to write about. If you find that nothing has been published in *Reader's Guide,* you may have a fresh idea worth pursuing. You may also want to check your subject headings in the *New York Times Index* for the past five years, or if your topic is regional, check in the library of the nearby newspapers. In large libraries, you will find newspaper indexes in the microfilm room.

When you ask yourself "So what?" list the people who might

be interested in your idea. Would it appeal to men or women or both? Would it be better for children? When you come across the name of a magazine or regional newspaper whose readers might like to know what you have to tell them, make a note on your idea page.

Don't discard ideas or notes or research material. If it is too late to use an idea this year, mark a note to yourself on a calendar so you'll have it ready for next year, and start a file with the months listed on folders. Keep an idea notebook, an idea to a page. When you clip material from newspapers and magazines or photocopy information, be sure to jot down the source and date.

A sense of timing is an elusive but real requirement for successful sale of manuscripts. A writer must recognize the trends of interest, the time to tell his story and consequently have a feeling (in advance) of the mood and life style of those who he hopes will read his material.

Dozens of books and articles about all phases of the American Revolution and founding of the United States are being published in the 1970's and will continue to be published.

But what will be the trend of social and political reforms in the decade to come? What will replace the campus rebels and the nostalgia for the 1930's?

Correctly gauging the answers is the history writer's challenge.

TYPES OF HISTORICAL WRITING

How do you decide whether to present your ideas as fiction or nonfiction, poetry or prose? Writing down a one sentence theme will give you a good start. Sometimes a manuscript starts out as an article and becomes a biography; sometimes a short story spreads wider and wider and becomes a novel. Some writers must be brief — and others have so much to say that they must use more space to say it. Disciplined writers of experience can use any form that fits the idea and scope of the material.

What if you find the same topic may be presented in several ways? Why not? I have used the same material, written in a different slant and with a change of wording, for several magazines and newspapers. For example, my article about Henry Knox was a long article, but I also won second prize in a poetry contest for a ballad about him. Sometime I'll write a book for teenagers about his adventures. I've had an article about the Battle of Baltimore in the War of 1812 published in *The Christian Science Monitor* — and a four-part fiction serial on the same material published in a teens magazine.

Just because an idea has been used does not mean that you cannot use it again, with a fresh point of view, a different style, and that special fire that only your personal enthusiasm can bring to any subject. Note how many times the story of Johnny Appleseed has been told, from articles to a children's book to a movie. How often are books published about Leonardo da Vinci, John F. Kennedy, Eleanor Roosevelt, Ben Franklin, Thomas Jefferson — and television and movies also use this same material.

The approach of any anniversary date is an invitation to the writer, which he has accepted a year ahead!

Are there any fields of writing or the visual arts which cannot use historical writing and research?

Here are just a few of the opportunities:

Short material: articles, fillers, short stories, essays, poetry, puzzles, quizzes; on both adult and juvenile levels.

Books: historical novel, romance novel, biography, autobiography, juvenile books, oral history, folk tales, ballads, folk songs, research for business firms, archives.

Dramatic arts: theatre, opera, films, radio, television, plays in printed form.

Local history: oral history, publicity, pamphlets for historical societies, newsletters, etc., regional writing for town, county, state, area.

Public relations: history of industry, preparation of pamphlets and books for all types of people and firms.

Visual arts: photo essays, pictorial history, art books, comics, film strips, documentaries, cartoons.

You should choose your ideas because they fire your imagination, because you lie awake at night thinking about them.

As a professional, you would ordinarily select those ideas that seem to be most publishable, because to do otherwise is often a waste of valuable time. But *dare* to be different, to "walk to the beat of a different drummer" if you are impelled to do so.

Remember, a writer must have integrity, must cleave to accuracy of fact and detail, must be above prejudice. But what pleases you most will stir your imagination and enthusiasm and bring precious new life to your writing. That must come *first*.

CHAPTER THREE

THE HISTORIAN AS DETECTIVE AND SCHOLAR

Everyone can't like to do research; many find it a dull and necessary step to writing. Those of us who truly enjoy research, finding a challenge similar to that experienced by a detective in seeking out elusive facts, need many a cautionary reminder to stop doing research and to start writing.

Beginning writers of history should be willing to give at least six months of their time before deciding that they can't "settle down" to doing thorough investigation of an interesting subject. Meanwhile, those of you who feel that way will be writing articles or fiction, based on material which doesn't require in-depth treatment.

Put aside ideas which require more concentration and effort than you wish to give them now. Keep the ideas in your files until you are ready. From time to time you'll come across information to add. But don't worry about the hard work that may seem to loom ahead. By the time the six months are over, you'll have so much experience that researching in depth will no longer seem formidable.

"Every man has a right to his opinion, but no man has a right to be wrong in his facts," Bernard Baruch once said.

Achieving accuracy of fact should be the first goal of those who write, and must be of those who write history. From the start of your work as a researcher, you must keep the light of facts shining on your labors. Guesses, "maybe's" and prejudices must be shut out.

When the Manuscript Division of the Library of Congress received 1,800 manuscript pages, maps and notes from Kenneth Roberts, it reported that the collection graphically revealed Roberts' devotion to historical accuracy, showing thousands of revisions, corrections, and annotations in the author's handwriting. They indicated a meticulous checking of the most minute details. Kenneth Roberts received a special citation in 1957 from the Pulitzer Prize Committee for his series of novels based on American history — which during the 1970's have fascinated a new set of readers of American Revolutionary literature.

It is imperative that you know the basic facts of your subject. For example, police officers, gun experts and even criminals have pointed out inaccuracies and mistakes made by mystery and crime writers in describing police procedures and the use of firearms in books, television and moving pictures.

THOROUGH RESEARCH TAKES GOOD DETECTIVE WORK

Since I very much enjoy pitting my detecting skills against writers of whodunits, I like to think of myself as a detective-historian while I search the records of the past for information and enlightenment.

Just as a detective tries to uncover new evidence, you set out to learn the truth about the subject you have chosen. It will become fascinating when you find one fact fitting into another, and your questions of "why?" and "when?" and "how?" answered one by one. Excitement may build up for you as it did for me one day in the New York Public Library, when after a search of several years, I found in a microfilmed newspaper of the 1830's the date a certain ship sank in New York Harbor. (I yelled "hurrah!" and then looked around in embarrassment, to meet the understanding smiles of neighboring researchers.)

Unless you become a real pro, you won't read 7,000,000 words of contemporary material as Jim Bishop did to find unique information for his book *The Day Lincoln Was Shot.* He also traveled Booth's escape route step by step. To say Mr. Bishop is a careful researcher is not telling the whole story: John Marquand, telling of this in his *Report* of the book for the *Book-of-the-Month Club News,* remarked that the finding of "a myriad of lesser-known facts lends the whole an amazing freshness." Mr. Bishop used his imagination — his detective-like skill — to seek out just the right ideas.

Anyone can parrot phrases out of old history books. Only those who care enough will go that longer, exciting road to new discoveries, which will give life and meaning to those known facts.

David Oakes Woodbury, writer of twenty-four popular science books — plus countless magazine articles and scholarly technical material — emphasizes the importance of finding that extra fact which will enable him to make a comparison or show a contrast. which will be within range of the layman's experience.

Readers need comparative examples to understand the vastness of the world, and its complications.

One of my favorite stories is this: Jimmy and his little brother were walking by the town reservoir. "Think how many billions of gallons of water are in that thing," Jimmy said. "How many squirts of my water pistol would that make?" his brother asked.

This is relevancy to a ten-year-old!

PAPER PLUS PEOPLE

There are two kinds of research: library study or reading, and "live" investigation, which covers dozens of ways in which you can learn more about customs, ideas and experiences. Countless books have been written about methods of doing research and it is not my intention here to burden you with numerous details. In any library, you will find a list of books to guide you further. You'll also find some suggestions in the Bibliography of this book.

You can read a letter reprinted in a biography or you can go to the source and see the letter for yourself. When you see the original manuscript, you can be certain of its accuracy.

You have to question what you might assume to be facts, and look further. You have to learn which historians are more objective and which write with bias. You must perceive whether a "debunking" is to achieve truth or to promote a writer's prejudices. This will become easier as you progress with your research.

As briefly and clearly as possible, I plan to list here the ways to start your research and the types of facilities you may explore. Take what you need and make note of the rest. Before you start, you will need to know how to record the information you find — methods which will be useful for any form of writing.

TAKING NOTES

Begin with the knowledge that you will take about eighty percent more notes than you can use for one article.

Begin with several notebooks, varying in size. Many professional writers use cards, but I consider it more orderly to keep my material in notebooks and a file, perhaps because I lose material that is not secured. You will need notebooks for the following:

Pocket-sized notebook in which to record your bibliography; that is, the titles and other information about the books, letters and other manuscripts that you read. Every source you consult should be recorded here. This includes books on your subject but which you found of no use to you, to avoid having to consult them again. Also use this notebook to record ideas, and other books and persons recommended to you as sources of information.

Large looseleaf notebook in which to keep sheets of 8½ x 11 notebook paper, on which you will record your notes from research. Use only one side of each page, in case you want to transfer notes on that page to another notebook or file folder.

I use index pages to divide this notebook into sections: dates, perhaps, or subjects. I also have cardboard slip pockets with punched holes in which to deposit travel folders, brochures and so on pertaining to the subject. Newspaper clippings may be placed here if you don't want to paste them on notebook pages. Bulky material, however, should be put in your file.

A file for beginners can be a shoebox manufactured for men's shoes, large enought to hold file folders. Any shoe store will give you several for the asking. A package of file folders and a cardboard ABC file divider will do fine for a start. If you prefer, you could buy a metal file for $4 -$10. I use both.

If you decide to take notes on *index cards,* you will need *a file box* of the proper size. The advantage of using cards is that you can shuffle them around more easily than you can notebook paper and so rearrange them in several kinds of order while you are writing. The disadvantage of cards is their small size which holds little information.

Another notetaking aid is the *tape recorder.* You need a recorder with a good hand microphone, a fast rewind speed both forward and back, a start-stop foot pedal. It should be operable both on battery and electricity. The foot pedal saves your temper when you are transcribing. For advice, go to a store whose clerks are knowledgeable or to another writer who uses a recorder.

Some of the ways you can use a recorder are: to read notes from books at home or when you can secure a nook in the library; to record documentary material from television; to record interviews; to take note of details of your observations while you are driving a car or visiting museums and other places.

Remember to state first where and what you are recording, and the date, whenever you are using the recorder.

When you have completed a tape, you either mark it for further reference and play it back when you need the information, or you transcribe the notes and use the tape over again. If there should be any question of authenticity in an interview, it is vital to keep the tape.

Whether you use notebooks, cards, a typewriter or a recorder, note taking technique is fundamentally the same. With a notebook, use a pen, for pencil sometimes smudges. When a library has alcoves for its use, a typewriter can be a boon. Make a carbon copy of your notes if you use the latter. Later the original can be placed in your file or notebook for permanent preservation, and the carbon can be cut up and the various subjects distributed to folders. Always include the *place* you find information, the *source* and *the date* in your notes.

RESEARCH READING

You have your idea, with its theme written in one sentence, and now you are ready to start your research. What do you need to know? Before you begin exploring the library, let's consider a method for reading and taking notes.

You have your book, your notebook or cards, and a pen. Open the book and read the preface, the introduction, table of contents, and the "blurb" on the jacket if there is one. This will give you a good idea of the author's purpose and the scope of his work. At the top of the first page of the notebook record the name of the library. Always put the date on your notes as a check for yourself and as proof for income tax records if you are claiming mileage and other deductions for your research. List the book's title, author, author's credentials (professor at, director of), publisher, city, date of publication. Note what type of illustrations and maps are used. Be sure to put down the library call number, so you can find the book again.

When you later record this book in your bibliography notebook, it is a good idea to include the call number and a key word to indicate which library the book is from. I've had trouble finding a book again when I've failed to do this and once went to three libraries before I found a book I needed.

Perhaps the list of illustrations will give you an idea of sources of photographs for your article. If so, copy it. You are groaning, for it is a long list. Don't overlook the greatest convenience a researcher can know: the photocopying machine. Most libraries have installed such a machine to be used by patrons. Those which have not, will be able to photocopy material on the office machine, at a slightly higher cost.

While you read, make note of material which you will want to photocopy before you leave. Probably the bibliography will be a good one for future reference. Perhaps there are some maps or illustrations you'll want to look at later. Make note of the pages.

Record the page number of the book beside your notations, for you must be able to identify the source if you use the material. Don't follow too closely the words of the author, but be exact in your summation of his ideas. What you are seeking is accurate information, not style. Knowing where to find what you need to know is more important than overcrowding your mind and notebook with too many details.

Watch the footnotes, for there may be a clue there more useful than the text itself. When you come across information that is vital, take fuller notes. If it is something you wish to quote exactly, and it is long, it can be photocopied. *Quotations must be copied exactly,* poor spelling and punctuation and all, and, of course, the source given. Writers alert readers to an error in the original from which they're quoting, by using the italicized word [*sic*] in brackets, directly after the mistake.

ORGANIZING MATERIAL

Sometimes you will be working on several projects at once and a method for organizing your material — notes, newspaper clippings, ideas — is essential.

Type the notes gathered during the day while they are fresh in your mind. I type with a carbon. If you like the idea of keeping current notes in a looseleaf notebook, type the original on notebook paper and use a yellow sheet for the carbon copy. Then you can file the original notes alphabetically by author or subject and cut the carbon sheet in sections, to file in other subject folders.

Try to sort your notes each day, classifying them, deciding on the sequence in your work. *Be sure each slip of a note has an identifying mark to show the original source.* Notes that cannot be classified at once, put in a "hold" folder or file under a general heading.

You may be able to paste several clippings of the same subject area on one sheet, with the subject title written at the top. This will prevent small slips of paper from getting lost.

You might choose to work by story sequence rather than by topic. Dates would be the important guideline and your notebook divided into calendar sequences, and your file folders numbered by dates.

The method is not important; knowing where to find your notes and knowing where those notes came from are the vital concerns. Occasionally, even after years of research experience, most historians lose track of a reference source. Sloppy care of your notes could mean a lot of re-reading and hours of searching which could have been avoided.

By the time you have found material in an encyclopedia and read some books, you should have an idea of how you wish to proceed with your material. It will be helpful if you make a tentative outline. An outline is a helpful tool to provide the writer with guidelines for his article or story, just as a pattern guides a dressmaker while she is making a suit.

Because of the current interest in this country about both Russia and heroes of the American Revolution, let us suppose you have decided to write an article on the subject of John Paul Jones and his association with Catherine the Great of Russia. Before thinking of a definite magazine for it or querying that editor, you might decide to cover the preliminary research like this:

1. A short resume of his previous experiences, which would entail reading a complete biography or two, covering more than just the section about his life in Russia.

2. What the man himself was like. To determine this, you'd watch for hints of characteristics, descriptions of his mannerisms, what he looked like, and so on.

3. You would need to know something of the times in which he lived, and you would jot down important dates, events during those times which concerned him, how he reacted to them, customs of the period, and the like.

4. You would need to know Catherine's background, something about Russian life, the status of the Russian Navy, and something about Russian history, customs, fashions and anything else which would help you to write knowledgeably.

5. Why did he decide to leave the American naval service?

6. Other material would unfold as you continue your research.

Because the emphasis would be on Jones and Catherine, your outline would give several paragraphs to previous experiences, most of the article to his Russian associations, and a brief bit of his life afterward. The outline helps you to explore what you need to find out, keeps you on the track, and ensures unity of your material. With the outline, you give yourself a guide for the rest of your study, to keep you from over-researching.

An outline should not be complicated. It is just a series of ideas or notes to yourself to keep you reminded of your goal, with space left between each section for recording references to help you find the details you require. Without a plan and a purpose, you tend to move in circles.

It is necessary to know a great deal about a subject if you are to be authoritative about a small part. Perhaps you will write only a few sentences based on notes which cover a dozen pages — but they will be sentences based on sure knowledge and judgment.

Remember that you can use the rest of this researched material on Jones and Catherine in other articles. In your study you will surely discover several other approaches to the various episodes in John Paul Jones' life. Some of them might be his experiences as a supervisor while his ship, the *Ranger,* was built in Kittery, Maine; the reasons he changed his name; the exciting mystery about his burial place; the account of his naval adventures in the American Navy. Most of this information you will have found – and barely mentioned.

How do you go about finding all this material? The next chapter will describe the many library sources which you, as a historian detective, will need to discover for yourself.

CHAPTER FOUR

LIBRARY RESEARCH

Allen Todd (author of *Finding Facts Fast*) says that a first-class research worker needs to combine the skills of four techniques: those of *a research librarian,* who knows where to find necessary material; *the university scholar,* who emphasizes thoroughness while finding new information or uncovering buried facts; *the investigative reporter,* who knows how to ask the right questions; and *the detective,* who imaginatively thinks through a research problem and then looks in the most promising places for his answers.

Librarians are a writer's best friends! I have never known a librarian who was not eager to help me find out what I needed to know. Go to the largest library near you and introduce yourself to the research librarian. Ask her to show you how to use reference materials, in addition to the catalogue with which you're probably already familiar.

Intelligent use of the library card catalogue is important. Some libraries have a separate subject catalogue, as well as the usual catalogues by title and author. If you have never used such a system, ask the librarian to explain its use, and how the library arranges its books.

Each library has its own way of marking the call number, the identifying number by which you ask for the books you wish. Most use the Dewey Decimal system to classify types of material, but some libraries now use the Library of Congress arrangement. This is why it is necessary to identify the library location of each book you list in your bibliography.

When you begin research, it saves work to go from the general to the particular. I try not to do research which has already been done for me.

Your first step, then, is to go to the reference section and look up "John Paul Jones" in the *Encyclopaedia Britannica* or the

Encyclopedia Americana. See what these books have to say about Catherine the Great, the history of the United States Navy during Jones' lifetime, about Russia in Catherine's time.

What you find here will give you the material for your outline.

Next, look up your subject in the card catalogue. For the Jones story, you would look under 'Jones, John Paul," "U.S. Navy, History of," "Catherine the Great," "Russia, History of," "American Revolution, Naval Battles." Each heading will lead to another. You would find the names of the ships Jones commanded and may wish to read something about them.

You make a list of the books available, with their call numbers, title and author, dates included in each book, and a brief description to tell you what each one covers.

In the reference section, you will find *The Reader's Guide to Periodical Literature,* mentioned previously. Look by subject in the volumes covering the last five years and see if anything has been published in magazines relating to your subject. List the magazines, title, author, date, page number.

Select from all the material you have noted three or four book titles, including at least one with a "j" in the call number. An abbreviation of juvenile — this will be a book written for children. I am a faithful reader of children's history books, both fiction and nonfiction. The language is simple, the facts are clear, the setting usually authentic.

Some libraries allow you to go into the rooms where the books are shelved. Look first at the directory of the library floors, which often is on a bulletin board in large libraries. Check the call numbers to locate your books. At the same time, see what other books are under the same call numbers; usually you will find other helpful material.

At those libraries where browsing in the book rooms is prohibited, you'll have to request your books at the desk, filling out the information on a card for each book.

If you use a library new to you, ask for a card. Neighboring towns will give you a library card and the use of the library for a year for a small sum, perhaps from $1 to $5. I found that I could take books on the history of my town from a nearby library, while my own library keeps these on reference shelves.

For background information you might decide to read a general history of the period in which you are doing research. You may find some books telling of customs of the period. Before you know it, you may get involved more deeply than you intended and love every moment of it. You might start thinking, *When I know more, I might write a children's book on The American Commodore and the Russian Empress.*

You will begin to see why you must keep all your notes, and start filing them in an orderly manner. No matter what the scope of your subject is, you follow the same pattern when you do research; for a longer article, you just do more of it. "In depth" is an appropriate term.

If you found some material on your subject was printed in a magazine or two during the past five years, read it. This will give you an idea of how much information can be used in an article, and it will add to your store of knowledge not only in research but in expertise. If nothing has been published you may have a fresh subject.

When taking notes from magazines and newspapers, be sure to record the name, date and pages.

REFERENCE BOOKS

You will need to learn as much as you can about the general reference books in your library. New ones are published every year. Sometimes a reference book will give you just what you need to know without further research. Reference sources in specialized fields can be invaluable in showing you where to look for detailed information.

Among the types of reference books to be found in a city library are indexes to magazines, newspapers, special subjects; encyclopedia for general information and in such subjects as world literature, art, music, sports; dictionaries not only for word meanings but for language use, the meaning of terms in various fields of interest, slang of past and present; almanacs for all kinds of miscellaneous information; biographical references including directories and many types of volumes like *Who's Who,* and listings of individual occupations and professions; publishers' book lists to be found in the *Cumulative Book Index, Books in Print,* and others under subject, title and author; atlases (maps) and gazeteers (places).

NEWSPAPER AND MAGAZINE SOURCES

If you really want to understand an era, dig into its newspapers! They are a vital history source, sparking story ideas and giving a flavor of the times in which they were published. Here you will find information often not available from any other source.

Some newspapers allow a reader to use the actual bound volumes of local newspapers. It is more likely that they will be on microfilm. It is easy to learn how to handle the machine after the librarian explains the technique.

Occasionally a newspaper will give its ancient collection of newspapers to a museum or historical society.

The American Antiquarian Society, Worcester, Massachusetts, has made excellent progress in its goal to secure a copy of every newspaper issue published before 1876. In 1974, it already had 1,496 of the 2,120 newspapers printed in the United States prior to 1821. Officials of the Society worry that historical societies and small-town newspapers might not realize the historical importance of newspaper preservation.

Suppose you need to know what type of hair-do was worn in the early 1900's. What better way to find out than to look at magazines of that date? This is an original source and can give you a wealth of material. Here you will find first-hand information about fads, fashions, foods, songs, architecture, vocabulary, literature and countless other items. The advertisements are as valuable as the articles, stories and pictures.

The Union List of Serials in Libraries of the United States will help you to locate the magazines you need. "Serials" means magazines. There are also indexes to periodicals of special interest subjects. For example, trade journals are indexed in the *Business Periodicals Index.*

Some periodicals have their own library, in addition to an indexed collection of past issues. More often, periodicals in modern times have their publications microfilmed and made available to many large public libraries. Regional magazines often have libraries of regional material, plus an enormous amount of resource material in their files.

TYPES OF LIBRARIES

Every state has its own library, its books giving prime emphasis to its history and culture. Some have museums in conjunction with the library, but often they are completely separate.

Your local library can borrow state non-circulating material for you to use in your own library. Less valuable material you can borrow yourself at the small cost of one-way postage.

Many private libraries were founded on collections made by individuals, later endowed or sponsored by a group of interested citizens. Among the most famous is the library of the American Antiquarian Society, Worcester, Massachusetts, mentioned earlier. In addition to its collections of newspapers before 1821, its half million manuscripts have proven a boon to innumerable researchers. It has the country's largest collections of early American fiction, children's books, almanacs, psalm and hymn books, cook books, city directories — and much more. For the historian interested in Americana, doing research there is like being in paradise!

There are many more like this throughout the country, each specializing in certain fields of interest, but having other material, also. You will find detailed information in the *Harvard Guide to American History.*

Policies differ among college and university libraries. Those who live near are sometimes welcome to use the university library facilities. When you live out of state, you may be allowed to use reference books and read in the library, but not to borrow books. You may be allowed to have material photocopied for a small sum. Your local library might be able to borrow books for you on inter-library loan, except for those in the Rare Books section.

Boston University, for example, invites the public to visit its Zion Research Library, which has a free booklending service for material related to the field of religion and Biblical history.

Most university libraries have a wealth of historical material relating to their own states.

It would be impossible to list here all the groups which maintain a library pertaining to a particular field. In New York City alone there are over a thousand special libraries. Prominent in this category are industrial firms, some of which have both a specialized library and a museum. Others have a library plus a public relations department which gives historical information about its own firm to writers. A great many also publish a house organ or magazine and issue pamphlets. The Federal Government publishes *Plant Tours,* a geographical list of firms which welcome visitors to their plants.

The National Association of Manufacturers, 277 Park Avenue, New York, New York 10017, can assist inquirers looking for information about industry and business.

There are banks which not only have displays pertaining to the history of finance, but sometimes encourage the study of Americana and art, and maintain libraries and publish pamphlets. One of these is the Federal Reserve Bank of Boston's Research Library, 30 Pearl Street, Boston 02106, whose manuscripts, maps and other holdings emphasize New England economy and finance.

The national offices of many religious denominations have libraries relating to church history.

Examples of the wide range of special libraries are the Folger Library in Washington, D.C., which has a Shakespeare collection unsurpassed anywhere in the world, and more than half the known books printed in the English language up to 1641; the library of the Hispanic Society of America, Broadway, between 155th and 156th Streets, New York City, which is an important center for research on Spanish and Portuguese culture; the Huntington Library in California, which has a large collection of early Americana, with emphasis on the American West; the Presidential libraries, each emphasizing a specific era of American politics and culture.

When you need bibliographies and specific information about the circus, agriculture, medicine, law, stamps, fashion, art or just about anything, there is almost certain to be an association to help you. The names and addresses of many of them are listed in the *World Almanac and Book of Facts,* the *Information Please Almanac* or other similar annual publications. One of the most comprehensive sources is the *Encyclopedia of Associations*. The public library reference room will have these and other sources.

Most writers of history, especially those working with biography, find it necessary to trace family trees. In addition to the genealogical information which you will find in state historical society registers, archives, individual family genealogies to be found in many libraries, information in other books, and similar sources, there are a few libraries which specialize in this field.

The one whose librarians have been cordially helpful to me is the New England Historic Genealogical Society, 101 Newbury Street, Boston, Massachusetts 02116. Going directly to the offices of your nearest genealogical society will open up to you many other sources. Usually only members are allowed to visit the book shelves, but congenial and helpful librarians are there to bring material to your desk.

The Genealogical Society of the Church of Jesus Christ of Latter-Day Saints, Inc., 107 South Main Street, Salt Lake City, Utah 84111, has earned for its genealogical library the title of "the genealogical treasure house of the world." Although a private collection of the Church, the library and its research facilities are available to the public without regard to race or religious affiliation. The Archives include over seven million alphabetized family group records from the United States and foreign countries. Its holdings are not limited to statistics of its church members. Copy service is available. Mail inquires will be answered. There is a charge for detailed research, but all are welcome to use the Temple Index Bureau files (these cover most geographical areas, nationalities and periods of time) — and to use the library's other resources.

The historian must be aware of the offerings of libraries, museums, historical sites and many other facilities to be found in countries all around the world. Most public libraries in the United States have a copy of the two-volume set *The World of Learning*, which lists the major educational institutions around the world, and also includes a brief description of the subject holdings of their libraries, museums, and so on. Opportunities are especially available to us in neighboring Canada. Moreover, the Canadian government is making a splendid effort to bring its literature to the universities of the United States, by offering a variety of publications and books to help us become acquainted with Canadian history.

OTHER RESEARCH SOURCES

In addition to the many types of libraries given here, there are numerous other research sources available to you. You will find some on your own to augment the information listed:

Historical Societies: Every state has a historical society, and on the local level the number is increasing each year. While there is little uniformity about them, most have a library or reference room and many issue publications.

State historical societies often maintain art galleries and impressive picture collections.

A membership list may be obtained from the American Association for State and Local History, Nashville, Tennessee 37203. The cost of the 1974 edition is $10, less to members.

Many local historical societies often hold such treasures as letters, journals, ship logs, store accounts and other items gathered from attics and lavender-scented boxes. Your town historical society may be the most helpful of all sources on local subjects.

You may find groups of amateur historians with particular hobbies have organized clubs of their own. Such a one is the Piscataqua History Club of Portsmouth, New Hampshire, which maintains a library devoted mainly to the history of the sea, but with other local and state material.

Some groups of this type also maintain one or two historic buildings open to the public.

Begun in this fashion, but so well established and professional through the years that its library and genealogical material are regarded with great respect, is the National Congress of the Daughters of the American Revolution, with headquarters in Washington. The Sons of the American Revolution maintain beautiful Fraunces Tavern in New York City, more a museum than a library.

Professional Organizations: To find the best-informed people in the field you are studying, turn to the professional groups, many of which maintain libraries. The American Medical Association, 535 North Dearborn Street, Chicago, Illinois 60610, is the chief source for information about health. The American Historical Association, 400 A Street S.E., Washington, D.C. 20003, publishes a catalogue and its dues include an excellent magazine. Refer again to an almanac for a list of professional organizations. Look under subject rather than the official name.

Public Relations Offices: There are numerous men and women in the public relations field, in business, industry and professional organizations, and as separate firms, which specialize in providing a "public image" for companies and individuals. They are eager to help writers if it will mean favorable publicity for their clients or employers.

Most manufacturers and large business firms have public relations offices. Almost all nonprofit organizations have public relations departments willing to help writers with historical material.

The Chamber of Commerce of the United States, 1615 H Street N.W., Washington, D.C. 20006, offers information in the field of economics and will assist writers with their research, supply some photographs and check manuscripts. The Chamber will also help a writer to find sources of information not directly related to its own interests.

Do you want to know something about the history of spices? Find a firm which packages spices and write to the public relations director.

State and local chambers of commerce, and state development and parks commissions have historical material and can often supply photographs.

It is your job to sift the genuine information from the exaggerated information received from public relation representatives, who might over-sell their product, company or town. Sometimes free photographs will have people in out-of-date fashions or an automobile of ten years back. Be alert to this.

Government: Our own government has many aids to help us in research, and it is ready to assist us free of charge. The United States Library of Congress will answer questions and direct you to sources. Don't be surprised to receive answers from more than one department. The Library will send you lists of its holdings in a particular field upon request. Its *National Union Catalog of Manuscript Collections* will help you to locate information about people and their personal papers.

Such reference information should be sought — only after you have exhausted your local resources — from the General Reference and Bibliographical Division, Library of Congress, Washington, D.C. 20540.

The National Archives and Records Service, Pennsylvania Avenue at 8th Street N.W., Washington, D.C. 20408, is the repository for official records of the Government, including treaties, proclamations, laws, war records, and many private papers. You may do research there and will find information about official affairs of government beginning with the founding of Jamestown, Virginia, in 1607. Photocopying service is available and could be helpful if you know exactly what you are looking for.

The Army Medical Library has the greatest collection of books in the world on the history of medicine and public health.

Military records are not always deposited in government archives. A roster of Colonel Benedict Arnold's army when it was encamped at Point-aux-Trembles, Quebec in 1775 was found in 1972 by Aldrich Edwards II in the archives at Yale University. However, each branch of the armed services has material available in its field. For instance, the Coast Guard can provide a great deal of information if you are doing an article on lighthouses. The Naval Academy at Annapolis, Maryland, has a vast amount of material on naval history, including the letters of John Paul Jones.

For statistics on farming write the Department of Agriculture. If you need information on national parks or historic sites, write the National Park Service. Address your inquiry to Public Information Officer. Some government departments have regional offices.

For a comprehensive listing of government agencies, the *U.S. Government Organization Manual* is available from the Superintendent of Documents, U.S. Government Printing Office, Washington, D.C. 20402. (The 1974-1975 edition was $5.75)

The Smithsonian Institution, with national headquarters in Washington, embraces many divisions, such as archives, libraries, museums, special sources. If you cannot visit its amazing buildings, send for a brochure to see what is offered. The Institution is the largest museum-gallery establishment in the world, and includes historical, scientific and cultural information on such a vast scale that it would take years to cover it all — and by then its collections might be doubled. It operates major facilities around the country and overseas.

A useful reference is *A Directory of Information Resources in the United States,* which gives government-sponsored information resources and information resources of the Federal government. You can order this from the Superintendent of Documents for $2.75.

The United States Government Printing Office, Public Documents Department, Washington, D.C. 20402, has hundreds of books and pamphlets for sale at small cost. Using its facilities can help you build up a good reference library for a minimum investment. Write to the Superintendent of Documents and ask to be put on the mailing list. Ask for a list of material available in American History or any other subject that interests you. Your request will be sent to the area office nearest you. Perhaps you will be able to visit a government book store near you to see some of the 35,000 or more titles printed.

State, County and Local Sources: Just as the Federal government offers all types of information to the public, so the departments within each state can help to answer questions within their scope. Address the appropriate department at the state capitol building, or ask your state representative or senator to help you. Some departments have county offices.

County records are an index to the state's past. You will have an interesting time if you visit the county seat to search old records in the Registry of Deeds, usually kept at the court house. By looking up a will written in the 1700's, I was able to find out when a person died. In county records you can learn when a town was settled and by whom, when its name was changed, population figures, and many other bits of information.

Your own town or city records, especially the annual reports, reveal much of a place's history. Old reports will have births and deaths, perhaps lists of teachers, town officials, reports of schools and other town business. Town libraries often have a complete file of local annual reports. The local cemetery office should have a file of burial information. Frequently, churches keep such records.

Vocabulary Sources: To get the aura of speech in a certain period, read documents and literature of the same dates, study orations and sermons, read historical fiction. (But never use fiction to establish facts.)

Study the *Dictionary of American Slang* or the *Dictionary of Slang and Unconventional English* and *Black English,* compiled by linguist J. L. Dillard of the University of Puerto Rico.

Reading plays of the proper era is also an excellent way to establish the flavor of the times.

Perhaps the best way of all is to read diaries, journals and letters, many of which are available in printed form.

Manuscript Collections: A great majority of existing materials about American history are in manuscript form and may be the historical writer's greatest boon. Many libraries and museums, both public and private, have valuable collections of manuscripts, including letters, ship log books, land sales records, military field reports, church records, journals, diaries, account books of stores and professional people, and other personal data which have been donated by those who originated them or by family or by other owners. Sometimes they are bought from the owner or at auctions. Today literary auctions are big business, as you have noticed in news reports.

Often an institution specializes in the original manuscripts it collects. For example, the Houghton Library at Harvard University has most of the manuscripts and letters of New England writers of the nineteenth century. The Huntington Library, San Marino, California, emphasizes the history of the seventeenth and eighteenth century. The Peabody Museum, Salem, Massachusetts, is known for its marine history collections. Each state and university library, of course, stresses its own history and literature in addition to other specialties.

Next to the Library of Congress, the Massachusetts Historical Society has the most important collection of American manuscripts, including the Adams and Jefferson papers.

The Library of Congress, state and historical society libraries, and others, are suffering from a change in the law, which previously allowed donors of this material to receive a tax benefit. A law passed in 1969 has seriously eliminated the flow of historical documents, except for those donated in a spirit of generosity. This situation is particularly true of papers gathered by officials or former officials. Lay people are still likely, however, to donate their family papers to the local or state library, to their college or historical society. Writers are especially generous in this regard.

What is needed are new laws which state that official papers belong to the public and not to the office holding them. A pending Federal Court case involving the requisition of former President Nixon's White House tape recordings is one example of this need.

Because literary thieves have stolen irreplaceable letters and other materials (even from the Library of Congress), current researchers are having a harder time securing original material to examine, and must be content with a copy or even a microfilm. Such material is always used in the library. Photocopies will usually be made upon request for home use, except of the very old manuscripts which are too delicate to be handled in this way, and which are always provided by copy or film.

The true researcher prefers to go to the original source, to see for himself the manuscripts of the times. Next best are photocopies or printed reproductions of the material. It is all too easy for inaccuracies to become "fact" in print, or in transcripts of original material. Careless transcribers — and even well-intentioned ones — can make mistakes which may change the meaning or a name.

I have found it helpful, for example, to refer from an eighteenth-century letter to an available transcript, since penmanship of early times is difficult to decipher because of the use of a type of f for s, the frequent use of a form of ampersand for *and,* and unusual spelling. Sometimes words and names in a transcript have been proved incorrect when compared with the original. The only sure way is to learn to recognize peculiarities! *The Harvard Guide to American History* has an excellent section on this skill.

To locate personal papers, consult the records of more than one library. There may be published or typed lists or records in a library card file. Sometimes manuscripts will be in scrapbooks or file folders known only to the librarian.

There are several guides to help you find manuscripts. One is the *National Union Catalog of Manuscript Collections,* published by the Library of Congress, already mentioned. Some state or state historical society libraries have listings of manuscripts from all local groups in the state.

We can thank early historians who realized the value of manuscripts and saved them, and wish that more individuals understood today the importance of preserving personal papers. My great grandmother burned all my Uncle Will's letters from the Civil War, because she considered them "personal."

Jared Sparks, a pioneer in American historical research, discovered two trunks filled with Benjamin Franklin's letters in a Pennsylvania attic, and another lot on a shelf in a London tailor's shop. Imagine the loss to historians of the American Revolutionary period if they had not been found. These and the letters of many other people important in our history have been published.

We are also indebted to the written accounts of soldiers and little-known private citizens for some of the most accurate, firsthand information of the past. You will find bibliographical material of available diaries and other personal records, printed or still in manuscript form, in the reference room.

Store and business account books give a picture of the economic situation of the time. A shipping book which I found at the Brick Store Museum library, Kennebunk, Maine, gave me important information about the work of two men I'd been researching. Notations in one log book gave us the clue as to why a merchant committed suicide. He and the captain had arranged a signal to bring word of the success or failure of the venture, but the captain died. Watching his ship sail into the harbor and not seeing a signal, the merchant killed himself. The mate didn't know about the arrangement, so the merchant falsely concluded that the project was a failure, and that he was ruined.

Family letters are to be found in many an attic, and the writer is truly a detective when he endeavors to find them. Character, customs, vocabulary, history — there is no end to the amount of information to be learned through these personal manuscripts.

The thrill of discovering manuscripts which bring you closer to the past is indescribable!

Weather Resources: In spite of the many jokes made about the weather, to the historian this subject is one of vital concern. It is important to know accurate weather conditions if actual dates are given either in fiction or nonfiction.

The weather, day by day, was of great consequence in the story of Henry Knox on the trek from Fort Ticonderoga. One of my heroes, young Sam, watched the burning of Washington in 1814 while a thunderstorm raged in the dark of night. Considerable research has been done to pinpoint weather conditions before, during and after the Battle of Trenton.

Changes of climate and the incidence of weather conditions have influenced the course of history. For example, General Howe's plan to attack George Washington's army near Boston was defeated by a severe storm, gave Washington time to mount defenses on Dorchester Heights and brought about the evacuation of Boston by the British.

The Ice Age impelled migration. Remember the tragedies of the Dust Bowl. In Biblical times, Joseph's elevation to high office in Egypt was influenced by years of drought.

The modern historian realizes the importance of physical factors, especially of climate or earthquake, as an influence in some of the great events of history.

The United States Government kept no complete records of weather history until the Weather Bureau was established in the Department of Agriculture in 1890. In 1940, this responsibility was transferred to the Department of Commerce.

How do historians and scientists learn about weather conditions of the past? Prof. A.E. Douglass of the University of Arizona in the early 1900's discovered that the thickness of the rings of annual growth in old trees of the forests on the Arizona plateaus were proportional to the amount of rainfall. He was able to carry such records back to A.D. 11. Through the study of glaciers and other forms of geology, scientists have been able to trace broad weather patterns and the greater forces of other forms of nature.

Such records are helpful in the broad scope of meteorological history, but the writer of history has to be able to pinpoint weather conditions closely — or to avoid mention of them entirely if they cannot be determined. This is not such a hopeless task as it seems, for through the years men have always been interested in the weather and numerous manuscripts have been uncovered which can help us.

The American Meteorological Society, 45 Beacon Street, Boston, has published four fascinating and helpful volumes, written by David Ludlum: *Early American Winters* I - 1604-1820; *Early American Winters* II 1821-1870; *Early American Hurricanes* 1491-1870; and *Early American Tornadoes* 1586-1870. (There will be more.)

Information about the weather of any period will be welcomed by the Historian of the American Meteorological Society. If you find a little-known letter or manuscript mentioning weather, make a photocopy for him, and you may be adding to the weather knowledge of the past.

Never "invent" weather conditions for convenience when you are writing factual material. Whenever a specific date is mentioned, the weather on that day must be reported accurately or not at all. This is true even if you are writing fiction without its being historical. Should you say that on September 27, 1938, it was a sunny day, you had better be sure it was sunny in the setting you have chosen.

Does this seem a lot of to-do about nothing? If accuracy is to be your goal as a writer, the reporting of the weather is just as important as the correct spelling of names. It could very well be your bad luck to have your story fall into the hands of a reader whose wedding day was September 27, 1938 — and whose reception was interrupted by the hurricane which occurred that day!

Microfilm Sources: While using microfilm is not the easiest way to gather information, it may be the only accurate way to see the original material. When a microfilm reproduction of a manuscript, newspaper, periodical or book is the only source available, you must use it with a machine, and this is often hard on the eyes. It is a necessary method of preserving brittle, ancient and valuable material.

The greatest drawback is that you must go to the library source, unless you know exactly the date and page of the newspaper you need copied, or the correct name of the manuscript or book you are seeking. A one-page copy of a microfilm costs about 10¢.

I have had a whole book reproduced in a paper facsimile when it was the only way I could read it. The cost was $22.

You may order a microfilm copy made at the source for use with a microfilm reader, but there may be occasions when it will be worth the extra cost to have the paper facsimile made. This is especially so when you need a manuscript or volume for detailed study.

Librarians can secure microfilm of almost any microfilmed research material for use in the local library on interlibrary loan.

Consult the *Directory of Microfilm Services in the United States and Canada,* published by the Special Libraries Association, 235 Park Avenue, South, New York 10003.

An invention is pending which will simplify the use of microfilm. It is a portable reader slightly larger than a cassette recorder, with which the student could read microfilm in the comfort of his home, taking the film home from the library just as he would take books.

To find the proper sources for research is not always easy. It is often a challenge to your ingenuity.

You can see that a beginning historian will find plenty of work as a detective!

CHAPTER FIVE

THE HISTORIAN AS EXPLORER: MUSEUMS AND PLACES

While library resources are the backbone of historical research, the personal touch is what makes your work unique. This means that you must consult "living history" sources, see for yourself the places about which you write whenever possible, talk with those who "remember when," steep yourself in the atmosphere of the past, be it immediate or long ago, put yourself in the shoes and on the footpaths of those about whom you write.

When you are writing about the places and people you know, this will be easy. You will visit the nearby historic buildings or the house where the town's hero was born or the site where Indians ambushed a family on its way home from church. Likely it will look quite different now; yet there will be a flavor about it that will shine out of this personal experience onto the typewritten pages.

This part of your learning to be a writer of history we may call "exploration." For many of you this will be more satisfying than pondering over books and manuscripts. If so, this will help you decide just what kind of historical writer you want to be. Many freelance writers write only of their explorations and personal involvement among reminders of the past.

Of one fact you may be certain: This on-the-spot research will stimulate your imagination and give authenticity to your writing.

Arnold Toynbee said that travel was always important in his life as a historian and should be a goal for all historians. It certainly is an important part of the research of writers like the world's foremost naval historian, Samuel Eliot Morison. Believing in seeing for himself the places about which he writes, he retraced by plane and motor launch the 40,000-mile route traveled more than 400 years ago by Magellan and his crew. He knew that this effort would give authenticity to his book, *The Discovery of America: the Southern Voyages.* No wonder the Morison books are so lively!

Try to visit the locale of your story — absorb its scenes, its sounds, its smells. Dispel the modern concepts from your thoughts and try to see it as it used to be: the noisy waterfront of the eighteenth century against the present industrial scene. Remember the ships and the bustling wharves described in the books you've read about this place. Do this, even if you have driven only ten miles.

If you are like me, after this imaginative research, you'll find yourself going back into the past almost every time you are driving by. When I cross the bridge over a winding estuary, I see not the macadam road on which I'm driving, but a narrow rutted road, and on the little river beyond, a boat with a young girl in it — though Sally lived two centuries ago, she and her surroundings *then* are very real to me *now*.

When we speak of travel, however, we usually mean going a distance from home. We mean carrying a notebook with many questions in it, derived from our study, to be answered along the way. We mean keeping a tax record of mileage, costs and places. We mean carrying two cameras, one for black and white pictures, one for color slides, and a small notebook in which to record the situation in which each photograph was taken. We mean making room for a box in which we have folders and notes and maps and lists which have come from state or travel information offices, chambers of commerce, and our research.

Every professional traveling writer is equipped like this. The number who carry a tape recorder is growing.

MAPS AND CHARTS

There's something fascinating about maps! They are a guide for the traveler — a catalyst for nomadic dreamers.

Knowing map or chart resources is a necessity if the historian is to have an authentic recall of a geographic area.

My preliminary research for the writing of *Young Sam and the Battle of Baltimore* included study of the terrain of Baltimore as it was during the War of 1812. I felt I must know the battle plans, the local roads, the surrounding waters, the length of the river, the width of the bay, streets in the city and other details.

Preparation for a Revolutionary War teenage novel I'm currently researching includes the making of a detailed map of the whole surrounding country, including street names as they were in 1776, and accurate mileages.

Maps and charts will graphically portray for you the growth and culture of a people, the routes of explorations, boundaries, the changing of world geography, a country's expansion or losses. Without maps we would find it hard to understand history, even though misinformation is sometimes perpetuated in map making, and the extension or cutting down of boundary lines keep cartographers busy.

Our National Archives have more than 1,550,000 maps. The American Antiquarian Society has many rare maps among its 11,000. You will find collections which specialize, like those of special-interest libraries. The American Geographical Society in New York City has prepared a catalogue of maps of Hispanic America and can help inquirers in other fields.

Nautical and aeronautical charts, maps of rivers, topographic maps and many other varieties of maps and charts are prepared by the federal government. There are map depositories in most of the institutions already discussed.

Regional, national, federal and world map guides found in the library reference room, will simplify your research.

MUSEUMS

What should the writer of history look for when he travels?

People are more interested in museums than they used to be, now that directors have become more aware of the importance of linking the facts of the past with the living present, and are developing imaginative, lively programs to help the public to appreciate its heritage.

There are about 6,000 museums in the United States, and more than half of them are devoted to history. Annual attendance will soon go beyond the current 700,000,000 visitors.

Most good-sized museums offer more than exhibits. They schedule films, musicals, period fashion shows and similar special programs to help visitors to relate to the history of their town or state.

Perhaps one objective of a trip will be to visit museums which can provide information about your subject. More often, when you travel with your family, your exploration will not be so carefully directed, and you'll have to see what the museums you visit can provide.

The Du Sable Museum of African-American History, Chicago, can help with the study of Black History. Toys of early American children will be found at the Antique Toy Museum in Philadelphia.

There are so many marine museums that a special catalogue is published. Old ships are becoming "floating museums" in increasing numbers. Indian life is depicted in a number of Western museums, one of which is maintained by the town of Sante Fe, New Mexico. Among the Halls of Fame are the Baseball Hall near the Farmers' Museum in Cooperstown, New York, and the Cowboy Hall in Oklahoma City, Oklahoma. Whaling is emphasized at the Sag Harbor Museum on Long Island, New York.

While the West Point Museum at the United States Military Academy is the largest and best known of the Army historical museums, it is only one of seventy-two under the auspices of the Chief of Military History in Washington. Some Army posts have their own museum.

Museums sometimes are found in towns famous for products which are manufactured there, like the Corning Glass Works in New York State.

At historic sites there is often a museum, like the American Museum of Immigration in the base of the Statue of Liberty, with some 200 exhibits and dioramas focusing on the flow of foreigners to the United States, beginning in the 1820's.

It is a good idea to begin your exploration of a museum by watching the short lecture and slide film presentation, describing the battle or event, to be found at a large number of museums and historic sites. The briefing at the museum at Washington's Crossing, Pennsylvania, is especially interesting to the historian.

Sometimes the museum is arranged in a series of displays outdoors, like the logging museum at Eureka, California, the National Hall of Fame for American Indians at Anadarko, Oklahoma, the Iron Works at Saugus, Massachusetts, and a number of railroad and trolley museums. The student of Civil War history can learn a great deal at Gettysburg, while American Revolution devotees will follow with delight the trails at Yorktown, Virginia.

Usually museums will have such aids as pamphlets, booklets, maps, postcards and other items for sale. Keep track of your costs for income tax purposes. From the museum library you may order copies of manuscripts and other material, to be paid for in advance and mailed to you.

You will find museums devoted to almost every subject. A list may be obtained from the American Association of Museums, 2233 Wisconsin Avenue, N.W., Washington, D.C. 20007.

Period fashions should not be overlooked. Peter Howe, in his column "Here's How," published July 7, 1972, in the *Boston Sunday Herald-Sunday Advertiser,* points out that historic events affect women's styles. He says that any great change in world affairs is usually followed by dramatic changes in style.

Copies of portraits, pictures, prints and etchings may be available, to help you recreate scenes and fashions. Watch diligently while you read to find picture sources.

Furniture and house decorations, sometimes regional, sometimes national in scope, may often be found in a special section of large museums, like the American Wing of the Metropolitan Museum of Art in New York City.

Still closer to living history are the houses and buildings carefully preserved by those who care so that future generations may know how people of the past lived. Having visited the homes of Thomas Jefferson, George Washington, Clara Barton and other historic figures, who would not feel closer to them, seeing them as real people rather than awesome names in history?

The Association for the Preservation of Virginia Antiquities, the National Trust for Historic Preservation, the Society for the Preservation of New England Antiquities have counterparts everywhere.

Such houses and their contents throw light on the popular taste of a period and enable us to learn about standards of living, manufacturing techniques, trade and skills. They provide us with the vicarious experience of the life of individuals and their time.

Individuals, societies, organizations, universities, towns, help to preserve the past. Historic preservation districts are springing up, aided by state and national government. In Paris, Kentucky, Daughters of the American Revolution lovingly care for the Duncan House. Mark Twain's study is on the campus of Elmira College in New York. The grand home of Albert Gallatin, treasurer of the United States under Jefferson, is opened by its owner for a fee, in New Geneva, Pennsylvania. Old missions are kept in condition by the Catholic Church. The Adams Homestead in Quincy, Massachusetts, houses the library of John Adams and is a national historic site.

LIVING HISTORY AT NATIONAL PARKS AND MONUMENTS

Living history demonstrations of various periods of American history are sponsored by the National Park Service. These help the writer to see for himself the crafts and trades of other times. Some show how a single craft or skill is done, while others show life at a frontier trading post or on a long-ago farm. These are often similar to a restoration village, but on a smaller scale.

One of the loveliest I have seen is the working Colonial farm at the George Washington Birthplace National Monument on the Virginia History Trail, about thirty miles east of Fredericksburg. Depicting the industrial skills of the early nineteenth century is the national historic site at Hopewell Village in Pennsylvania. Run as a real ranch — working cattle, baking bread, grinding corn and all — is the Pipe Spring National Monument in Utah.

The booklet, *Living History in the National Park System,* is available from the Government Printing Office. Travel guide books can be very useful in finding such projects.

OTHER RESOURCES

Towns and Landmarks: For authentic background for a story, "Young Sam and the Battle of Baltimore," published as a four-part magazine serial, I went three times to that city. Your setting will be much more believable if you can explore the town where your story takes place.

Find newspapers published in the era you are researching. Learn the names of restaurants, inns, hotels, amusements, shops and so on by looking at the advertisements. Note their location.

Hopefully, the local historical society, newspaper office, library or town office can be of help in locating old newspapers. Be sure you have a list of the items for which you need answers. Perhaps you will want to write for information before you visit the community; this would save time, and put you directly in touch with the best source.

Take both black and white photographs and colored slides; you'll regret it if you do not. Your color film must be slides; editors accept only transparencies – not color prints.

The recognition of historic landmarks is increasing all the time; they vary widely in type and historical period. Be alert for inscribed boulders, signs and other clues which might lead you to an unusual and little-known story.

Cemeteries and Churches: Another source of information is the old cemetery, with its crumbling, lichen-covered stones, and its air of mystery and serenity. Those doing genealogical study secure considerable assistance from cemetery and church records.

The Daughters of the American Revolution have performed a valuable service in making available lists of the Revolutionary military personnel, often with clues originally furnished by old gravestones.

Seeing for yourself the grave of your biographical subject, and noting the dates and the names of relatives on nearby stones, is to achieve almost complete authenticity. I say "almost" because it is possible, if improbable, that remains could be removed from beneath a gravestone and reburied elsewhere. One of my story subjects, "Sally's" husband, for example, was buried in York, but his name is on her gravestone in Kennebunk.

Church memorials and records are a similar type of source. When you visit churches, look for wall plaques and other evidences of the past which may give you a clue to the names you are seeking. Church membership lists and other church documents like those issued for marriage bans and for funerals may give you other clues.

Historic Trails, Rivers and Canals: Following the towpaths or water routes of active or restored canals can be an adventurous way to learn local history. The history of the canal is an important part of our transportation lore. Many men went broke, and a few got rich, while backing this system of connecting existing waterways with artificial canals. Canada, Michigan, Ohio, New York, Maine and the District of Columbia are only a few of the areas which have interesting opportunities for exploration.

Think of the courageous explorers whose ships have followed rivers: John Smith, Champlain, Lewis and Clark and numerous others. Think of the nostalgia of the Swanee River, the Mississippi, the Columbia in our history.

While I was researching the life of Henry Knox, my husband and I followed the Knox trail from Boston to New York State, stopping at each commemorative boulder along the way. Without this personal exploration, I could never have truly understood Henry Knox's ordeal, when he brought artillery from Fort Ticonderoga through deep snow and over tremendous hills to Boston.

Following such trails is not a new idea. Francis Parkman did it in *The Oregon Trail,* and other historians have followed the progress of Lewis and Clark, and other explorers.

Some states, especially in the West and Midwest, have made it easy for us by issuing maps with trails carefully described.

Historic Sites: Forts and battlefield sites, lighthouses and places commemorating important events in a community are preserved everywhere you go.

Fort Necessity, south of Uniontown, Pennsylvania, is a reproduction of the fortification erected in the French and Indian Wars under the direction of a young George Washington. Some forts like Fort Kaskaskia, Illinois, and Fort Boonesboro, Kentucky, are absorbed in local, state or national parks.

Typical of many areas are the commemorative plaques marking the long-gone birthplace of Benjamin Franklin, and the site of the Boston Massacre.

Lighthouses, always a favorite historical topic, have lost much of their aura of adventure with the coming of automatic, unmanned beacons. Lighthouses continue to attract people to seacoast towns, however, and Edward Rowe Snow of Marshfield, Massachusetts, continues to sell large numbers of his books about lighthouses, shipwrecks and ocean adventure out of New England ports. Rose Labrie of Portsmouth, New Hampshire, has sold more than 10,000 copies of her self-published booklets on the lighthouses of Nubble Point, York, and Pemaquid, located in Maine.

Restoration Villages: Your appreciation of ancient crafts and skills may first be aroused when you go with your family to see such places as Old Mystic Seaport in Connecticut or Westville, the re-creation of a Georgian village of 1850. The more than 125 such villages are either restored buildings already in place or reproduced by bringing together buildings and artifacts of similar periods and of historical importance, and often featuring artisans skilled in crafts of the period. These are listed in *Directory of Historical Societies and Agencies* published by the American Association for State and Local History.

Delightful in themselves for the atmosphere and charm generated by evidence of a past era, they can also be a magnificent source of information. I have watched oxen being trained at Old Sturbridge and learned how Colonial women dyed cloth at Strawbery Banke and how an eighteenth century man would fashion a broom for his wife at the Farmers' Museum in Cooperstown.

Whether you explore a Victorian house in Portland or walk through the gaslit Latin Quarter in New Orleans or watch artisans blowing glass at Jamestown or visit a gold mine in Lead, South Dakota, you are participating. Nonfiction writing requires this aura of reality just as much as fiction.

Pageants, Dramas, Musicals: You can journey back in time by seeing annual or occasional historical presentations in towns across the country, and abroad.

"The Stephen Foster Story" immortalizes this poet-composer's work in a musical drama written by Paul Green, Pulitzer Prize-winning playwright, and presented each summer at Federal Hill, Bardstown, Kentucky — known as "My Old Kentucky Home."

Kate Douglas Wiggin *(Rebecca of Sunnybrook Farm)* is remembered each summer by the regionally-loved "Old Peabody Pew," re-enacted for two days in August at its church site in Buxton, Maine.

"Unto These Hills," an exciting drama of the Cherokee Indian Nation, is shown nightly from June through August at Cherokee, North Carolina. Every summer at Williamsburg, Paul Green's "The Common Glory" portrays the drama of the American Revolution. Each evening throughout the summer and fall seasons "The Shepherd of the Hills" is played in Branson, Missouri, bringing to life Harold Bell Wright's classic story of the Ozarks.

Similar vacation experiences will be found in nearly every state.

Safaris and Such: There are countless synthetic, commercial developments which can provide an aura of the past, a taste of reality, so long as you remember these are tourist attractions and often not completely authentic.

I knew Old Tucson, and Virginia City, Nevada, were glamorized for tourists — yet I could see Wyatt Earp and Doc Holiday cantering along the dusty Arizona road, and watched over Sam Clemens' shoulder while he worked on the Nevada newspaper and wrote *Roughing It.*

Yes, we must cultivate imagination to live vicariously in the past, perhaps even cultivate the simplicity of a child to winnow out the true from the brassy make-believe.

CHAPTER SIX

EXPLORING THROUGH PERSONAL INVOLVEMENT

Personal exploration which will enable a writer to speak with authority can be enjoyable. Elizabeth Yates spent many days in a rural school to obtain background for *Nearby*. She took her knitting and sat quietly listening and observing, until the children forgot she was there.

Loula Grace Erdman had to know how a young woman would feel when she fired a gun for the first time, for her book *Far Journey*. She went to a shooting gallery, she relates, and succeeded in "frightening the living daylights out of the young attendant;" but she *did* experience the feeling she needed. Another time she built a fire of cow chips on the prairie, so she would know the shape and texture as well as the smell of them as they burned. On that trip of exploration she checked terrain, judged distances and, back home, spread out maps and made drawings to scale. When a small prairie fire was in progress, she jumped in her car and saw for herself "the licking flames and the rush of the wild things rushing for safety."

When you make candles as a Colonial woman would or learn other required information by personal involvement, you will not only be more convincing and accurate in your writing, but your life will be enriched as well.

An Environmental Living Program inaugurated by the National Park Service in 1969 is a literal "live-in" experience for young historians and their teachers. Adults can find similar opportunities.

At an ancient *heiau* or temple on the island of Hawaii, at the Arizona Tubac Presidio school of 1850's at Tumacacore National Monument, at the John Muir Historic Site and two other sites in California — the ELP idea is spreading and students are reading their history books with new appreciation and understanding.

The coordinator encourages interested groups to contact him for information at the Bolton Institute, 1835 K Street N.W., Suite 302, Washington, D.C. 20006.

Adults are offered many opportunities by the National Park Service, restoration villages and other historical preservations for work experiences in old-time farming, crafts and similar demonstration programs.

. You may also enjoy your own type of "live-in" by attending seminars or classes, some of which offer actual experience in crafts and skills. These might be at university level or short courses offered by a historical association or individual craftsmen. Ask to be put on the mailing list of universities within commuting distance.

Seminars or workshops in American culture are offered for several weeks in summer or winter and might lead into further study in the museum or art field. Unless you live near a cultural center of this type, attendance would require room and board as well as tuition.

One of the best known in this field is the program at Cooperstown, New York, sponsored by the New York State Historical Association. Graduate students across the nation can apply for individualized museum training internships at Old Sturbridge Village in Massachusetts, as part of the new $1.7 million museum education building designed to give in-depth understanding of the past to young and adult alike.

INTERVIEWS TO SECURE INFORMATION

Wherever you go, to a library to study or to a distant state to secure background and first-hand information, the personal contact is of primary importance.

An interview to secure information is more than a conversation with a hostess in a historic house, though that could be important, too. It begins with an arrangement to talk with someone who knows the answers to your questions. It is better if it is a planned meeting, by previous appointment made by telephone or letter. Wherever you live and wherever you go for information, it is a good idea to secure, before you start, the names of the people who can help you when you get there. You might write to the town librarian or public information officer if you cannot find the name of the curator of the museum or of the expert in an institution.

In your letter, state that you are a writer and need specific information and ask for an interview with someone who can help. Tell when you are arriving, or if you can arrange it so, leave the date to the other person. Enclose a stamped return envelope.

Your planning should include a list of specific questions easily understood by the person granting the interview. You would not, obviously, ask to learn "everything about housekeeping in Colonial times." With proper homework completed by reading, you would already know the basic steps in making candles, how food is dried, that a crane was a necessity for cooking over an open fire, and so on. The more thorough your homework, the more specific your questions will be.

While you are reading, jot down questions that you must have more specific answers for, or operations that you know you should see in person: "How does a spit operate?" "What does the board used to smooth down a feather bed look like?" "How did Indians grind corn?" "Can I see a grist mill in operation?" "Where can I see a horse car?" "What do dried herbs smell like?"

Why couldn't you just walk in and see for yourself? Perhaps you could, but it might be that the expert would be busy, or away for that day — or that a busload of school children is scheduled to arrive just then. (This has happened to me several times when I could not plan ahead, and it is a frustrating experience.) It is more professional not to leave your specific research to chance.

Always record the name of the person, his telephone number, date of telephone calls, place of interview and date, and other pertinent information with your files. You will want to send a note of appreciation to each person who helped you as soon as possible.

After you have had such an interview and you come home and start to type your notes, you might discover that you can't read a certain important name or that you forgot to obtain a significant bit of information. Take care about the names by printing every letter of every name.

If you have a deadline, use the telephone person-to-person. Have the exact questions you wish to ask written out. If it is not urgent, type the questions on a self-addressed postal, and clip it to a short note requesting the answers. This thoughtfulness will be welcomed by every busy person.

USING THE MAILS

A valuable research tool is the use of the mail to secure information. Always enclose a stamped self-addressed envelope except when you are requesting help from government sources.

When you need more than a single answer, your letter of inquiry must be a good one. Use friendly, informal language. Always address your letter to an individual not a company, and to the "top" man if you have no name: "Attention of Public Relations Officer" or "Attention of the President." If you have talked with the person before, remind him of this.

Explain in your letter exactly why you need information. Your correspondent may want to know how you plan to use his answer. Ask specific questions, not generalized questions that require a great deal of thought to answer. He might not reply if you ask too much of him.

Later, be sure you write and thank him for his help. Always keep his reply on file, stapled to a carbon of your letter of inquiry.

The mails are a great help in securing books from the state library. You pay only return postage, perhaps 15¢ for a big stack of books, marked "library rate." (7¢ for the first pound, 3¢ each additional pound were the 1975 rates.) Often your state library will have information which cannot be found elsewhere, and its regional material will be more complete than that in most local libraries.

When you ask for books, type your request and keep a carbon. I failed to do this once and never did remember what I had asked for that brought the response, "Do not have the other book." It will be helpful to the librarians if you give author and title. When you ask the state library for books on one subject, be specific: Do not ask for American History when you mean Civil War History. Upon request the library will send a selected bibliography of holdings in a single field of interest.

CHAPTER SEVEN

THE INTERVIEW: ORAL HISTORY

A primary source involving people is the interview, one type of which is called oral history. Oral history interviews aim at obtaining reminiscences from people who can describe events as participants or viewers, contributing new information and fresh insight to history that would not otherwise exist.

The oral history technique is intended to add to, not repeat, historical source material. (Writers have to remember, too, that a person's memory is not always accurate, or it may be colored by a view he wishes to give an event he saw or participated in, so multiple versions of a single event are a more likely avenue to the historical truth.)

In contrast to the journalistic interview, which is used for immediate publication, the oral history interview is intended for use in the future by a variety of researchers, to help explain the *why* and *how* of events and personal relationships.

Probably oral history would never have achieved the status of a professional technique without the development of electronic recording equipment. Its greatest use is not, however, that of tape cassette, cartridge or reel, but in transcript from these. Usually, the original recorded interviews are transcribed, edited, indexed and bound for the historian to study.

The story of the narrator's life, his memories of a prominent figure of society, his relationship to an institution or his views of a past episode or political regime, his description of life of the past century — any or all of these and many other kinds of material may be included in oral history memoirs. It is paradoxical that the only time a researcher will hear the sound of the narrator's voice will be when he wants to hear the flavor of speech or intends to verify a statement he questions.

Oral history as a professional technique began at Columbia

University in 1948, under the direction of the late Allan Nevins. Although it had been in his thoughts for a long time, Professor Nevins brought the idea to public attention in the preface to *The Gateway to History* in 1938. He had a difficult time those ten years trying to convince other historians of the practicality of launching a program upon a regular basis for the benefit of future researchers. Without doubt, the greatest obstacle was the task of taking notes.

George McAneny, a prominent civic leader of New York City, was the subject of Professor Nevins' first official interview under the Columbia University oral history program on May 18, 1948. He talked about former mayors of New York, the World's Fair of 1939, the construction of the subway, among many other topics. In his account of this occasion, Dr. Louis M. Starr, director of Columbia's oral history program, pictures a graduate student, Dean Albertson, struggling with his pencil and pad to keep up with the flow of words, and then going home to read his notes, trying to remember what he had left out while he transcribed the interview.

This was the first of several thousand interviews to be conducted under the auspices of Columbia's oral history program. The work was eased with the development of recording devices, first the Webster wire recorder, and then the tape recorder, which became what Dr. Starr calls "the salvation of oral history." Great strides have been made in recording equipment since those early days.

From Columbia the technique spread to other universities and then to institutions and historical societies.

An example of the extensive government program in oral history is that of the Archives of American Art, begun in 1959, which has in its files more than 1,500 interviews with persons in the visual arts.

Many publications are available from the Oral History Research Office, Butler Library, Columbia University, New York, New York 10027. Your local libraries and university history departments may also have information on this subject.

INTERVIEWING TECHNIQUE

Dr. Starr points out that interviewing is as old as history itself, and that Herodotus, the father of history, relied on interviews in the writing of his history of the Persian wars. Retired teachers, because of their background, often make ideal oral history interviewers. Others are drawn from a wide range of occupations, with presence as important as scholarly background.

James Billie, a Vietnam veteran and manager of the Okalee Indian Village in Florida, plans to tape an oral history of the Seminole Indians, who once ruled the vast Florida Everglades, using the older members.

Asking questions is a natural way to obtain information. In the Bancroft Library at UC-Berkeley is material gathered by Hubert Howe Bancroft, who in the 1880's sent aides on horseback over the Western plains to talk with cattlemen, miners and others, gathering first-hand information for the Bancroft history of the American West. Through the years all kinds of writers have been doing much of their research through interviews.

I once interviewed a ninety-year-old man who while a lad watched a Lincoln parade. Another man with many stories to tell drove a coach for Dr. Elizabeth Blackwell, our first woman doctor.

Your personal contribution to this field might be made through recording the "recollections" of elderly folk in your area. Not only can they relate their own experiences, but they may be able to tell you of particulars passed along to them by their parents and grandparents.

Some of the best sources will be older businessmen and civic leaders, who have participated in significant events of community life. Individuals whose careers are noteworthy can also provide material.

This type of project is called "oral history" only if you preserve the tapes and records for posterity, either as they are or in transcribed form, and deposit them in the library of your historical society or in the collection of another institution.

The writer must have some background knowledge of the subjects to be discussed.

If the farmer or business man is to furnish you with satisfactory information, you must be informed about those special subjects. If not, how are you to know whether the narrator is giving you accurate or imaginative information? How will you know what questions to ask? Unless your knowledge of the historical background of events is similar to your elderly narrator's, his references to them will have little meaning to you.

Schedule the interview several days ahead and mention the significant topics you would like to discuss. You would give the prospective narrator a list of the subjects or a few of the major questions you have prepared. This would prompt him to look for scrapbooks, letters, pictures and other material.

Unless the person to be interviewed already knows you or has been introduced by a mutual friend, you will need to take some time to become acquainted and to assure him of your integrity, (that you're a professional researcher — not a gossip). This will make both of you more relaxed and able to converse easily.

Your questions, prepared in advance, may be written out in detail to fix them in your mind, but it is well that they not sound rehearsed. It is likely that the trend of the interview will bring other ideas into focus, perhaps change the scope of the talk.

There are two broad types of interviews: autobiographical and topical. For the former, let your narrator talk freely about his life and memories. For the latter, you limit the interview to certain topics, and your advance research must be done carefully if the interview is to be productive.

When you are interviewing the older people in your community, you would be likely to stress the autobiographical, and then through the transcripts of a number of interviews, select material covering specific subjects, like school history, transportation in the area, business of the past.

Most oral history projects center around a single subject: a political movement, an individual biography, the history of an institution, a presidential administration, a particular field of interest like agriculture or crafts. Interviewers try to guide the narrators into the proper area by well-researched and specifically-stated questions. It is wise to tell those you interview that you are planning to talk with others on the same subjects or period of history; each will be more careful of his facts if he knows they are to be checked with others.

Ask positive questions, and use questions which emphasize *how, why, when.* Associate periods of time with events to make it easier for the narrator to place the dates. Ask for the definition of technical terms and for the spelling of names.

Strive for drama, human interest, enthusiastic response, as you lead from simple beginning questions to those which require more thought. By that time you may both have forgotten the little tape recorder microphone.

Fallibility of recall may make some of this material inaccurate. Charles Morrissey, Director of the Vermont Historical Society and associated with an oral history project about the Ford Foundation, says, "Interviews can do great harm if they result in misinformation or perpetuate myths. The historian should feel responsible for testing their accuracy." If you cannot check out facts, identify the material as "legend" or qualify it with "as Mrs. Doe recalls."

The person to be interviewed may be uneasy speaking into a microphone, even at a distance, and it might be helpful if you explain how the recorder works. Start with the introduction to the talk: date, place, name of narrator, name of interviewer and the subject to be covered. Then play it back. Emphasize the importance of the project to future generations and as a means of *enriching history.*

An interview should never be longer than two hours, shorter if the narrator is elderly. Several short interviews will be more productive than one that is too long and too tiring.

Oral history projects vary in the way the rights to the taped material are handled. Although Columbia University allows the speaker to retain ownership, it may request him to assign the copyright years later so that it may share the transcript with other libraries through micro publication. Most institutions try to secure assignment of the property and then when the material is quoted in publication or used in other ways, a royalty may be paid to the narrator or his heirs.

Always make a carbon of the interview, so you will have a copy of the original transcript. The completed transcript is usually given to the narrator for review. The handling of the transcribed material by researchers may be earmarked "Permission required to cite or quote," which protects sensitive material. Occasionally, written permission may be required before a researcher may even look at (or hear) the material. Sometimes no one is allowed to use the tapes or transcripts until a certain number of years after the subject's death.

The person interviewed might be asked to sign a statement that the information has been supplied by him, and that it is to be available to the historical society, institution or individual interviewer for reference purposes or for use in articles or a book.

When the tape is transcribed, there should be only factual editing. To correct grammar or colloquialisms is to destroy the very flavor for which the recording was intended; but if there is an inaccurate statement, note should be made of it on the transcript.

The technique of oral history has been applied at many institutions like Duke University, North Carolina, as a means of capturing the experience of the poor and ordinary who have no other kind of documentation of their lives. This goes back to the depression years when the Federal Writers Project sent out 300 interviewers to talk with more than 2,200 former slaves — material which has been almost forgotten. Duke's method combines investigative reporting with oral history methodology, and is aimed at getting answers to *specific* social questions, e.g., patterns of disenfranchisement in particular elections in the 1920's and 1930's.

ORAL HISTORY AS SOURCE MATERIAL

Next best to talking with a person is to hear what he has to say on tape or record. Using a transcript will often be the only choice given to you, but if the tape is available, you may want to listen to it, to catch the nuances in important passages.

It is difficult to take notes from the tape, so use both if they are available, just as you would examine an original letter and use a copy to help in deciphering the handwriting. The index will help you find the particular information you need. The chief value of oral history as a research source is that it provides personal, first-hand information about a person or event which is not available elsewhere. The vernacular, the excitement of an eye witness, the opinions of one who may be a bigot, are a treasure to the historian in search of authentic information.

Since 1970, the Library of Congress has included oral history collections in its *National Union Catalog of Manuscripts Collections.* In 1971, the Oral History Association published a directory, *Oral History in the United States,* listing some 230 projects by state with brief descriptions of contents. This is expanded in R.R. Bowker's 1974 publication, *Oral History Collections,* to provide more detail and include some projects in Canada, England and elsewhere.

Some of the major collections also publish their own catalogues, the most striking example being Columbia's *The Oral History Collection,* 1973, edited by Elizabeth B. Mason and Louis M. Starr, a 500-page volume published in both soft and hardcover. (Oral history has grown rapidly — Columbia's first edition in 1960 had only 120 pages.)

Researchers and others who have a special interest in the work may want to join the Oral History Association, a young and vigorous group which now has over 1,000 members. It publishes a newsletter and an annual, and holds a workshop prior to its annual meetings. For further information, write Oral History Association, Box 20, Butler Library, Columbia University, New York 10027.

Some books are based entirely on oral history, like the autobiography *Felix Frankfurter Reminisces.* Another is *Plain Speaking, An Oral Biography of Harry S. Truman,* by Merle Miller, based upon some 200 taped interviews made in 1961 and 1962, plus the candid comments of friends, relatives and colleagues who knew him well.

During the last four years of his life, former Soviet leader Nikita Khrushchev dictated his reminiscences into a tape recorder. Transcripts translated and edited by *Time* correspondent Strobe Talbott, have resulted in historical documents of great value: *Khrushchev Remembers* and *Khrushchev Remembers: The Last Testament,* were published by Little, Brown & Co. in 1970 and 1974. Time Inc. gave all 180 hours of tape recordings (nearly 800,000 words) to the Oral History Collection of Columbia University, where a verbatim transcript has been prepared.

CHAPTER EIGHT

EXPLORING THROUGH AUDIOVISUALS

The term "oral history" is not usually given to collected speeches, orations, sermons, literature read aloud, music, films, radio and television and other audio-visual aids, but I think they are at least distant cousins. All of these are research sources concerned with people speaking aloud, although their purposes differ.

Aided by the speeches of the past, a writer of history can learn much about the emotions and trends of thought and also get the flavor of the time. Through inflections you may also discern something of the orator's character, even though speeches are more formal than conversation.

Sources to lead you to both printed and recorded material as well as that in manuscript form will be found in the reference room at the library.

Recording studios are beginning to appreciate the significance of these and we find recordings of Churchill, FDR and such events as President John F. Kennedy's inaugural speech, in record shops and libraries. In the early 1900's phonograph records were made of the speeches of Theodore Roosevelt, Woodrow Wilson and others on the campaign trail, and then shipped around the country to be played on the victrola at political rallies. A far cry from the impact of television today!

Some years ago I was privileged to help the librarian at Middlebury College, Vermont, obtain additions to the college's collection of old ballads and folk songs. We went to Brunswick, Maine, to record the voice of Robert P.T. Coffin singing sea chanties. It was a wonderful experience. Folk songs have been recorded in the homes of many elderly folk to preserve for this program a heritage fast dying out. Foreign sources are naturally centuries older than those in North America, except for traditional Indian melodies.

The world's first history lessons came through the relating of sagas, and the singing of ballads. These and music and drama continue to record the tempo of the eras through which mankind moves. Snatches of song can give identity to a period as quickly as any other clue. Study of the numerous anthologies of the past centuries of song can help to give authenticity to the history of an era.

As a part of its oral history, members of the faculty of Tulane University have recorded interviews with key figures in the evolution of New Orleans jazz. On West 55th Street in New York City is the New York Jazz Museum, the first in the country devoted to the history, legend and legacy of jazz from its African origins to the modern era.

Most poets and dramatists, as well as writers of fiction, have used historical themes and spoken out against injustice. Often the study of a period's literature and music, and the other arts, will reveal the spirit, wit, social criticism of the era. Patriotic and religious songs and ethnic and regional ballads will help you to understand the sentiment of its people. Anthologies have been published to cover just about every type of song and poetry from firemen to sailors, from cowboys to lumberjacks.

The Library of Congress's latest edition of *Literary Recordings* was prepared in 1974 and is available through the Government Printing Office. Included are theatre experiences of actors and actresses, and items like *Stage Struck* — the story of Florenz Ziegfield, with his own voice and those of people identified with him.

Many universities and city and town libraries also have similar oral history programs.

Collectors of mementoes of the performing arts are numerous. Thousands of theatre buffs, movie and circus fans are drawn to the New York Public Library and Museum of the Performing Arts at Lincoln Center for its "Giant Bazaar and Auction" of duplicate materials from its collection. The Performing Arts Research Center has collections of theatre magazines and programs, photographs, posters, prints, autographs, theatre props, albums, sheet music and other memorabilia.

Similar centers will be found across the country in major libraries, art centers and museums.

POPULAR CULTURE

The Smithsonian has recently produced a comprehensive collection of classical jazz, drawing on the archives of all major recording firms. The set may be bought from the museum's shops or ordered by mail. Write to the Institution for information about other periods of music and the performing arts.

Constantly increasing are the numbers of history teachers who use oral history and audio-visual aids in their classes.

Dime novels, comic books, picture post cards and other items showing how people lived in "bygone days" are in great demand in an era of nostalgia. The Center for the Study of Popular Culture at Bowling Green University in Ohio, has amassed over 200,000 such articles for its library since it opened in 1969. Popular music, films and artifacts are now prized as documentary material. The audio center contains over 50,000 old records, and their tape collection includes old radio programs, interviews with popular authors and musicians, and sheet music, pamphlets of religious sects and much more. The Center also produces a quarterly magazine, *Journal of Popular Culture*.

Sound recordings, as I have mentioned, are being made in other fields than poetry, music and drama. The phonograph, once used only for entertainment, now plays records of public speeches, accounts of newsworthy events and other phases of public life.

The Department of Classics and Comparative Literature at Brooklyn College (N.Y.) is looking for historic phonographs and for discs from 1877-1913 for *The Antique Phonograph Monthly* and other projects.

Stanford University, California, has an Archives of Recorded Sound, patterned on the impressive collection of William R. Moran. Stanford has the largest collection of records in the western United States and has served as a model for sound libraries in other universities. Half of its collections of more than 100,000 cylinders, records, tapes and player piano rolls were donated through the efforts of Moran, and in time the latter's collection will find its home there — including scores of campaign speeches, recordings of major historical events such as the wartime speeches of Churchill and FDR — in more than 40,000 discs dating back to the 1890's.

Catalogues are published by all commercial record companies. You will find helpful material in the American Archives of Folk Song at the Library of Congress, the *American Record Guide* and the series of music recorded in 1951 by New Records.

It takes some adjustment in thought to consider the world of motion pictures a part of historical research unless one remembers the once-popular newsreels which preceded every movie show. I'll never forget the newsreel which recorded the pulling down of the American Flag by the Japanese soldiers at Corregidor.

The movies we take of our children record family history. Documentaries, newsreels on television and all cinematic material have recorded, and will continue to record history in the making — and will provide historians with illuminated material of the past.

Movie nostalgia is all the rage in the mid-70's. A New York movie book club offers fans such material as *Pictorial History of the Western Film, Sixty Years of Hollywood, Detective in Film from Sherlock to Klute.* Illustrations run to the hundreds.

In all honesty we must admit that the British have us beaten in the field of historical drama for both television and theatre. "The Edwardians" of the 1974 television summer is fascinating. They have cared about history for a longer period of time and it shows! By adoption we can claim Alistair Cooke and his "America," with its fine attention to detail, and accurate interpretation.

And now for the next decade, at least, American and Canadian television will often feature documentaries on the American Revolution and its aftermath. The field is wide open for the alert, imaginative writer willing to learn the techniques of this special field of authorship.

The Library of Congress has information on films of all varieties and its collection of factual movies goes back to 1897. The Library, the National Archives, and the Museum of Modern Art in New York City, are leaders in the preservation of films. The Museum of Modern Art maintains a card file of important films produced since 1889. National Archives has more than 34,000 sound recordings.

Information on films, filmstrips and other materials produced by the government has been published by the United States Office of Education, 400 Maryland Ave., S.W., Washington, D.C. 20202, in a descriptive catalogue and a directory.

The audio-visual aspects of library work are expanding rapidly and many libraries are accumulating collections of films from television shows, news programs and movies, adding to these often. See also in your nearest library the directories of films, filmstrips, etc., categorized by subject, published by the National Information Center for Educational Media (NICEM).

Many radio sound records have been preserved for permanent use. The Federal Communications Commission has broadcast scripts and tape recordings on file. A variety of material may be obtained from the national offices of the radio and television networks.

Beginning writers of history would not be doing research in depth enough to require exploration of some of the sources mentioned here. It is important, however, that you have knowledge of them. Beginners have a way of turning into pros!

Into such a pro as James B. Sweeney. He reports that for his book, *Pictorial History of Sea Monsters and Other Dangerous Marine Life* (150,000 words, 350 photographs) his research involved the following: "careful study of 82 journals published by learned societies; 243 newsletters printed by various nautical organizations; 74 commercially-published journals released by universities, the government and industrial firms; many hundreds of trade journals, innumerable house organs and thousands of newspapers . . . the screening of many scientific motion pictures, the writing of almost 1,000 letters of inquiry, visits to 12 large aquariums, 54 museums, 76 libraries, 4 zoological parks, and trips to 8 foreign countries. Furthermore, over 150 fishermen, sailors, sea captains and yachtsmen were interviewed with a tape recorder and generally at some length."

Remember, though, he and all writers do just one interview at a time, go slowly step by step — and expect it to be interesting all the way.

CHAPTER NINE

WRITING HISTORICAL FEATURES AND SHORT ARTICLES

Much of my reporting and writing experience has been writing articles and news stories for state and national newspapers and for regional magazines. This training is good discipline for beginners, because it often requires working toward a deadline. Of the more than 5,000 or so articles of mine which have been published, about 500 have been on historical subjects.

I began reporting for the *Quincy-Patriot Ledger* in Massachusetts while I was in high school. Early in my experience I learned that jotting down a few notes before typing the material was a welcome guide for quick reporting, and it was not long before I could write the original with a carbon without having to rewrite. When one has a newspaper deadline to meet, there is no time for a second draft.

For the freelance writer, however, there *has* to be time to write with accuracy and completeness; and the mini-outline — where names, dates, figures and facts were checked — helped me to achieve this skill.

Many writers hate the thought of an outline. When you are a professional writer, with some expertise in following a mental outline, it may be all right to skip this chore. For the present, you do need an outline or a summary of each phase of your work.

First, read over your notes, and then jot down in a few words your thoughts as you consider what your aim is in writing the article or story. You may use the journalistic approach, listing the *Who? What? Where?* and jotting down one-sentence answers beside them.

You may jot down some human interest anecdotes you want to give to illustrate some of your points.

Probably while you have been working, various ways to begin the manuscript have come to your thought. If you are like me, you will be thinking of this while you are going to and from your regular work, before you go to sleep and whan you wake up. Now the "outline" will give you ideas for the first paragraph, the development of the story, the conclusion you intend to reach, and you will know what type of reader you want to reach. Your outline will provide you with direction.

THE QUERY LETTER

Most professional writers write an article only with the assurance of an editor that he is interested in the idea. The editor knows that writers whose work he has read or bought can be trusted to do a reliable job. You have to sell him on your reliability through a query letter.

Before you write a query letter, examine your material as an editor would: will it be of interest to his readers? Are the elements of emotion, drama, inspiration present?

A query letter saves the writer time and effort and a lot of rewriting when he aims at a top magazine. Address it to an individual editor by name, selecting this from the masthead of the *latest issue.* (Editorial turnover is frequent.)

An article query is a sales letter. Take time to make your presentation sparkle. Be brief; one page, if possible. State your central idea, your theme, your point of view, the way you plan to present the material. Be specific, but do not exaggerate. Don't promise more than you can deliver.

Arouse the editor's interest and curiosity by starting off your letter with an amusing anecdote or a provocative question or several eye-catching, thought-provoking statistics.

You must convince the editor that your idea is right for his readers, that it is important and interesting to them.

Give your qualifications for writing about this subject, and name your sources of information. Assure the editor that you are in a position to give him or her authoritative facts, embellished with anecdotes, and give several. The editor has to be sold on *you* as well as on the idea. Enclose a self-addressed stamped envelope. Keep a carbon copy.

If the material needs illustrating, tell what kind of photographs or prints or drawings you can provide, or where they can be found.

Present your letter as you would a manuscript, carefully typed on good bond paper. Watch grammar, spelling, punctuation.

Send only one query in a letter.

Don't expect an immediate answer. Check with the editor at the end of six to eight weeks if no answer comes by then. This is tough on writers, but often seems necessary from the other side of the desk. (If your article query went to a newspaper editor you might telephone; these editors often get swamped with the details of their work and never do get to answering letters.)

Before you query at all, you must know your market, read the magazine in question for several issues, check in the *Reader's Guide* and be sure your idea has not been used in recent months. It is what the editor has not used — but is appropriate to his audience — which will interest him.

Although some far more experienced writers and teachers do not agree with me, I believe that the beginning writer must learn his trade by selling to the smaller markets, regional periodicals, newspapers, the "little" magazines with editors who have more time to encourage a beginner, who do not expect an in-depth treatment but a good story, simply told. The "big time" writers don't send material to these markets, many of which do not require a query letter. Why not try to be a big fish in a little pond until you are ready for deeper water?

Professional writers still receive rejection slips. Don't let one NO on a query discourage you; try another editor. If you get a good many rejections on the same idea, give it a close look; it may not be a good one, after all.

You have only one opportunity to receive a *yes*. Make the most of your presentation the very first time out.

Never send a query unless you are prepared to follow through with the completed manuscript.

HOW TO PREPARE YOUR MANUSCRIPT

Since your manuscript is your introduction to an editor, make sure it represents the best you know how to do. Use a standard type and be sure it is clean. The ribbon should always be black. Paper should be a medium bond and you must make a carbon copy of your work, two carbons for a book. Allow at least an inch of space all around. Double space unless the editor requires triple spacing.

At the top left of the first sheet type your full name and address. In the upper right-hand corner type the approximate number of words. Never put an exact count like "1556"; use "approx. 1500." Figure out the average number of words to a page and multiply by the number of pages, plus the amount on Page 1.

Begin your story halfway down the page and center your title. Under that, center your name as you wish it to appear in print. Drop down four spaces and indent your first sentence five spaces. If you're writing for a newspaper, most prefer a 65-character line length.

Watch the bottom margin. Mark each page lightly in pencil at the place your page should end. Formerly when writing for newspapers writers always stopped each page at the end of a paragraph, even if it meant leaving a wider margin at the bottom. The reason was that pages of a manuscript may be divided among several linotype operators and the type later reassembled. Now with optical scanners and photocomposition that's not a problem. It's still important that your title or an abbreviation of it and the page number be at the top right of every page: "A New Dawn — 2." Type your last name only in the upper left corner.

Up to five pages of manuscript can be folded in thirds and mailed in a #10 envelope. More pages should be mailed flat. Keep several sizes of envelopes on hand, including 9x12 manila envelopes. When you send photographs, you may prefer to use a photo folder which will also hold the manuscript.

Enclose a letter only if the manuscript is sent on request or you need to establish your qualifications for a specialized subject. Nothing you say in a letter will help to sell your manuscript if it cannot stand on its own merits. Editors abhor "cute" notes.

Proofread your manuscript with care, looking for typographical errors, spelling and so on. Read each page of this final draft before you take it from the typewriter; if you find a mistake later, you may have to retype the whole article. Erase carefully. Do not strike over. (An investment in erasure tape will save many anxious moments.)

I have been told that editors put aside manuscripts that come to their desks with faint typing, many visible erasures and sloppy typing, and also manuscripts typed in unusual script or on hard-to-read colored paper.

We writers need all the help we can get to catch an editor's attention and must send him the best-looking, best-edited, best-written manuscript we are capable of preparing.

Every writer has a unique approach to his work. My writing classes have proved that even when a group of writers is given the same facts or plot, each will create a story of his own, quite unlike that of any other member of the group.

Because readers like drama, conflict, emotion in articles as well as in fiction, the article writer often adopts the fiction writer's techniques: setting the scene, using dialogue, flashbacks, transitions, specific description and characterization — everything which will *show* rather than *tell* the reader. An article writer who expects to do more than report news needs to learn these techniques.

In addition, the use of suspense, swift pacing, simple language, an informal style and the selection of relevant anecdotes will challenge the creativity and ingenuity of the writer.

In his book, *Writing and Selling Non-Fiction,* Hayes Jacobs writes: "Of particular value are the fiction writer's ability to bring people to life on the page, and his skill in recording sensory impressions — the sight, sound, smell, taste and feel of things. Nonfiction focuses on facts, but to impress the reader with facts, one must become aware of his emotions — how he *feels* about things, as well as what he thinks of them. Good storytellers do that naturally, almost as if by instinct. Writers of nonfiction often have to work at it."

Reading a wide variety of material — poetry, history, drama, biography, fiction of the past as well as of the present — will help nonfiction writers to acquire a feeling for rhythm in writing and an understanding of methods required to give a fictional touch to nonfiction.

Sentences and paragraphs should vary in length for a pleasing effect. Nothing is more disconcerting to a reader than a paragraph which fills a whole page, or a sentence which goes on and on, sometimes without active verbs to provide direction.

Examine construction in your reading and note the difference in treatment between newspapers and magazines, and between short fiction and book-length material.

Confusion about similar words or words that look or sound alike; failure to understand the difference between antonyms and synonyms; and failure to understand a word's connotation — these are some of the ways in which mistakes can be made in word usage.

If you are not sure, look it up. Look it up, anyhow, and add to your vocabulary! No woman likes to be called "skinny" when she thinks of herself as "slender" or "svelte," but "a skinny old hen" may be just the term an angry boy would use. "Marshmallow-faced" or "granite-jawed" give a word picture hard to beat with twenty words.

We need to take particular care that our words are meaningful when the accuracy of factual information is at stake. Our town has had some hilarious results from the comments of a dearly-loved minister who came to Maine from South Africa, where the same words have quite different meanings. Such differences would be vital in writing.

We must make certain that what young people sometimes call "dull old facts" come to life in a new and lively form. The modern writer of history knows that his work must be creative and imaginative and vivid if it is to be enjoyed.

FOOTNOTES

It seems to me that these little numerals which require a break in our reading and a glance at the bottom margin slow the reader's thinking; indeed, it may confuse him. But some publications prefer this style.

Certainly, in fiction and in most articles footnotes are not necessary. Some editors require an accompanying bibliography or listing of source material, sometimes just for their reference, sometimes to place at the end of the article.

Copyright acknowledgement of a quoted song would be an exception.

The carbon of your manuscript should bear the needed references, page numbers, book title or author or all three, in readiness for the writer to answer questions about his sources.

WRITING THE NEWSPAPER FEATURE ARTICLE

A feature article may have its beginning in the news, but it goes beyond that, to answer the *why* suggested in the news. It embellishes the material of the news story or it reminds readers of events and people who have made news in the past.

It is important to relate the past to the present with what article writers call a "news peg".

Where once newspaper features were very short and completely reportorial in style, they now may be written in a more dramatic, creative way. Frequently newspaper features vary from magazine articles only in length and immediacy.

Here is a newspaper feature lead with a "news peg":

Every American school child knows the name of John Paul Jones, the famous captain of the *Ranger,* the Kittery-built ship of the Continental Navy which received the first salute ever given to the flag of the United States. Jones, who lived briefly in rented quarters in Portsmouth, N.H., lies buried in a memorial crypt in the chapel at the Naval Academy in Annapolis, Md.

But mention the name of Hopley Yeaton, even in his native Portsmouth, and the most you're likely to receive is a puzzled look and a "Hopley who?"

. . .Yeaton, for his lack of fame, deserves no less a place of honor in our history than Jones, however. (The Coast Guard Cutter Eagle) will be bearing Yeaton's remains from their original gravesite in North Lubec, Maine, to the Academy where they will be interred in a memorial suitable to the first commissioned officer of the Revenue Marine Service, forerunner of the Coast Guard.

"The Coast Guard Honors Hopley Yeaton"
Jim Martin, Kennebunk, Maine *Coast Pilot*

WRITING FOR MAGAZINES

Magazines have space for and usually require more in-depth treatment. This means writing the article in greater detail. For example, a newspaper would print a short article about the birth anniversary of a famous historical character, and would also publish a short profile of a local celebrity. A magazine would require some *new* information about the too-familiar historical figure, or a fresh approach, and would accept an article about the local person only if he had accomplished something of national interest.

Magazines print articles with considerably more specific information about a person's life than a newspaper has room for. The former would allow for development of character in some detail — information news editors can't include for their readers, who frequently read on the run.

Magazine deadlines are set several months in advance and an article whose subject matter has a short time span of interest would be more likely to be accepted by a newspaper or weekly magazine. When you begin writing for magazines, you must select your subjects with the question of timeliness in mind: a timeliness which has a longer period of relevancy than a newspaper requires.

This means that historical material which is tied to current events must be foreseen, perhaps even written in readiness for future submission. The numerous articles which will appear about events of the American Revolution were begun months, even years, ahead.

Magazine editors who use historical material say that much of what they receive is "dull, dull, dull." Lionel A. Atwill, editor of *Adirondack Life* (New York) says that manuscripts are often poorly researched, facts not substantiated and limited references used; yet, like many editors, he plans to increase the amount of historical material in the months to come. Davis Dutton, editor of *Colorado Magazine,* publishes an Old West history piece in every issue, sometimes more, and says that much of the material he receives is "basically too dry, and lacking in historical imagination. We want pieces that will draw the reader into the past completely, not ones that will make him a mere spectator. Research should involve the whole context and a feel for it — not just a bundle of facts, even if they're well told."

CHAPTER TEN

THOSE OPENING PARAGRAPHS

After you have selected your audience: newspaper readers or magazines published for boating enthusiasts or whatever; how you use your facts will be determined by your choice of reader.

Choose the point of view from which you can best tell your story and remember to make the vocabulary fit the narrator. Most often, you will select the usual third person approach. Don't be cute, but dare to be different if your subject matter allows it. The thoroughbred Secretariat himself tells the story of "A Century of Derbies" through an "interview" with Starkey Flythe, the creative editor of the *Saturday Evening Post*.

The hardest part of writing is getting those first words on paper. You must catch your reader's interest on the first page or you won't keep it. Unless you are working from a good outline, you may, in revision, find your real beginning on page two or three!

In the first paragraph or two should be a hint of your theme, the introduction of the event or the main character, the establishment of the setting. You might begin with an exciting moment in your story and then, through flashback or other technique, fill in the necessary background information. Try a variety of openings or "leads" before you decide on your final beginning. Do you see that you can change the slant of your material by your choice of a first paragraph?

Here are some examples of published article leads:

1. *Startling statement*
Historic Old Boston has a lot of famous attractions that don't really exist. But it's still fun to visit them.

Take Bunker Hill Monument, for example.

"Debunking Bunker Hill"
Richard O'Donnell, *Ford Times,* Oct. 1971

2. *Summary*

Dr. Emanuel Herrmann is not exactly a household word, but perhaps he should be. A young professor at the Austrian military academy, he felt that the mail service of the 1860's was expensive, and that most letters said in two pages what could be said in one. He designed a thin envelope-sized cardboard which would weigh less than a letter ....

The Austrian Postal Service liked the idea. On October 1, 1869, the first official postal card (Correspondenz-Karte) appeared...

"Story of postcards goes back a century"
J. Timberlake Gibson, *Smithsonian,* April 1974

3. *Personal*

We went on a pilgrimage to historyland on a bright May day, eager to see the birthplaces of three Virginians who had a hand in the making of American history.   "Houses of History"

Philip and Doris Marston, *Campfire Chatter,* July 1970

4. *Drama* - Sometimes it will take several paragraphs of narration to build up suspense, like this one:

Except for a gusty westerly wind that rattled shutters and tossed loose objects about on the ground, the night of Saturday, November 18, 1973, was quiet on Monhegan. The men had been busy all day working on their traps and gear ...

About 9:15, Barbara Hitchcock was looking out the living room window ... and saw what she thought was a brightly lighted ship lying off Green Point ... but when they heard no ship's bell or horn as a signal of distress, they assumed the lights to be those of one of the herring boats ....

... On her way to bed Dot stopped to shut off the radio, and as her fingers touched the switch she heard the call, "May Day from the J. H. Deinlein. We have struck off the northern end of Monhegan and are sinking!"   "A Tale of Two Tugs"

Alta Ashley, *Down East,* November 1974

5. *Description*

The tigress listened. In the darkness she heard the big male tiger call. Carefully she made her way through tropical thornbush, over the mud of irrigated rice fields, past the thatch of farmers' houses and the wary barking of their dogs.

Now, close enough to hear the breathing of the male, she leapt a fence, paused, then sprang again.

Only then did she see her error. Bars still separated her from the male — and a wall of wet concrete now stood between her and freedom.   "Orissa - Past and Promise in an Indian State"
Bart McDowell, *National Geographic,* Oct. 1970

6. *Anniversary Tie-In*

This is a very special Christmas for a certain jolly gentleman. One hundred and fifty years ago this month ... that grand old man of the North Pole made his literary debut into the pages of American folklore.

"All About Santa Claus and How He Grew and Grew"
Charles J. Jordan, *Yankee,* Dec. 1973

7. *Mystery*

One of the unsolved and perhaps unsolvable mysteries of early American history is what happened to the first English colony in the New World ... They landed on Roanoke Island, off the coast of present-day North Carolina, in July 1587 — and disappeared from the pages of history. "The Lost Colony of Roanoke Island"
Walter Spearman, *American History Illustrated,* May 1969

8. *Curiosity*

Historians who don't believe everything they read in old history books have lately been taking another look into the American Revolution and asking why this revolt against a mother country succeeded.   "The Defeat of King George III"
John L. Kent, *Catholic Digest,* July 1970

9. *Quotation*

A young person is supposed to have asked Justice Felix Frankfurter, "And how do you know the human race is worth saving?" The Justice answered, "I have read Anne Frank's diary."

"Anne Frank Revisited"
Robert Taylor, *Boston Sunday Globe,* Jan. 9, 1972

10. *Suspense*

At daybreak on the morning of December 6, 1775, Henry Knox, twenty-five-year-old aide to General George Washington, left his bunk at Fort Ticonderoga and climbed to the stone wall overlooking Lake Champlain. His gray eyes searched the lake 100 feet below. It was ice-rimmed and rough water tossed the boats at their moorings. He wondered whether he would have time enough to get General Washington's guns the thirty-three miles down to Fort George before Lake Champlain and Lake George became ice-locked. "A Noble Train of Artillery"
Doris R. Marston, *New England Galaxy,* Winter 1970

11. *Question*

Women in the Casino locker room? Why, Newport had never seen the like! For the first time in over 90 years, men were excluded from the locker rooms where Sears and Dwight, Hovey ... had each prepared himself for The Big Match.
"My Word! Women in the Casino Locker Room?"
Ira Dember, *Yankee,* August 1972

12. *Anecdote*

On the night before Christmas, 1971, Lyndon Baines Johnson played the most improbable role of his varied and controversial life. Protected from public view behind the gates of his Texas ranch, he donned a red suit and false beard, climbed aboard a small tractor and drove to the hangar adjoining his airstrip. Assembled inside for greetings and gifts from LBJ were the families of his ranch hands. They were so stunned at the sight of the former President ho-ho-ho-ing aboard a chugging tractor that they greeted his arrival with disbelieving silence. Undeterred, Johnson disembarked from the tractor and unloaded toys for the children.
"The Last Days of LBJ"
Leo Janos, *Reader's Digest,* Sept. 1973,
condensed from *The Atlantic Monthly,* July 1973

Note the titles used in the articles quoted. See how important a title can be in attracting attention. Did you notice that a quotation, a suggestion of suspense, a question, the use of "you" bring the reader right into the story? Editors often change a writer's pet titles, but you might find such a bright one that the editor will let it stand.

Take care not to use 3,000 words to tell a 1,000-word story. One of my grandchildren once said to me, "I asked my father a question, but he told me a lot more than I wanted to know."

Knowing when to stop is almost as important as knowing how to begin. A craftsman will do well to read and write many essays, for the essay format is the most satisfying one for article writing, too. You make a statement, you give illustrations or anecdotes about that statement or subject, and then you reword the statement in a forceful summary which refers to the beginning theme. Sometimes you will read printed material which ends with less emphasis than it began. Don't you feel let down? Don't let your "steam" die down as the end approaches.

Examine the way published articles begin and end, and see whether your own conclusion is good enough to compete with them.

CHAPTER ELEVEN

TYPES OF ARTICLES AND MARKETS FOR THEM

Here are a few suggestions for newspapers and magazines which publish historical material, arranged under categories. Remember, however, that editors and editorial policies change from time-to-time. Always check the latest issue of a publication to which you want to submit.

ADVENTURE

This includes true crime, mystery, sea stories, pirates and such, treasure hunts, explorers, space technology, biographical tales of courage. Editors of men's magazines are looking for true stories or fiction about shipwrecks, buried treasure, dashing spies and exciting battles, usually with plenty of rugged action, often with a new twist and told in colorful, brisk language.

Argosy is one of the best markets for adventure articles. They expect the unique, something new in science or exploration, archaeological discoveries of magnitude. Always query. Some published there are "I Found the Richest Shipwreck in the World" (Robert Marx); and "Watergate Plane Crash Mystery" (Milt Machlin).

Sea adventure is a favorite theme of *Down East* and the boating magazines. *The Saturday Evening Post* prefers United States locales for its articles on mystery, adventure and espionage.

The military and men's service magazines *(V.F.W. Magazine, Kiwanis, American Legion)* lean toward tales of combat and other war-related subjects, but also use other types of action stories. *Saga, Stag* and other men's magazines like true adventure and exposes.

Regional magazines like adventure of their own area, especially the Western ones.

Editors of magazines for children and youth use adventure, both true and fictional history, like *Boys' Life. Grit,* a news weekly, frequently publishes adventure stories on its children's page. Some adult magazines in the religious field also use children's material.

Women's magazines seldom use historical material, but when they do, the chief characters must be women. If you have a good story about a courageous woman, try them. If she is a shady lady, try the men's market. In a currently history-minded America, the women's field may broaden dramatically in the years ahead.

AMERICANA

Covered in this field are many topics about America: folklore, antiques, home decorating, foods, travel, architecture, arts and crafts, nostalgia, fashions, the days-of-old.

You must study the magazines which publish Americana, for they differ widely. *Early American Life* covers the period from 1700 to 1850. *American History Illustrated* and *Civil War Times Illustrated* seldom emphasize home life, but they might. *Smithsonian* covers every subject the Institution does, including natural history. *Americana* (American Heritage Publishing Company) features crafts, architecture, exploration, food, home life, gardening, inventions, and differs from *American Heritage Magazine,* which leans more toward biography, historical events and social culture.

National Antiques Review may use a brief history of an old house (sometimes with many pictures), reports of current antique shows and information about special subjects like the history of old silver, but it is aimed at the amateur as well as the professional antique buff, while *Antiques Journal* appeals mostly to the latter. *The Antiques Dealer* is written for dealers and show managers and is a trade magazine. Other hobby and craft magazines have their specialties and you must read them to find out what is acceptable.

Women's magazines like *American Home* use folk art, architecture, furniture crafts, regional crafts and folk history and biography related to these. An example: *American Home* published in its American Treasury series "All My Wishes End at Monticello" (Mary Evans), illustrated with photographs of Thomas Jefferson's home, and a profile of him *in relation to that home.* Magazines of this type also use material on regional food and travel. Newspapers, particularly in their Sunday editions or magazines, use regional Americana articles of the same type as regional magazines, usually shorter. Travel and regional magazines use a great deal of Americana, including the auto clubs magazines like *Away* (ALA — Automobile Legal Association).

Magazines published for senior citizens are good markets for Americana, and for "I remember when" stories and similar material. They demand thorough research and the same high quality of writing as other national magazines.

ANNIVERSARY TIE-IN

Newspapers are good markets for articles which give the history of an event or the biography of a person having a birth or death anniversary. Watch for information about the vital statistics of historical figures, and events whose anniversaries are coming up. During the coming decade, the writers' market will be wide open for material on the American Revolution and the founding of the United States, including history of foreign countries associated with these events, the Loyalist side as well as the Patriot.

Using oral history techniques, you can secure valuable information about your town's history, which local newspapers would like to publish, if you interview elderly neighbors and friends about to celebrate their golden wedding anniversary.

Keeping a calendar book in which you note forthcoming events and anniversaries will help you to look ahead several years and to plan accordingly. As mentioned earlier, a helpful publication is *Chase's Calendar of Annual Events* ($5.00), published by Apple Tree Press, Box 1102, Flint MI 48501.

Here are a few examples: "They All Discovered America" (Robert Marx, *Oceans*) and "Fifty-Two Years After Columbus" (*The Sewanee Review,* from the journal of Friar Tomas de la Torre, translated and edited by Frans Blom) — both reprinted in the October issue of *Catholic Digest;* "Murder on Independence Eve" (Olive Tardiff, *Exeter* (N.H.) *News-Letter*); "The Hell That Was Peleliu" (Leon Lazarus in *Saga*).

ARCHAEOLOGY

Nearly every part of the country has "digs" of amateur or professional importance. New emphasis has been given to the subject since the production of the moving picture, *Chariots of the Gods,* taken from the book and based entirely on archaeological research and the mysteries surrounding it.

There are several magazines devoted to the subject. *Archaeology* articles are written by trained professionals, but *Grit, The Christian Science Monitor* and *Argosy* among many other newspapers and magazines, carry considerable information by non-archaeologists about exploration and discoveries. Look up the term in *Reader's Guide* to see what periodicals are accepting articles on the subject.

A report on the progress of a regional excavation would be of interest to many. *Maine Times* ran one called "Gradually, the Lost Pemaquid Colony Emerges," with photographs of the area and of artifacts found in the digs.

THE ARTS

While writing about the art world often requires a certain expertise and professional knowledge, there are phases of art history and biography, of architecture or historical buildings, comments on a certain painting, stories about art museums and their founders, which would be within the scope of a layman.

For example, I once sold a story about the Thomas Jefferson painting at Bowdoin College, which was used for the 2¢ stamp, to *Down East.* I have sold articles about local and national artists, writers and musicians to regional magazines, and can no longer count the number of articles about historic buildings in our area and which we have visited while traveling, which I have had published. One unlikely magazine which takes much of this material is *Campfire Chatter.*

Reader's Digest is a good market for the unique approach to art. It has published "Our Little-Known National Treasures" (Don Wharton, reprinted from *Early American Life,* "Those Magnificent Gothic Cathedrals" (Ernest O. Hauser) and "Washington's Prayer

at Valley Forge" (Thomas Fleming), based on a painting by Arnold
Friberg, well known for his historic works of art.

Remember the face of Uncle Sam painted by James Montgomery
Flagg for Army recruiting posters? *Away* used this for a lead in
its article "The Real Uncle Sam," a biography of Sam Wilson.
Away frequently prints articles about historic houses. Most regional
magazines and newspapers accept similar material. *Yankee* published "The Old Family Business" — the history of the Vose family,
founders of the famous Boston art firm (Jack Post). *American Home*
ran "Pennsylvania Dutch Perfection" (Rosemary L. Klein), tracing
the history of Amish art through architecture and crafts.

Antiques in one issue published "The Arts and Crafts Movement
in America 1876-1916" (David A. Hanks), "Jonas Chickering: 'The
Father of American Piano Forte-making' " (Helen Rice Hollis),
"Cup Plates in America" (Jane Shadel Spillman) and "Sewing Tools
in the Collection of Colonial Williamsburg" (Sandra C. Shaffer).

Some newspapers accept art and architectural history and commentary, like "Preserving California's Heritage" (John Muir House)
which was written by Larry Wood, published on the Real Estate
Page of *The Christian Science Monitor.*

BIOGRAPHICAL ARTICLES

Biography seems to touch every other category of writing, and
why not, since history is made by people! We may write of a single
adventure in the life of a man or woman or about one section
of his life (childhood, manhood, influence on society) or a sketch
of a whole career. It might be written to emphasize a single
characteristic like the humor of Lincoln or the single-mindedness
of Peary in his search for the North Pole. Remember the faithfulness
of Ruth and the patience of Job?

The lack of modern heroes and heroines is so great today that
Time devoted half of its July 15, 1974, issue to a survey called
"In Quest of Leadership." Thumbnail sketches of two hundred
men and a *few* women were given. Some Americans in the mid-70's
are looking longingly for heroes to believe in for the future.

We do not seek perfection, however. Catherine Bowen didn't

try to make John Adams over, but showed him as "a blunt man, passionate, willful, vain, and honest to the farmer-Puritan marrow of his well-covered bones." She never lost sight of the *man* even in the midst of historical events which could have overpowered the character she stressed.

A historian tries to be objective and fair, but what he selects as the meaning of a life will be what he himself believes. He must make it clear that what he tells about his hero (or villain) is his interpretation, based on the facts he has gathered.

You present the picture YOU see as well as you can. Select significant details to help the reader understand and appreciate your character, but don't try to cram into an article what one would expect in a book-length biography.

What are some of the methods used to tell stories about people and their past? In the *Post,* Julie Eisenhower talks about her childhood memories of Alice Roosevelt Longworth. A full page article in *The Christian Science Monitor* emphasizes the architectural triumphs of Frank Lloyd Wright, written by William Martin. The fiftieth anniversary of the football debut of Red Grange is told by Jerome Brondfield in *Reader's Digest,* which also published a story about "Bull" Halsey by Admiral Arleigh Burke USN (Ret.).

American Forests accepted a story of John Wentworth, last royal governor of New Hampshire as a *colonial forester* (Robert S. Monahan). "The Lancaster Eagle" in *Yankee* describes John Bellamy's work in carving the eagle for that ship's figurehead and what happened to the eagle later. Yvonne B. Smith, the author, wrote this as a chapter in her biography of Bellamy.

One issue of *New England Galaxy* shows several methods of writing biography: John Hancock's struggle with Great Britain over shipping taxes (Francis H. Hacker); Samuel Flagg Bemis' memories of his Harvard professors; the story of Henry Knox's adventures in bringing guns from Ticonderoga to George Washington in Boston, based on Knox's journal (Doris R. Marston); William K. Bottorff showed the cultural life of Boston in the 1720's to 1750's through the biography of Peter Pelham; Betty Rivers approached the life of Harriet Beecher Stowe from the point of view that she was not an aggressive fiery woman, but a loving woman whose early background had given her a concern for humanity.

Opera News carried the story "Sousa Marches On," reprinted in the *Reader's Digest.* (Its author, Ann M. Ling is well known for her musical writings.) *Away* accepted a story about Johnny Appleseed from Keith Hodgdon. *Guideposts* began in 1974 a series of "first person" articles by American Revoluntionary "eye witnesses," written by the editors.

Argosy did a little "muckraking" in its "Goodbye, Buffalo Bill," but Bill Slattery ends it "He *was* a dear old man and they ought to leave him alone." In *Modern Maturity,* Edna M. Graff wrote about "The Day They Nominated a Woman For President" (Bella Lockwood) and Walter Monfried wrote "The Man Who Brought Us Alice" (Lewis Carroll).

Reader's Digest compiled the writings and remarks of many for "Henry Ford: The Man Behind the Genius," and published a new view of "Machiavelli: The Man and the Reputation" by Ernest O. Hauser, who says that while his name has become a synonym for intrigue and deviousness, Machiavelli was in fact one of history's foremost patriots and political analysts.

I have gone into more detail in this category to show you that biography can be used in many ways to bring freshness and a unique point of view to the lives of historic personages often treated routinely.

ESSAYS - CREATIVE COMMENTARY

Essays are based on your personal views of past experiences or events, and can be articles of protest, commentaries on history, you own interpretation of events and people of the past and the like. It differs from other types of historical writing in that the reader knows that what you are saying is your own opinion. Many literary figures are discussed in this type of writing, with personal commentary and evaluation.

Blake Clark wrote an article in protest of the "Wanton Disregard of our Heritage," published in *The Diplomat. New England Galaxy* printed Alan Seaburg's article "A Typical Thoreau Summer." On the Home Forum Page of the *Christian Science Monitor* is a daily essay which may be on an author's favorite book or commentary on the history of the English language and frequently on art or nature.

The late Robb Sagendorph of *Yankee* once told me that he regretted the lack of attention given to essays by editors, including himself. He said that the essay was the cleanest, finest, most inspiring form of writing and there should be a place for it in the publishing world.

The Atlantic Monthly, Harper's Magazine, Saturday Review, Christian Herald and the literary magazines are possible markets IF you're an expert on something or your writing is "clean and fine" and what you have to say is fresh and convincing.

FOREIGN HISTORY

Many remember the very popular "Twin" books, small readers which described the life of twin children in countries around the world. Who will write a modern version for today's children? The American press publishes considerable material about foreign countries, including articles about foreign travel and history.

On its travel pages the *Boston Sunday Globe* published Olive Tardiff's articles on May Day in Russia and Christmas in Belgium, both combining customs of the past with action of the present. Other newspaper travel editors accept such material, expecting first-hand knowledge and not travel guide information.

Foreign magazines will accept articles which have information about American ties with the country concerned. Although most of its authors are British, *History Today* (London) published "Theodore Roosevelt and the 'Special Relationship' with Britain" by D. H. Burton, professor of American history at St. Joseph's College, Philadelphia.

Americas, published in English, Spanish and Portuguese, prints articles on history, art, literature, music and travel for readers interested in inter-American relations.

By studying several books about a country, or doing research on one phase of foreign life, you could write an acceptable article or filler. I have had newspaper and magazine articles published on the origin of St. Patrick's Day, Orangeman's Day, St. Valentine's Day, Christmas customs around the world and similar material.

PERSONAL EXPERIENCE

Nostalgia, travel, remembering bygone days are some of the areas of personal experience articles. Nostalgia is very popular, perhaps because many people live so much longer and make an audience to share memories with, or it may be escape from much of the ugliness which this decade has faced. Among the joys of childhood for many of us was sitting on Grandpa's knee while he talked about what he did as a boy.

Travel published "Remember When — Everybody (or so it seemed) turned out to welcome or wave goodbye to the passenger trains ...?" J. B. Truscott took a trip into the land of Nostalgia when he rode a steam train and visited museums of railroadiana, and railroad sites. Several regional magazines run series under the heading "I Remember—," with contributions by readers. *Modern Maturity* publishes "I Remember—" articles, too, and *NRTA Journal* carries similar material. One in *MM* was "When We Rode a Sleigh," illustrated with photographs which carried many of us back a long way. Sometimes they publish ". . . was my hero."

Other titles found in my reading: "Learned by Heart in a One-Room School;" "Living It Up in Oldtime Maine" (with blueberry recipes); "In the Heyday of Tourist Business;" "My Friend Buffalo Bill;" "Following The Trail of Zane Grey;" "Cooking on the Old-Time Log Drive;" "Remember The Ice Man?"

This type of writing is most effective if the personal experience is your own or the reminiscences of someone you are interviewing. However, you may recall tales told you by your grandparents or stories of local history, or you may find a diary or a country store customers' account book and embellish these with further details of past customs.

PHOTO ESSAY

This is a story told in pictures with a short accompanying text or with expanded photo captions. One cover of *Salt* shows a variety of barns, with a cover story inside, and more pictures. *Modern Maturity* published "That Gorgeous Gibson Girl," with two inches of text surrounded by pictures created by Charles Dana Gibson eighty years ago. *Maine Life* filled a whole page with pictures and brief stories of old-time hotels, no longer in business.

The Christian Science Monitor once published "Knock! Knock!" which featured knockers from old houses, captioned only with the town. *The Boston Sunday Globe* featured doorways from historic houses in Wiscasset, Maine, each with architectural detail in the caption.

Other ideas I have found in my reading: railroad stations, railroads *(Yankee);* the brick masonry on Main Street, a composite of ancient brick buildings in Michigan *(Ford Times);* derelict ships with a poem as commentary *(Maine Life);* baby carriages of early times *(Modern Maturity).*

SOCIAL CONCERNS

The current mood of America leans toward articles and books which stress the history of, and solution for, such social concerns as mental health, social reform, environment, the morality of government officials, personal morality, crime, the problem of nursing homes, minority groups, poverty, prison reform and many more.

This is a category in which a writer needs to move carefully and selectively, and is certainly not an easy one for the writer not thoroughly experienced in this field. It *is* a subject which needs to be explored and given prominence in our literature.

For example, *Lithopinion,* a quarterly which goes to what the editors call "opinion makers," emphasizes "the elucidation of the changing patterns of public affairs." It is interested in "the contemporary world — politically, sociologically and historically." One recent article was "On the Waterfront" by Alex Gordon, covering the decline and rebirth of New York's waterfront. Another discussed "America's Imperial Presidency."

Black History fits this category, like the article by Jeannye Thorton on Frederick Douglas (father of the civil rights movement) in *The Christian Science Monitor,* which "reveals that his ideals and actions are as relevant as they were a century ago," and "LBJ and Civil Rights" by Charles L. Sanders in *Ebony.*

Some approaches to education belong here, too. An article by Walter Monfried in *NRTA Journal*, "Father of the Public School" points out that Horace Mann believed that universal education is the "great equalizer."

There is great poignancy and a strong reminder that past atrocities must not happen again in articles like "Anne Frank Revisited" by Robert Taylor in the *Boston Sunday Globe.* I shall never forget this one.

Indians and other minority groups need their stories told, like "Magnificent Were the Iroquois" (Wallace Brown, *American History Illustrated)* and "The Continuing Massacre at Wounded Knee" (Terri Schultz, *Harper's Magazine).*

Dreams of Utopia, realized or smashed, are a social concern like "Utopia in American Literature" (Maury Klein, *American History Illustrated).*

Improvements or stalemates of all kinds in society can be considered social concerns: Dorothea Dix's lifelong crusade to change the plight of the insane; Elizabeth Blackwell's one-woman fight for women's recognition as doctors; all the spreading roots and vines begun by Watergate; the continuing exposes by newspapers like *The Christian Science Monitor* and magazines like *The Nation* and *The New Republic* about the past and present problems of nursing home care, the abuse of children, prison reform; the continuing struggle for a good environment for all — the subjects are endless in number.

An interesting study can be made of the work of "specialists" in expose or *muckraking,* as it was called by Theodore Roosevelt: Ida Tarbell in the past century when most of what are now called "investigative reporters" were women; the Queen of the Muckrakers today, Jessica Mitford (See August 1974 *Writer's Digest);* and other modern ones like Drew Pearson and Jack Anderson, his successor, who prefers to be called a *Muckraker.* (See "How I Became a Muckraker" in *Argosy,* May 1974.)

Objectivity is a must for those writing about social concerns, if they wish to avoid the maudlin, "sob sister" efforts used by some journalists of the past. There is enough excitement inherent in the activities of reformers, inventors, social workers and those who for centuries have opposed reform, in just giving the facts.

TOPICAL TIE-IN

While the United States was buzzing over President Nixon's visit to China, *Life* came out with an illustrated historical article called "When the U. S. Sailed to China." One writer, disturbed by the civil war in Ireland, wrote a story of an event which happened on Orangeman's Day when she was a small child in Scotland.

Articles appear every day with a topical tie-in, and there are countless more waiting to be discovered. If you keep files, as suggested, material like this will come in handy during the years ahead.

Note the thousands of articles, books, television and play scripts, written about the American Revolution and the Civil War.

WRITING A COLUMN OR A SERIES

One writer, a Marine wife, decided to write a column of advice for military wives and suggested this to the editor of a county-wide newspaper, who agreed to the idea. It was very successful. When her husband was transferred to another base, she carried her scrapbook of clippings to the editor of a newspaper there, and soon was having her column published in it.

Newspaper editors might be interested in a column of material about history; biographies of local people, background information on area churches or historic buildings and sites. Other ideas are a "Do You Remember" column, a calendar of historical events day by day, 5-10-25-50 years ago. Those with much historical information in their files will see this as an additional way to use researched material.

To start, prepare a calendar book divided into months and years, with plenty of room to paste in or note events, anniversaries, and so on. Then decide what subject or series of subjects appeal to you, and do the necessary research. Prepare five or six columns or articles with pictures. Make an appointment with the editor of the largest newspaper in your area, perhaps a Sunday edition. You may want to send the articles to him several days ahead of the appointment. If he is interested, let him set the fee; however, be sure it is high enough to cover the cost of photographs, or arrange with him to have a staff photographer take them.

Once you agree to furnish the material, you must produce on time and regularly for an agreed length of time: three months, six months, once a week for a year. The editor will probably decide on a trial run to be sure his readers like your material.

If you find a unique angle, your work could develop into a national column, with subjects selected from around the country. To make this happen, after your series has run for a time and you have a representative set of clippings, query a syndicate editor. A list of syndicates and the material they handle is given in *Editor and Publisher Syndicate Directory* ($5.00 from *Editor and Publisher Magazine*, 850 Third Avenue, New York, N.Y. 10022), and in *Writers' Market*. See also the chapter "How to Syndicate Your Own Column" in *The Creative Writer* (Writer's Digest).

Grit carries a column "Wonderful Women." Within days after Gerald Ford became President, "Gerald Ford: the man from Michigan" (Ed Kudlaty and Bob Cochnar) was appearing in papers across the country, from the Newspaper Enterprise Assn. *Rudder* carries a continuing series on "The Great Solo Circumnavigators and Their Boats," a specialty presentation by Jerry Cartwright.

Our state newspaper has published two books, the contents of which first ran as a daily series on the history of the sea. Our county newspaper, a weekly, carries a column of local history and another of reminiscences, both by historical writers, and has just begun serialization of a local history book. Your articles could become a book, too.

FILLERS

Fillers are short articles of under 1,000 words, but usually much shorter. The quiz, puzzles, the anecdote, short quips and such material come under the filler heading, and range from ten words up.

Among the many magazines which accept short historical material are *Amerco World, Enka Voice, Presteel Press* (with a picture or two), *Travel and Leisure, Vulcan Varieties, Argosy* (Adventure column), _Modern Living, Exhibit_ (art history), _The New England Guide, The National Guardsman, New Mexico Magazine, Guideposts, Boating, Football News, Grit, Reader's Digest,_ and most juvenile magazines.

Read with pen in hand, watching for anecdotes in that biography, an unusual fact in that travel book, and scanning newspapers for ideas.

Like poetry, fillers must be written tightly, using the fewest possible words required to tell the story, to paint the picture. Active verbs, thumbnail description, simplest vocabulary cut the word count yet make a complete presentation possible.

CHAPTER TWELVE

HISTORICAL POETRY AND SHORT FICTION

The sensory appeal is often neglected by historians and overlooked by poets. There is poetry in the past — lyrical, heroic, dramatic — for the past is filled with episodes of adventure, with folk sagas, balladry, to stir the imagination and arouse empathy with our ancestors.

Unquestionably, a knowledge of the literary heritage we have both from home and abroad — Whitman, Shakespeare, Browning, Emerson, the Bible, Carl Sandburg, Milton are a few voices that come to mind — will feed our emotions, nurture our thoughts and prepare us to express our enthusiasm in poetic form, in verse and song.

"America is a poem in our eyes ..." Emerson wrote in 1843. Patriotism has risen and waned and in the mid-seventies is rising again. Perhaps there will be a new American Renaissance in the coming decades, a re-awakening, a new appreciation of the world's heritage, a new national heroic literature.

There is no better way to express this growing pride than through poetry.

In *Daniel Boone,* Stephen Vincent Benet wrote of his hero who "walked by night when the phantom deer arise and all lost wild America was burning in their eyes." *Poet Lore* is keeping the narrative poem alive, offering top money prizes for the winning poems in the Stephen Vincent Benet contest held annually. Its late editor-publisher, John Williams Andrews, succeeded in reviving the traditional historical narrative poem. In 1970, he published *Triptyck for the Atomic Age* (Branden) which includes "A Ballad of Channel Crossings." Mr. Andrews' final work, a lifetime effort, is a saga of the life of Charles Lindbergh and the world he lived in, a book-length, *The Round World Under.*

Duncan Emrich's *American Folk Poetry* (Little, Brown, 1974) covers 300 years of history, tragedy and comedy. He is the former chief of the Library of Congress' folklore section.

Lyrical poetry, also, tells of man's dreams and heartaches, the spirituals and hymns, for example. Poetry is the purest form of writing in which to tell the story of mankind.

If you have such a story to tell, even editors who do not usually accept poetry may be receptive. *The Saturday Evening Post* published a definite exception: a full-page poem, "The Fathers and Sons Banquet" by Ray Bradbury.

Have faith in your work and dare to approach an editor if you think his readers would share your enthusiasm for your story.

William Packard, editor-publisher of the *The New York Quarterly,* is a history scholar. Study "The American Experience" in the *Quarterly* for Spring 1973 for a lesson in the writing of poetry about America. He says, "Of course this American character is infinitely variable, just as the American experience itself is endlessly open and continuous. And perhaps the true subject matter of contemporary American poetry is this open flow of experience — how it all goes on and on and on, as if we could define ourselves indefinitely." Mr. Packard is receptive to poetry written with insight and careful craftsmanship.

Finding a market for poetry of a specific type requires research. Here are some which accept poetry with history themes: *New England Galaxy, The Christian, War Cry, Seven, The Christian Science Monitor, New Hampshire Profiles* (about New Hampshire), *North/Nord* (Canada), *Texas Metro Magazine, Westways, Beau Cocoa* (black experience), *Conradiana* (Joseph Conrad and his world), *Kansas Quarterly* (Mid-Plains region), *The Virginia Quarterly Review, Hyacinths and Biscuits, Major Poets, Poems from the Hills* (Appalachia). You will find more as you study the market.

HISTORY IN SHORT FICTION

When a serious writer of history decides to write historical fiction, he finds himself struggling between his scholarly leanings and his sense of creativity.

Although I have discussed using fiction techniques in nonfiction, these are, of course, developed more fully in writing fiction. You must be familiar with methods of characterization and plotting, of using flashbacks, description and transitions.

Viewpoint is important in writing historical fiction. You must be certain that your characters think and act *in their own time and situation.* In their speech or customs or reaction to any situation, there must be no hint of events to come or of changes in mores. They can know only what they see or feel or are told or have experienced.

In the early part of our American history, the slowness of communication must be remembered, for people seldom got the news of towns other than their own for several days, perhaps weeks.

When writing fiction, start out with a few fundamental rules in mind:

1. Don't distort history but weave your fictional theme into the historical background. Use your research material sparingly.

2. Give a faithful picture of customs, housekeeping, business procedures, cultural pursuits, pastimes and whatever else will enable your reader to feel he is a part of the story. Often a few details will be enough, but to find just the right details will require careful research.

3. Present whatever historical figures you use with accuracy. It is preferable to use popular heroes of the past as background or supporting characters rather than as hero or heroine. Never place a real person in a situation or place he could not have been according to history.

4. Whatever historic events you use as the setting for your story must be accurate in detail, in time and in location, but here, again, avoid loading your story down with too much information. Remember, you're telling a *story.* Fiction achieves realism through the use of sensory perception. This means your research must be done with awareness for details which will convey to a reader of the present what people of the past saw, heard, smelled, tasted and touched. (People are people in every century, so this is usually easier than it seems.) Watching for anachronisms is a constant challenge.

5. It is legitimate to create your main characters and set them

into a period of history, using exciting events as a part of their lives. Many nameless figures have participated in historical events, and this is a favorite ploy of fiction writers.

6. Avoid selecting a period or event about which it is difficult to secure information. The locale you choose should be one you can describe with accuracy. It is best if you can visit it, for the quality of historical fiction depends greatly on the writer's ability to create an authentic atmosphere in another time, another place.

Although the general women's magazines seldom publish historical fiction, there are other markets. Among them are these: *The Saturday Evening Post; Grit,* especially for children; *Black World* (dealing with Black America, Caribbean, African experience); *St. Louisan; War Cry* (Biblical, church holidays); *The Philatelic Reporter; Dimensions; The Sample Case.*

Some literary magazines use historical fiction: *The Above Ground Review; Negro History Bulletin* (folklore, myths, and brief historical plays – American or foreign); *South Dakota Review* (Western setting preferred).

Among the men's magazines using fiction are: *Action for Men; True Action* (adventure, crime, World War II, profiles: "all story backgrounds should be carefully researched"); *Argosy* (the sea, mysteries, war, but the editors prefer nonfiction); *Cavalier; Ellery Queen* (mystery based on historical background).

A few regional magazines use fiction: *Bucks County Panorama Magazine* (must be oriented to Bucks County); *Connecticut Magazine* (Connecticut humor, history); *Western Fiction* (wild West only); *Zane Grey Western Magazine* ("authentic, realistic western background"); *Yankee* (New England).

A REMINDER

Don't send manuscripts to any of the magazines or newspapers listed, without studying several copies. If in doubt, query even if the market requirements do not say you must. Magazine titles mean nothing, for each periodical has its own slant, its own preferences and you must *know* them.

CHAPTER THIRTEEN

ILLUSTRATING YOUR WORK

History is recorded not only with words but with brush and camera and chisel, with pen and needle and carving tools. Many who could not write at all have left their mark in handcarved furniture and colored paintings on cliff walls, priceless jewelry and pieced quilts, pottery hardened by sun and towns hacked out of wilderness.

The Flowering of American Folk Art: 1776-1876 by Jean Lipman and Alice Winchester (Viking 1974) is full of the spirit of a young nation. Through all civilization men and women have found joy in creative expression and added through the artifacts of even their small world a sense of beauty and their personal history.

The writer will grow in awareness and appreciation of his heritage while he does research to find illustrations to help give more meaning to his ideas. He will come to realize that the history of sculpture or home decoration or cartooning is an important part of the history of a people.   The narrative of art history reveals not only the evolution of style, but the evolution of peoples. Illustrations of all types tell the story of society.

Just as the successful writer is one who can change with the changing market, writing new subjects in a new style, so he must select his illustrations to comform to new ideas. Emphasis today is on reality rather than the "pretty." Unity and coherence are as important in illustration as in writing.

You must think of illustrations for your material from the date you select a subject. Perhaps much of what you expect to publish will not require illustration. How do you know for sure? You might be doing a newspaper feature which you think would require only one simple photograph, if any, and then when the research and first writing are done, find that you have a "sleeper" — material which can be of national interest. That is not the time to scramble around looking for illustrations.

Finding illustrations may require as much research as your writing. I have always thought it worth the effort. In your reading and explorations be alert to the possibilities of using more imaginative illustrations to complement your photographs. Sometimes catalogues offered primarily to artists will have good suggestions for writers.

You may get involved in considerable correspondence and detective work. I remember one time, after months of research, finding the paintings I needed to illustrate an important article. I had seen one first on a calendar. The paintings were in a private museum and it was necessary to clear the permission to use with the artist. It took some doing to secure his address, and then a wait of a month or more before a gracious letter came, granting permission.

The letter was given to the museum, an order placed for copies to be photographed, and finally the precious pictures were in my hands. The editor paid for having them photographed that time. If you want to keep the photographs for further use, you should pay for them yourself.

In addition to the usual photographs of people and places taken on the spot or bought from a museum or other source, there are numerous kinds of material you could use as well. Among them are advertisements, business catalogues, calendars, postcards, paintings, playbills, placards, etchings, sculpture, maps, hundreds of kinds of decorative arts and unusual artifacts.

Before the coming of photography, silhouettes were popular. To produce these black paper cutouts pasted on white cards, the artist would place his subject in shadow against a white background and with scissors snip a likeness. A silhouette of Jane Austen's sister, Cassandra, was painted on plaster and bronzed by John Miers around 1812. One of the loveliest of crafts, etching on glass, is related to this art. The likenesses of many famous people will be found in silhouette and make an interesting contrast in illustration. Hans Christian Andersen was a skillful silhouettist.

Probably the most popular types of illustrations are cartoons and caricatures of people in the news. These tell much about social conditions and political persuasions of the times. Paul Revere was famous for the caricatures he made in the Revolutionary period.

This was sometimes referred to as "lampooning." The American Antiquarian Society has a complete set of Revere prints.

Another strong influence in this field was Thomas Nast. While his political cartoons were better and effective, he also created the concept of Santa Claus. Often eighteenth and nineteenth century newspapers and periodicals used cartoons to give visual and humorous expression to their political bias — as still done today.

ILLUSTRATING ARTICLES

Good photographs accompanying a manuscript will help to make a sale which might otherwise be lost.

Some articles depend more on the illustrations than the text. For example, an article in *Modern Maturity* prepared by the editorial staff, "The Way We Looked," features photos most in demand during the past 74 years of all those made by Brown Brothers, stock photographers. Without the pictures, there would have been no story.

American History Illustrated prefers to have a hand in finding illustrations, although it welcomes suggestions. An article "Who Was Gutzon Borglum?" by M. Samuel Cannon and Gabriel Palkuti used fifteen illustrations, most of them provided by the latter. "The Outer Space Beauty of Maxfield Parrish" by Julie Eisenhower in *The Saturday Evening Post* would have had less impact without the striking Parrish pictures, each with its identifying caption, accompanying the biographical text.

In the May 1974 issue of *Antiques,* the article on "Some Eagle-decorated Furniture at the Department of State" by Clement E. Conger and Jane W. Pool was considerably enchanced by the nineteen pictures showing eagle-decorated furniture. The April 1974 issue of *Antiques* is a treasure, for it is almost completely devoted to the history of Kentucky, each article beautifully illustrated, covering all phases of the state from the Kentucky Derby to log houses, from historic preservation to portraits of Kentuckians, from heirloom quilts to glass and silver. Prints and photographs came from museums, state archives, private collections, the Kentucky Historical Society, and many from the Helga Photo Studio.

WHERE DO WE LOOK?

To find illustrations, you use the same techniques as for nonpictorial research. Here are some leads. Each will open up another source.

1. *Books.* Use your library's card catalogue to find books on your particular subject. Those that contain a list of illustrations will carry the abbreviation "Illus." on the card, or actually spell out "146 illustrations."

Read the list of illustrations in each book and the acknowledgment of their origin. Make notes of those you can use.

Depending on your subject matter, books like *The Story of America in Pictures* by Alan C. Collins, and perhaps the older the better, can be useful. I found my copy in a secondhand store. You will find pictures of fashions, household equipment, architecture, pictures of events and places in numerous books of each historical period. The indexes of *American Heritage* and *Time-Life Books* will be helpful. Look for leads in the library reference room where lists of collections and other compilations are kept. Study book club brochures and catalogues from "remainder" book firms like the Publishers Central Bureau, which offers reasonably priced books on countless subjects.

2. *Periodicals and Newspapers.* Every issue of current and past history magazines is filled with illustrations, which also give their origins. You will find pictures in all types of magazines from *Ladies Home Journal,* which occasionally publishes an article like the biography of Mary Todd Lincoln (October 1972), to *Argosy,* which publishes adventure features frequently, to regional magazines which use many old-time illustrations.

To find out whether magazines have published photographs or drawings of a particular subject, look first in *Poole's Index to Periodical Literature* or *Reader's Guide,* and in periodical indexes like that of *National Geographic.* Most libraries keep back files of magazines for many years. In the *Reader's Guide,* for example, the entry for a particular magazine article will usually indicate "Por." for articles which have accompanying portraits of the subject, and "Ill." to indicate the article has accompanying illustrations.

Advertisements in magazines may be important sources. Among

examples I have found for reproduction as illustrative material, are fashions (hats, hair styles, gowns, shoes), pictures of Georgian silver, period furniture, clocks, artifacts, sketch of a whaling boat, many paintings offered for sale by art galleries, war posters, a 1793 portrait of Empress Catherine the Great, patent medicines, period paper dolls, automobiles. Magazines in the antiques field are especially useful.

Some magazines publish collections of their photographs. Yankee Publishing Company, for example, offers several collections, including *That New England*, which has 225 photographs, including sailing ships, classic autos and trains of old-time New England.

The news services keep files of their photographs and will sell one for about $20. Look first in newspaper indexes under your subject for dates of events. Newspapers will make you a print of a photograph taken of a local event for a smaller fee. Inquire at newspaper libraries. Your best bet is to study the newspapers themselves for the period you are researching.

3. *Government Sources.* The Library of Congress, Prints and Photographs Division, Washington, D.C. 20540, the National Archives, Still Picture Branch, same address, and most departments of government (agriculture, armed services, forestry) will help serious writers to locate illustrations.

The Smithsonian is preparing a Bicentennial *Inventory* of American Paintings executed before 1914. A collection of photographs and reproductions will be developed along with the written-record *Inventory*. The complete *Inventory* will be produced by artist, present location and subject. You may have direct access to the complete *Inventory* (not a catalogue) by visiting the office or by writing to it beginning in late 1976. Researchers may write to Miss Abigail Booth, Coordinator, Bicentennial Inventory of American Paintings, National Collection of Fine Arts, Smithsonian Institution, Washington, D.C. 20560. Duplication of pages pertaining to an inquiry will be supplied by mail, starting in late 1976. Information about federal collections of other kinds may be obtained by writing to the other places given here.

The National Archives have the Mathew Brady Civil War collection, *New York Times'* Paris office archives and the works of many prominent photographers. The Smithsonian has published several helpful books like *Portraits of the American Stage 1771-1971,* and has at least thirteen museums and galleries of art. Archives of American Art (with branches in several cities) has more than 70,000 photographs and other information on artists.

I have obtained photographs from the National Park Service and from the Naval Library at Annapolis, and information about historic ships with photographs from the Department of the Navy. There are catalogues published by several Federal departments listing available illustrations including maps.

Among other useful reference books furnished by the government are the *Guide to the Special Collections of Prints and Photographs in the Library of Congress* and *Image of America, Early Photographs 1839-1900.* Some libraries have a collection of government booklets and catalogues, and most national sites have booklets on battles and other events, and historical personages.

Check for further government holdings under *Government* in the library's catalogue card index.

4. *Cities and Towns.* The City of Philadelphia is only one example of many communities which offer free photographs to writers. Philadelphia's two sources are: (1) the office of the city representative, which supplies black and white prints and color transparencies on the city and urban subjects without charge; or the representative will direct you to the correct local source; (2) the city archivist, City Hall, who has a large collection of historical photographs on many subjects to lend without fee, or he will have prints made from valuable glass negatives for a nominal fee. Address: 1660 Municipal Services Building, Philadelphia 19107. Other cities and some towns have similar holdings.

Chambers of Commerce may not offer such complete service, but they often supply photographs of local historical interest free.

Sources not often considered but useful are city tour guides and local travel bureau guides, and city street directories, which might have old maps and photos. A good example of this source is *Man-Made Philadelphia* (M.I.T. Press 1972) prepared by Richard S. Wurman and John Gallery, local architects. (If no such guide exists in your city, there lies an opportunity for you.)

5. *State Archives.* State archivists usually answer inquiries about their holdings relative to the state's history. A small fee may be charged for photographs of documents, portraits or other material. These are better quality than photocopies, which cannot be used for reproduction. Photographs suitable for reproduction are printed on glossy stock. Be sure to ask for this type if you plan to use them for publication. Color, if available, would be transparencies and would have to be purchased.

State offices which supply photographs and information to writers use varying titles for their departments: Development Commission, Department of Tourism, State Publicity Bureau and the like. Some state publicity bureaus are maintained by business firm memberships, but most will furnish photographs of historic sites and give information free. Write to the state office building in the state capitol for information. The chief requirement is the mention of the state in a credit line. Be specific in your queries.

Material mentioned here is seldom given exclusively to any one writer. When you use photographs from such sources, it is courteous to send a tearsheet of your article to the person providing the material.

Another type of state-sponsored source is the State Council on the Arts. For example, the New York Council has prepared "Main Street — The Heart of the American Town," a folio of fifty black and white reproductions of photographs illustrating architectural details through street scenes and close-ups of the individual buildings. It has also produced a series of exhibit portfolios showing aspects of the Erie Canal history and canal life through maps, broadsides, prints, documents, photographs and so on.

Maine's Sea and Shore Fisheries Department has published an excellent free booklet, well-illustrated, describing the history of the fishing industry. Each state department (agriculture, forestry, parks, etc.) emphasizes its specialty and usually has free photographs and printed material available.

State libraries and state historical societies are invaluable sources of information.

6. *Museums.* There is no general procedure employed for cataloguing museum collections for public information. Browsing in museum

sales rooms, studying the guidebooks and reading catalogues of current shows may provide good leads. Watch the newspapers for current listings of exhibits. One example of a show catalogue is *A Century of Illustration 1850-1972*, issued by the Brooklyn Museum, showing examples from novels, periodicals and other publications.

Most museums publish booklets like the Boston Museum of Fine Arts' "Great Americans From the Revolution to the Civil War."

Museums usually answer questions promptly and might offer suggestions for further research. The cost for securing a black and white print of a portrait or etching would be under $5, unless it is a special order. You will be permitted to use such copies in articles but must include a credit line mentioning the museum as well as the title of the painting and its artist.

The Smithsonian's Division of Postal History has a large collection of postcards, including a series used as political propaganda. One reference source in this category is *Picture Postcards* by Marion Klamkin (Dodd, Mead 1974).

Remember that illustrative material in museums is not limited to paintings and sculpture but also includes architecture, fashions, artifacts, prints, posters, lithographs, drawings, cartoons, color slides, among many others, and often books, pamphlets, postcards, documents and maps, which can be photographed or copied for publishing.

A milestone in the history of photography was the establishment in the Fall of 1974 of the International Center of Photography in New York City. Its purpose, director Cornell Capa says, is to provide a center for the dissemination of "documentary commentary photography that is deeply involved with man and his environment."

Long established and the first museum of photography in the country is the International Museum of Photography at the George Eastman House, Rochester, New York. This important source is very kind about answering inquiries.

7. *Historic Buildings and Village Restorations.* You will usually find good files of materials and old photographs, and information about additional sources in libraries here. If there is no librarian, the

director will have ideas for you: individuals with photographs, what other houses or villages might have on your subject. Most will have books, pamphlets, catalogues, slides and postcards for sale. Many will offer information from their files.

Ask the librarians or curators for suggestions for illustrations other than photographs. You may be able to secure copies of broadsides, posters, Victorian valentines and a good many other types you would not know about. It is a good idea to read publicity brochures first.

Sometimes a director will gladly furnish free photos since he is eager to spread news of holdings. Your thanks can best be expressed by sending him a tearsheet of your article or giving credit to the source in article or book. More often, the director requires payment for one-time use of photographs or the publication of color slides which you buy. Occasionally you will be allowed to take your own photographs.

Make certain of the procedure in each case before you begin research.

8. *Libraries.* State, local, special, historical societies and museums often have tremendous historical collections. For example, the New York Public Library has more than 100,000 prints, many relating to the history of the United States. Displayed on a wall at the New York Historical Society building was the print of a waterfront scene of the 1800's, which was just what I needed for background information, and I ordered a copy for $2.50.

If your smaller library does not have indexes of special collections, you will have to travel to a city library. In the latter there will be a Rare Books Division, an Art-Photography Division, periodical indexes, a great many expensive art books which smaller libraries cannot afford, and special catalogues of illustrative material. The larger library's card catalogue will also be comparatively better since it contains more holdings.

It is always better to go in person to a library, for most librarians don't have time to do research by mail. Most important, a librarian often has in his or her head a vast amount of knowledge which can only be shared personally.

Reference desk attendants at university libraries can guide you to state and town archive collections, and to the holdings of other facilities throughout the state.

9. *Industry and Business.* From photographs of antique cars to diagrams of the hand-cranking telephone, public relations departments will have treasures of illustrative material. You must be specific to give personnel a clear idea of your needs.

Banks and insurance companies often use historical material on calendars and are especially likely to sponsor publications of local history pamphlets. Some firms invest in art treasures.

Most firms keep files of information and photographs of past history. Local branches of national firms can get you photographs from the head office.

10. *Special Interest Organizations.* There are hundreds of groups like the American Red Cross, the Cowboy Rodeo Association, Daughters of the American Revolution, the National Safety Council, the Appalachian Mountain Club, the General Federation of Women's Clubs, the Boy and Girl Scouts, the National Recreation Association and more listed in the *World Almanac* or *The Encyclopedia of Associations.* Most will provide photographs of their programs, or give you guidance to other sources. Again, be specific.

11. *Stock Photographers.* Huge stocks of photographs are filed under every conceivable subject in the offices of professional firms. Most of them are in New York City. A list appears periodically in most photographic magazines. A recently published one, in paperback form, is included in the book *Where And How To Sell Your Photographs* (Amphoto Books $7.95).

Writers can't afford to purchase photographs from these agencies in the hope of selling an article; but editors may purchase photos from them to accompany an article.

Local photographers sometimes have a file of photographs or negatives of the area. One in our town makes prints for $2.

12. *State and Local Historical Societies.* These are excellent sources for old-time photographs and other illustrative material. Your local society can lead you to others which might be helpful.

In Maine — and probably in other states — state and town historical societies are cooperating in the establishment of a general listing of holdings in an effort to identify and preserve these records of the past.

13. *Private Firms.* For 50¢ you can order the *Dover Pictorial Archives Catalogue* from the Dover Publishing Company, 180 Warick Street, New York 10014. This is a catalogue of this company's books of copyright-free art and photographs on businesses, decorative arts, early American costumes, heraldry, armour, architectural design, seventeenth century games, etc.

14. *Private Collectors.* What do your friends have in their homes in the way of old photographs, valentines, postcards, programs from the theatre and other keepsakes? Several people in our town have outstanding collections of regional photographs taken at the turn of the century and before. One has a complete collection of *Saturday Evening Post* covers. Another collects railroadiana. A man in a neighboring town has a museum-like collection of material about Abraham Lincoln. A trolley museum nearby has a great collection of photographs and one of the largest collections of trolley car booklets, postcards and books on trolley history.

Among business firms which have important collections is Parke, Davis & Company, which commissioned a series of paintings on the history of medicine. The artist was Robert A. Thom of Birmingham, Michigan. These are of great interest to historians because they are accurate in detail of costume, hair styles, furnishings and so forth, achieved through the artist's painstaking research.

15. *Artists, Illustrators, Commercial Artists.* A few magazines like *Ford Times* employ artists to illustrate their articles. Editors of some children's magazines use drawings instead of photographs.

You may decide to illustrate your own material with drawings. However, most editors prefer to select their own illustrators. Never jeopardize a sale by sending inferior art. If a friend wants to illustrate your material, be sure to tell the editor that the drawings are only suggestions, and make sure your friend knows that editors have their own preferences in illustration style.

Although it is difficult to do, you must be as sure as possible that the illustrations you use are historically accurate. A letter written by a seventh grade boy was printed in *The Christian Science*

Monitor. The young man pointed out that a recent political cartoon of President Gerald Ford showed him using his right hand, when he is left-handed; and, he added, Benjamin Franklin was left-handed, too!

16. *Films and Slides.* Uncle Sam is the country's largest producer of films, video tapes and audiovisual material. Documentary films by the thousands are at the National Archives: World War II, polar exploration, development of the United States and its people, the Ford collection, the March of Times series, are a few. The Library of Congress also has a huge film library. The United States Office of Education offers a catalogue of motion pictures, film strips, and slides which are available for public use from federal agencies, and a national list of other places (called depositories) where material can be obtained, with brief notes on their holdings. Write to the Office of Education at 400 Maryland Avenue, SW, Washington, D.C. 20202.

Some libraries, museums and historical societies have film collections. All universities have special audiovisual departments.

The Museum of Modern Art in New York City is another leader in the preservation of films, and has a card index of important films since 1889.

Photos of old-time movie stars and information on the moving picture industry may be obtained from the Screen Actors Guild, 7750 Sunset Boulevard, Hollywood, California 90046. *The Great Movies* by William Bayer (G. & I. Publications) and similar books have hundreds of photos as well as information on the history of films.

Color slides of historic events, sites and people are on sale at most shops in historic buildings, museums, national parks, village restorations and other places receiving historical emphasis. Permission for publication must be arranged with the management of the historic location. You can also get ideas for illustrations by studying these.

Investigate collections of stereopticon pictures and lantern slides, also, as source material.

There are many audiovisual firms and film producers throughout the country which offer filmstrips, moving pictures, still pictures and other items, from which illustrations might be available for a reprint credit line. See *Artist's Market* (Writer's Digest) for a list of these.

PICTORIAL HISTORY

Any article or book whose success depends on illustrations as much or more than on words may be called "pictorial."

In the 1970's publishers are going all out for lavishly illustrated books, many in color, some using both color and black and white. Among the history-oriented types are arts and crafts, art history, folk art, photography, biography, fashion, social cultures, regional history or art, history of events or places or symbols told graphically with more illustrations than text.

Like any writing, you begin with an idea. Many of the suggestions in Chapter II and Chapter V can be carried out with a maximum of illustrations and a minimum of words. An idea's effectiveness for this type of writing can be determined by the quality and number — and originality — of the illustrations you find after a little research.

Since it could be expensive in both cash and time to find enough illustrations, you will want to query publishers before going too far with an idea. Don't start a pictorial history project unless you are sure you have several possible buyers, can maintain interest in it and find sufficient material to complete a worthwhile piece of work.

Pictorial history books may take double the research and leg work required for books with only a few illustrations. Most publishers prefer the work of professionals, expert in the field of the book. Yet there is no reason why an experienced writer — or an enthusiastic amateur willing to learn the necessary techniques and to devote himself wholeheartedly to the project — cannot put together an acceptable book. But be sure you have some interest from a publisher in the subject matter before you spend too much time in useless research.

If you decide it's worth pursuing, here are some suggestions:

Step 1. Research your existing competition in already published books — studying all illustrations and their sources. What new contribution could *your* book make to this subject?

2. Make a one-page outline of the idea you have chosen and your aim as soon as you have done enough research to know where you are going. Make photocopies of the outline to send with queries.

3. Start a card file index of illustrations — not only photos but every type of illustration which could be associated with your idea. Each card must include the title of the illustration, its type, its creator (painter, photographer, cartoonist) and the date created, where the original is, place you found the illustration (book title, author, page; museum, its location, direction for finding it again), short description. If possible, make a photocopy and put it with the card. Later, transfer to the text file.

4. Carefully record research information, using whatever method you have chosen from those suggested in earlier chapters. Coordinate information with illustrations in the card file wherever applicable, so you have a cross index. This will prevent illustrations and text from becoming separated — and buried.

5. Write letters to those sources brought to light through your research. You may also decide to write to certain historical societies, libraries in major cities, newspapers, etc., which you think might give you leads.

Each letter should be addressed to an individual and be typed, not mimeographed. Send a photocopied outline to give the recipient an idea of the scope of your work. Ask for suggestions for other sources.

Assure your source that you are willing to pay for charges for copying or having prints made for the right illustrations, and that you will give credit for pictures used.

6. Several months later, check your progress. To find material not yet available, you may need to plan a trip for on-the-spot research. Plan it well, try to combine with other writing research, and remember research trips are tax deductible if good records are kept.

7. When you have an attractive package of interesting illustrations

supporting your basic theme, send a query letter to a publisher who has shown an interest in pictorial history or in your particular subject matter. If he says "not interested," try the next publisher on your list. If a dozen say no, you may not have a marketable idea at this time. But when a publisher says, "Let's see the rest of the book," you have a worthwhile incentive for the balance of your research effort.

PUBLISHED PICTORIAL HISTORIES

Because it is the natural way to communicate beauty to many people, the art world is the largest group to publish books with a great many pictures. Art books are priced much higher than trade books, due to the tremendous expense of color reproduction. Conversely adding to the cost — often in the $25 range or higher — is the fact that comparatively few are sold. Most you will find only in large libraries.

The trend in nostalgia is bringing forth a number of photographic books, filled with priceless pictures of the past. Among these are: *Farm Boy,* the photographic history of Bill Hammer Jr., taken by Archie Lieberman (Abrams 1974), and *The Way Life Was* by Jeffrey Simpson, picturing aspects of American life from 1880 to 1915, as photographed by sixteen photographers (Praeger 1974).

Some biographies are being published with an amazing number of illustrations, like *Churchill: Photographic Portrait* by Martin Gilbert, written to coincide with Sir Winston Churchill's 100th birthday (Houghton Mifflin 1974). In the course of his research Gilbert gathered some 5,000 photographs and cartoons, — many from Churchill's private albums — and has selected 364 for this volume, many reproduced for the first time. Accompanying the photos are detailed captions with quotations from Churchill's speeches, books and papers.

What famous person's personal photo collection might *you* have access to for a book?

What can happen when insufficient care is given priceless material is exemplified in *The American Heritage Century Collection of Civil War Art,* edited by Stephen W. Sears (McGraw). This rare visual record of the Civil War appeared nearly 100 years ago in three years of successive issues of *Century Magazine*. The originals dropped out of sight when they were sold at auction in 1915. They were recovered in New Orleans in 1973. Scores of selected engravings made from sketches by combat photographers have brought art and history together in this volume. What other "missing" source material like this is waiting to be discovered by writers and historians?

Among the numerous regional offerings from all across the States are *Own Home* by Bob Adelman (McGraw 1972) who captured the life of Camden, Alabama, and its citizens in 129 photographs, with text in the residents' own words; and *Martha's Vineyard* (Viking 1970) where 79 photographs by Alfred Eisenstaedt and brief text by Henry Beetle Hough tell the Massachusetts island story from earliest times. Few regional books like these are nationally know, but they do very well in their own areas, and are usually published by regional publishing firms.

Relating past to present with hundreds of black and white and color illustrations are *Who's Who in the Old Testament* by Joan Comey, and *Who's Who in the New Testament* by Ronald Brownrigg. Published by Holt, Rinehart and Winston in 1971, both books are alphabetically arranged references to the men and women of the Bible, set in the context of history and geography, and enlightened by recent archaeological discoveries in the Holy Land. Seen in *The Faces of Jesus* by Frederick Buechner (Simon & Schuster 1974) with more than 150 full-color photographs by Lee Boltin, are the most beautiful and unusual portraits of Jesus' life produced by various cultures over a period of 2,000 years.

Anyone's hobby or special interest might result in a book of this type: In 1973 the first illustrated history of the musical box, *Clockwork Music* by Arthur W.J.G.Ord-Hume, was published by Crown. This tells in an unusual way the story of the instruments of mechanical music from the music box to the pianola by interweaving the history of the instruments with early advertisements, catalogues and newspaper articles.

There are 577 illustrations telling the history of painted decoration on American furniture in the first book of its kind: *American Painted Furniture 1660-1880* by Dean A. Fales Jr. (Dutton 1972).

So, in finding an original idea and deciding to write pictorial articles or a book, you can draw on all that has been written in the past as well as your own experience, and you will find that just about every field of interest can be developed into such material. It may take much more work, but it may also result in greater satisfaction for both writer and reader.

CHAPTER FOURTEEN

THE WRITER AS PHOTOGRAPHER

Illustrations may make the difference in the sale of your article manuscript. When choosing between two articles of equal merit, an editor will often select the one with the best pictures.

If you can take professional photographs, you have an advantage. While you are learning the craft, you might find a local talented amateur photographer to work with you on speculation, sharing equally in the sale. Sometimes a professional photographer would work with you on the same terms. Often he would prefer to take the pictures you need and sell them to you, which can be expensive.

Occasionally a newspaper or regional magazine editor will send a photographer to take the pictures while you do the story, but the most successful writers have taken photography courses or taught themselves well enough to become their own best photographers.

An editor of a national magazine who assigns a story to a professional writer after a query by the author, usually assigns a professional photographer to do the illustrations.

Daily shooting rates by members of the Society of Photographic Communicators are $200 with prices for publication of individual photographs varying from $50 on up, depending on the circulation of the magazine.

When you are working on a story, think out the scenes carefully to avoid a return trip or less than satisfactory pictures. The photographs and other illustrations should coordinate with the important points of your material. Give the editor a good choice of subject.

If you decide to take your own photographs, you will need *two* cameras: one for color transparencies and one for black and white pictures. Professional photographers don't agree on the best cameras. Some prefer the 2-1/4 x 2-1/4 twin-lens reflex for color transparencies or slides, and a 35mm for black and white. Others prefer larger or single-lens cameras. Until you can afford a good camera and know how to use it effectively, plan to work with a photographer, for mediocre pictures are worse than none at all,

You must have two cameras if you plan to sell material with color illustrations. You can sell the same material to more than one noncompetitive market, using black and white only for some, and color at other times. You might get some beautiful color slides which you could sell as magazine covers. Only a few editors of very small publications will accept Polaroid pictures.

I find the experts in a camera shop most helpful in deciding on just the right equipment, and most give discounts to professional writers not only on equipment but on supplies and developing. They can recommend books to guide you in the use of the camera and in taking pictures for the best effects.

Editors want color transparencies or slides, not color prints, since the former reproduce better. Black and white prints should be 8 x 10 unless an editor says he will accept 5 x 7. Larger prints, unless especially ordered, belong only in the photography salon. Some newspapers will use 5 x 7, but learn editorial preferences.

SIMPLE TECHNIQUES

You don't need a lot of expensive equipment to take good illustrations. Later, when you have become competent, you will want to take photographs for covers and the top magazines. That is another story.

Your most precious tool is your mind. A little thought in planning the photograph makes a great difference in the results. Just as you use an outline as a guide in writing, you need a planning phase in taking photographs. The best editing is going on at the moment you are taking the picture.

Look for the "symbols" of your subject. Ask yourself, "What is a visual symbol of this?" An example that comes to mind is the photographing of George Washington's birthplace site in Virginia. One symbol is the graciousness of plantation living, which suggested a picture from the house across the expanse of meadow to the river. Look for the drama in both the story and the scene before you and select shots to convey this to the reader.

Watch also for unusual views: the half shadows on a roof, the sparkle of light on water, the halo effect of back lighting when taking inside photographs of furnishings, the use of reflection, the effect of modern people in action against the historical background.

Plan for a variety of shots: close-ups and distance, changes in angle, framing by a branch in the foreground or trying for an unexpected lighting effect. Check before you click the shutter to be sure no post or tree comes out in the wrong spot, no mirror or window pane is reflecting your flash for an indoor scene. Take both vertical and horizontal shots to give more latitude in editorial make-up.

No pictures are of any use unless they tell a story and capture the spirit of the occasion. The story must stand alone, but the photographs also should be able to tell a lot of the story without a text. Take many more shots than you think you will need.

Keep a record of all expenses for tax purposes and to estimate the cost of this particular manuscript.

You will need to carry photo releases for times when you have people in your scenes.

Most magazines and newspapers do not require releases on photographs to be used strictly for editorial illustrations. But a model release *is* required from all recognizable persons in a picture which is to be used for advertising purposes (including photographs appearing in sponsored publications, company brochures, etc.), or which *may* be used for advertising purposes (for example, a magazine cover).

The release protects the photographer against possible suits for invasion of privacy or legal damages, since many states have laws which forbid a name, picture, or quotation from being used for commercial purposes without the subject's authorization. If the person in the photograph is a minor, the release must be signed by his parents or guardians.

You can type up a simple agreement form and have copies run off at your nearest photocopy or letter shop for use as needed.

Here's what a sample model's release looks like:

In consideration for value received, receipt whereof is acknowledged, I hereby give (name of firm or publication) the absolute right and permission to copyright and/or publish, and/or resell photographic portraits or pictures of me, or in which I may be included in whole or in part, for art, advertising, trade or any other lawful purpose whatsoever.

I hereby waive any right that I may have to inspect and/or approve the finished product or the advertising copy that may be used in connection therewith, or the use to which it may be applied.

I hereby release, discharge and agree to save (name of firm or publication) from any liability by virtue of any blurring, distortion, alteration, optical illusion or use in composite form, whether intentional or otherwise, that may occur or be produced in the making of said pictures, or in any processing tending towards the completion of the finished product.

Date_____   Model_____

Address_____

_____

Witness_____

The "value received" varies from a professional model's fee, down to the simple gratification for the subject in seeing his or her photograph published.

Each photograph, and that includes all illustrations, should have an explanatory note or caption. Except when the photo is used without accompanying text, the caption is intended to identify the picture or other illustration, not to tell a story about it. Describe it as briefly as possible. Include a credit line, giving the name of the photographer or the individual or organization which furnished the photo.

You must note how the magazine or newspaper or publishing house handles its captions to know what style to use for yours. Some newspapers use phrases, some complete sentences.

Each picture should be numbered or clearly identified.

I type captions on onionskin paper, backed with carbon paper and second sheet. Type captions single space on your 8-1/2 x 11 page. Leave space between each caption, so that you have at least two inches at the top and half an inch at the bottom of each one. Cut each caption apart. Tape the slip, face forward, to the back of the black and white photograph, so the caption can be read beneath it. Before the material is mailed, fold the caption up over the front of the picture. I attach a carbon of the captions to the carbon of my manuscript. Others prefer to simply number the photographs and supply a typed list of captions with corresponding numbers.

On the back of each photograph place a gummed label on which you have typed the credit line ("Used by permission of the Museum of Fine Arts, Boston" or "John Jones, Photographer, Greenville, N.C.") and your return address. Never write on the back of a photograph (it leaves indent marks on the front of the photo) but you could use a rubber stamp lightly inked.

To caption color transparencies, you can use the same method of typing, inserting the caption slip inside the plastic sleeve used to protect each slide; or number each slide or transparency and make a master list of corresponding captions, with carbon.

In addition to the captions, you should type a master list of the illustrations you are sending with a manuscript, for the convenience of the editor and for your own protection, again with carbon. This lists the photographs with identifying numbers and descriptions but not with the whole caption.

Never, NEVER, should you use a photograph originating with someone else without first securing permission to print it, and giving a credit line.

MAILING PHOTOGRAPHS

If your photographs are valuable or irreplaceable, send them in a special photo envelope, with manuscript enclosed, and by registered, insured mail.

Ordinarily, use the proper size manila envelope and enclose the pictures front and back with cardboards the same size or a size larger than the photos. Address the envelope before you put them inside. I prefer typed labels, but if I do use a pen, I make mighty sure there are no photographs inside to catch the imprint. Never use paper clips to hold captions or cardboard protectors to a photo.

When you are mailing a great many black and white pictures, use a typewriter paper box, with manuscript also enclosed.

If you are sending color transparencies, place each between two pieces of cardboard of the correct size and tape the edges, leaving space between sections of tape so they can be separated easily and without damage. Type a descriptive label and stick it on the outside of each cardboard cover.

When you send more than two or three slides, it is easier to mail them in the plastic box in which they came from the photo lab. This will fit inside the manila envelope, but you must mark the outside "Hand Stamp." Or you can buy sheets of plastic with pockets in which to slip the slides.

On all envelopes in which there are photographs be sure to print (or buy printed labels) "Photographs. Handle with care."

You will need to be both detective and explorer to find just the right illustrations for your work. Build up a list of sources and your own file of illustrative material as you find it through your reading and study of the sources given here. It is easy to make a photocopy of an illustration found in a book or periodical, or to clip a suggestion to keep for future reference.

A picture may not truly be worth a thousand words, but it certainly helps to tell — and to sell — a story.

An article which depends on illustrations for its impact can often be presented with captions rather than a longer text. Sometimes captions are two, three or four lines long, giving historical details and the source of the picture; sometimes they are phrases and only a few words.

Maine Life is one regional magazine which publishes frequent photo stories. One was "I Recall Steamers on Sebec" by Leon Hall. This was a double-page spread of lake steamers of the late 1800's, with captions giving two or three lines of history. A story about weathervanes in *Away* by Sidney Barnes has twelve photographs of unique vanes. Caption phrases are numbered to match the photos and centered in a box.

Some material in *Foxfire* and its Maine offspring *Salt* and *Furrows* comes in this category, for they use many photographs and little text in comparison.

The photo story seems an easy type to prepare, since it requires only captions or a paragraph or two of description. The selection of just the appropriate illustrations must be done with skill to achieve unity and to tell a complete story. You must have many more illustrations than you can use to allow a proper balance of subjects, and you need not limit yourself to photographs but should consider engravings, prints and posters as well.

Captions must tell each picture's story clearly in the fewest possible words — not such an easy task, after all.

To the professional historian, the photo story may seem a long way from the writing of history, yet this presentation is often what arouses a reader's interest in the past for the first time.

A FEW WAYS TO SELL YOUR PHOTOGRAPHS

It is always the dream of a photographer to sell a cover picture. There are many opportunities for this, which each photographer must find for himself as he explores magazines in his special interest field. This takes imagination and creativity, for you have to learn to SEE the possibilities on every hand. Study every type of magazine carefully and make note of its photography and its photographers.

I know several writers who are good photographers and who prepare lectures of color slides or motion pictures, which they offer to clubs, historical societies and other groups, at fees from $10 to as much as $100.

To do this, plan a lecture of about 60 slides with typed commentary, usually on 3 x 5 cards, or prepare a half hour sound film: The Covered Bridges of New England; Historic Churches in Windsor County; Gardens of the Past; The Wild West in Song and Story; Writers of the Nineteenth Century. The possibilities are endless and it is fun to do. There are lecture bureaus which schedule such programs for a percentage fee. They must be expertly prepared for the latter. For local lectures good technical quality and a well-planned presentation will suffice.

Slides of historic sites, monuments and similar places might be sold to historical societies or the directors of historic buildings for resale in their shops. See what your area offers now and if there are no slides available, prepare some and visit every shop.

I bought "A Literary Calendar 1974" (Universe Books) in which Susan and Thomas Cahill combined photography associated with literary history, quotations and the birthdates of literary figures. (This is a good resource for biography ideas, too.)

A similar project is the creation of filmstrips with audiotapes and a printed version of the text. Prepared by Seaverns W. Hilton, with a humorous touch, "Pictorial History of Maine" has been reproduced several times by the University of Maine, Farmington. The 117 color-coordinated pictures are divided into four sections, to run approximately one-half hour each. They are popular with historical societies as well as with teachers throughout the state.

This project requires techniques of historical research, art, writing and photography, a fine example of using one's full talents, and could be an excellent by-product of the historical writer's work.

Documentary films demand expertise. You might begin by preparing a regional documentary for the local television stations, which feature a number of these in a year's time. I have seen Bill Caldwell, a well-known Maine writer, going on a cruise along the Maine coast, telling the history of islands, and the story of the fishermen. Town histories are sometimes filmed by local photographers, using local residents as actors. The films could be rented to organizations for programs as well as shown on local television.

Is there a battlefield or other important historic site in your area which does not have an introductory program for those touring the area? Perhaps you could prepare and sell the manager of the area such a program. It would include a brief history of the region with slides to illustrate the text. In our travels across the United States, we always look first for get-acquainted programs, such as those at Colonial Williamsburg, Washington's Crossing and Strawbery Banke.

On her own, paying the full printing costs, one of my friends has published the pictorial history of a bridge, based on photographs and articles which she had prepared as a newspaper reporter. She also published a postcard. These have been distributed to the state information center and to local merchants throughout the city and two-state area on which the river borders, giving them a percentage on each sale. It has been financially successful.

Using these few ideas as a stepping stone, go on and discover other ways that those photographs taken to illustrate your manuscripts can be used again and again. See Writer's Digest's *Artist's Market* for more ideas.

When you send out photographs or color transparencies without a manuscript, you may want to include a *photo release* form. Have slips printed or typed to read: "This photograph release is for a single, one-time publication use only. All other rights are reserved to the photographer unless specifically negotiated for." This assumes, of course, that you're submitting to a magazine publisher which hasn't already forewarned contributors that it only buys "all rights."

CHAPTER FIFTEEN

WRITING THE BIOGRAPHY

If you like to write about real people, find it stimulating to do the research already outlined here, and have patience enough to complete what you begin, you will enjoy writing factual or fictional biography.

Your choice of a biographical subject is very important. Not only must it be the life of someone who interests you strongly, but it must be a life worth telling about.

It is a challenge to the biographer to find people whose story should become better known, or to find those whose right to fame has been lost through the years. Harriet Beecher Stowe is known everywhere, but Dorothea Dix, whose life was dedicated to the elimination of the horrors of insane asylums and battleground hospitals, is hardly known at all. In fact, her name is less known than that of Dorothy Dix, who used to write a newspaper column of advice to the lovelorn.

It will surprise you to note obituaries in newspapers and in news magazines like *Time* reveal impressive accomplishments of persons who have been little remembered.

A few successful books have been written by people who never had anything published before. It is more usual to serve an apprenticeship by writing shorter material. A backlog of published articles or short stories will help to sell an editor the idea that you are qualified to write a successful first book. Personal knowledge of your subject or a treasure trove of historical family letters will help a lot.

When you find a subject which fills you with enthusiasm, you will have to decide whether you are going to write factual biography, fictional biography or historical fiction, and for what age group. This will determine your approach.

The scholarly approach is to find all available material, exhausting every possible source, then weighing the information, making a selection of material for a balanced piece of work.

The *nonacademic approach* requires going into research deeply enough to learn a great deal about your hero, but not in quite the painstaking manner of the scholar. You would look for primary sources, read several biographies if any have been published about him, at least one comprehensive history of the times to give you authentic background information, perhaps several volumes of historical fiction or biographies of other people of the same period. Read several books written for children, both fiction and nonfiction. You must study enough to get the feeling of the era. Make use of newspapers of the period whenever possible.

You must constantly seek answers to WHY your hero acted as he did, HOW he lived, WHAT he did that people will want to know about, WHO he really was as a person worth knowing.

Perhaps, like most writers, you will be thinking of writing an autobiography. This will take as much research as a biography, but at least you will know your sources personally. Organizing and writing autobiography are the same as for any book. The one thing to remember, of course, is that unless you have had a truly extraordinary life and are a very talented writer, it's much harder to find a commercial publisher for your autobiography than that of an already famous or historically important person.

WRITING A BOOK

Books in your home library will show you how to start organizing thoughts about *your* book. Note lengths of books, numbers of chapters, objective of the author, organization of material.

Make a tentative outline of your book chapter by chapter. Chapter headings will relate to the significant theme of each chapter. The research material will begin to make sense.

As you progress, there will be a "boiling down" of data, a revision of outline, perhaps a change in the number of chapters. Time spent organizing like this will save you writing time later.

A chronology chart is the best way I know to keep a hero's life properly "classified." Make a date by date listing of the events in your subject's life on a large piece of paper or a poster board. Jacqueline Susann used a blackboard to keep track of her cast of characters in her novels. Write all the important events of his life beside the proper dates, noting his age in a circle at the side. You may change your mind about the scope of the book when you see the whole life in perspective.

You have probably already separated your research notes on his life into convenient folders.

Now it will be easier to take out the section of the subject's life you intend to write about, and you can file the rest away for future reference. You may want to refer to happenings in the past by use of transition, so keep the material handy.

Some biographies are written in "life patterns" instead of in chronological order, just as articles often emphasize one area of a person's life.

The procedure for this is to have your folders marked to cover phases of your subject's life, titled something like "influence on his community," "interest in art." These "life patterns" illuminating the personality and character overlap in time, perhaps covering a person's teens through his middle years. Each section may emphasize a different phase of character or a variety of events covering one pattern of his life style.

For example, consider Catherine Drinker Bowen's biography of John Adams. After the Boston Massacre, the people of Boston were ready to sacrifice the lives of the British soldiers to their anger. Here is the way Mrs. Bowen illuminates *his* life pattern as John Adams decides to risk his future for a principle:

Forester (a friend of the British officers) raised his eyes wildly; John watched him without speaking. . . . So the crown lawyers would not defend Preston! Their own man, and they dared not. They were afraid of the mob. Thousands would be on the streets today, hundreds had already gathered round the stone jail. Coming down Queen Street this morning, John had heard a name called again and again, in a kind of roaring chant. Now he knew the name had been Preston. . . .

Color rose in John's face. So far, he had felt nothing but anxiety, a great dread and horror that such things could come to pass in

his own town, his own country. Now, suddenly, he was angry. Here in Massachusetts Bay, where the English law gave everyone fair judgment by trial of his peers — here a man, an Englishman, lay in jail in peril of his life, and the bar denied him counsel! ...
... Outside in the street the clamor increased; the square before the State House was filling with people. A man ran heavily past the window; there were shouts. ...

I will take this case, John thought suddenly. *I will defend Preston if it is the last thing I do.* ... There were things at stake greater than a man's life — greater than nine men's lives, for if he defended Preston he must *ipso facto* defend the soldiers with him. And if what he had gathered since morning were true, this would prove as important a case as had been tried in any court of any country in the world.

John was suddenly swept with emotion, almost with awe, at the thing he had undertaken. The implications of it staggered him, towered higher than he could see. He got up, cleared his throat. "If Captain Preston," he said, "thinks he cannot have a fair trial without my help, then he shall have it. Here is my hand."

"Educating" your reader may be a by-product of your work, but you must never forget that the *story* is what is important if you want your words read.

The best biographies are written because a glowing idea inspires a writer, gives him impetus to go patiently through months of research, to reach the joy of creation and the satisfaction of bringing a worthy person "back to life."

Often a writer learns a greater joy: the joy of reaching and influencing the minds of men, of stretching their imagination, perhaps with "new patterns of thought, useful new insight," as Allan Nevins has suggested.

Leaving out genius — which is rare — and youthful inexperience — which can be overcome — perhaps the only difference between writers is in the degree of dedication which each is willing to give to the learning of his craft. Elizabeth Yates tells her students in writing classes on biography that skill is the result of discipline.

Imagination plays its role — the kind which enables us to live in the scene we recreate, to feel for a time that we are right there.

Perception plays its part. Catherine Bowen assures us that practice counts in achieving perception as it does in learning the craft of writing.

You will never know whether you have the necessary talent unless you begin.

Biography is not the place for eulogy; let each reader assess for himself the value of your subject. Personally, I believe that biography is not the place for "debunking," although in recent years there has been a trend in that direction. Why should a writer wish to spend his days of work giving vent to anger or carrying on a literary association with a person he despises? Yet some enjoy this and write best-sellers!

Critical writing must be clearly justified, not fed by twisting facts or leaving out favorable information. Mrs. Bowen has said that the biographer shows his bias by what he leaves out as much as by what he puts in.

Barbara Land, in reviewing Lynn Z. Bloom's biography of Dr. Benjamin Spock, commented: "Mrs. Bloom obviously admires him and respects the New England conscience that led him into the Peace Movement, yet she doesn't hesitate to mention his weaknesses, as seen by members of his own family and by outsiders."

Some writers successfully present the reasons WHY a criminal or traitor or other antisocial person had become what he was, without justifying his actions. For example, Roy A. Medvedev's book *Let History Judge* sketches the outlines of the Stalin epoch and attempts to analyze its meaning. A reviewer, Harrison E. Salisbury *(New York Times)* said: "Not a history in the conventional sense. . . . What he presents is not so much an indictment as the raw stuff from which an indictment can ultimately be drawn."

Such presentations would be beyond the capabilities of a beginning writer. Passion needs to be tempered with experience, balanced with the knowledge of history. Nevertheless, the thoughtful young writer has much to offer to current interpretation of history. The danger lies in writing into the work an emotional involvement instead of facts.

If the work is well written, the reader will understand the writer's point of view, although he need not agree. You may, for example, write from the point of view of a radical and thus castigate the conservative; but the point of view must be clear enough to allow the reader to judge for himself. If it is not, the work is propaganda. In *Oliver Wiswell,* Kenneth Roberts writes from the point of view of an American Revolutionary Tory, purposely to tell the other side, to show that those colonists who stood with the king were just as dedicated and sure of their position as the Patriots were of theirs.

A writer has a great responsibility not to mislead his reader through prejudice. When the bias is inherent — like the opposite points of view of the pre-Civil War Southerner and the Northerner in regard to slavery — the writer must make his position clear.

Perhaps our problem as Americans may be a failure of perspective — a tenacious subjectivity — because we are too close to our beginnings. Perhaps some of us have an inability to see our history as it *was,* as it *is* and to project impersonally what it *might be.* We must try!

Here are a few suggestions I have found useful in writing biography or historical fiction. You will find these in more detail, as well as many other instructions on the craft, in other writing books.

An anachronism is the use of some article, custom or word which is placed out of its time. There is also danger in anachronism of *feeling.*

Beware of using your knowledge of the present to interpret the past. Don't put anything in your manuscript which would show a knowledge of what will happen years later. You should have some understanding of the inner nature of the way history has of changing from period to period, from regional area to area.

Some writers tell in an "afterword" or "epilogue" what will be happening in the future: "The mentally ill of future generations were to live happier lives because she cared, although few would know the name of Dorothea Dix."

Tone and mood should be appropriate to the period in which the heroine lives. Study the Gothic romances to see that even those set in modern times have a touch of the Victorian. Ladies in Victorian times were seldom aggressive. There were rebels then and in Colonial times, but what was daring for women then would not be considered daring today, and their actions and thoughts must be interpreted from the standards of their own contemporaries.

To understand the differences in ideology, customs and speech to be found in periods of time and in regionalism, read literature written and published in that period. We history writers owe a debt of gratitude to dedicated researchers who have made our way a little easier by writing books which faithfully depict the past, but we must not lean too heavily on their research when we can do our own.

Slang, inventions, customs and foods and fashions must be checked carefully. Gundalow—schooner—dugout—clipper—sloop—freighter: which is correct? The beginner might just use "canoe" or "boat" but this would never satisfy Samuel Eliot Morison.

THE FICTIONAL TOUCH

Fictional treatment of nonfiction makes your material more interesting to read. There is a difference in writing factual material in a vivid way and in inventing description and other information which you are not sure existed.

It is the use of specific details—the use of the impressions of the senses—which makes your material come alive. Use words of color, specific words: *white birch* not *tree*. This does not mean that you need to "catalogue" or write pages of detail; sometimes it takes only a few meaningful words or apt phrases.

Burr, a novel by Gore Vidal (Random 1973), is brimming with personal observations by Charles Schuyler, the clerk who is the raconteur of the story. Without cataloguing details, they seem to pull the reader right into every scene. An example:

Instead of going inside the hotel, the Colonel (put off by a group of Tammany sachems standing in the doorway) turned into the graveyard of Trinity Church. I followed, obediently; I am always obedient. What else can a none-too-efficient law clerk be? I cannot think why he keeps me on.

"I know—intimately—more people in this charming cemetery than I do in all of the Broad Way." Burr makes a joke of everything; his manner quite unlike that of other people.... But if we seem strange to him, he is much too polite to say so, as he lives on and on amongst us: full of the devil, my quarry.

In the half-light of the cemetery, Burr did resemble the devil—assuming that the devil is no more than five foot six (an inch shorter than I), slender, with tiny feet (hooves?), high forehead (in the fading light I imagine vestigial horns), bald in front with hair piled high on his head, powdered absently in the old style, and held in place with a shell comb. Behind him is a monument to the man he murdered.

The senses have not changed since the history of man began. Only the multiplicity of man's experience has. You know the odor of wood smoke, the saltiness of tears, the joy of success, the bitterness of failure, and so you can experience a kinship with the men and women about whom you write, and learn to convey this to your reader.

Specifics in your writing will make all the difference. Your characters, living or created, are more believable if the reader can see how they look and move, hear their speech, understand their emotions, see the places they lived, not as shadows populating a dim past, but as people living and breathing now.

BACKGROUND

Background includes information about family, education, religious training and so on. Often it will require only a paragraph or two to orient the reader, or the information may be presented through a flashback or dialogue.

What do you do if you cannot find definite information about some part of your hero's life? Find (not invent) material with which to build a bridge: What was happening in the world around him; where he was living at this time; what he would naturally be doing—going to school, working as an apprentice? Reconstruct the pattern of his days by finding out how boys of that period played and worked.

Learn how people lived, worked and played during the hero's era, and in the region in which he lived. There would be differences in food and customs and activities from north to south and from town to city.

From his known habits and interests you can recreate scenes with a degree of authenticity. Study Esther Forbes' *Paul Revere* (which won a Pulitzer prize) to see how an expert has done this in a biography. Then study *Johnny Tremain,* which won the Newbery Medal, to see how she uses the same historical material in fictional form.

Victoria Holt wrote *The Queen's Confession* (historical fiction) from the point of view of Marie Antoinette, who tells her story when the shadow of the guillotine looms. The author begins this way to establish background:

It was said that I was born "with the vision of a throne and a French executioner" over my cradle, but this was long after ... My birth caused my mother little inconvenience. It happened just as the Seven Years' War was about to break out, and almost as soon as I was born she was carrying on with state affairs, so I am sure scarcely gave me a thought.

The following paragraphs describe her happy childhood, her education, her family. Deftly presented are background details which show Marie's character: "We were happy, carefree children." "She clicked her tongue and said I would never learn. I put my arms around her neck and said I loved her. Then she wrote out my exercises in fine pencil and I went over them with my pen, so that in the end it seemed as though I had written a very fair essay." "I had always been feather-brained and full of high spirits."

SETTING

Biographer Catherine Drinker Bowen says that when she tells about a lawyer giving a speech, she describes the place where he speaks, his manner and the weather outside. Here is an example of the way Mrs. Bowen described the day Oliver Wendell Holmes, Jr. was accepted to the Massachusetts Bar in *Yankee from Olympus* (Little, Brown 1944):

Monday morning was dark and gusty, with a threat of rain.

Peleg Chandler, his ears entirely hidden inside his shirt collar, walked to the courthouse with Holmes. It was barely a block, on the same side of the street. The pillared granite portico was dark and high. Holmes always entered the place with a quick sensation, not so much of excitement as recognition. This courthouse was a part of him, of his background and childhood. Here Judge Loring had sentenced the runaway slaves, Sims and Burns. Manacled to these very benches, they had waited the verdict. Up these wide granite stairs, Higginson had led the mob that tried to rescue Sims. Holmes had been eight years old. He had stood at his bedroom window on Montgomery Place, three blocks away. There had been shouts, feet running on Tremont Street....

Holmes and Chandler were early. Court sat at nine-thirty. Behind the Judge's Bench the new oaken panels shone yellow in the gaslight. There were five lawyers in court, they sat facing the Bench. Holmes recognized two of them; they nodded to him....

There was a rustling of papers among the members of the Bar. The Clerk stood up. His voice was loud, monotonous. "The Court will attend to the taking of the oath."

Holmes came forward. It was like graduation, like walking up for your diploma, like the Brevet-Colonelship given him three years ago on the Common. It was absurd to feel so solemn....

Then with his hand on the Bible he took the Attorneys' Oath.

In *Fiona,* the British writer Catherine Gaskin describes the setting as the heroine arrives in the West Indies to become governess to Duncan Maxwell. At the same time she shares with the reader not only an "undercurrent of fear" but hints at her theme: the treatment of slaves which is an important theme in the plot, and which leads to an uprising when Great Britain's Emancipation Proclamation is announced:

They had sent an elegant carriage for me — shining black with yellow-spoked wheels, and gold tassels on its cushions. Its Negro driver was clad in white duck with yellow epaulets and wore a black tricornered hat bound with gold. But no one of the household had come to welcome me. I felt alone and almost afraid in the midst of all that bright bustle of the ships at anchor, the carrying of the bales and barrels, the singsong voices of the slaves speaking in their Gullah language. .... It was a cheerful chaos of movement and color and light, and yet I felt a cold undercurrent of fear.

One of the ways through which you can achieve familiarity with the setting in which your characters move is by obtaining maps of the area and then drawing a rough map on which are located all the important landmarks of the story.

Emilie Loring wrote "young love" stories which were not historical at all, but she used real places as her settings. She subscribed to a newspaper of each place for several months before she completed her book, so she could use the names of streets and stores and so on.

A good example for achieving accuracy of detail in setting is given by Faith Baldwin's methods of research. She not only uses reference books and maps, but for one story set in the Adirondacks she obtained booklets on the weather, flowers and animals of the region, bought secondhand books describing the New York mountains and consulted people living there — to be sure of a few facts. If you are not sure how a place you are describing looks, visit it, or write asking for specific information and a photograph.

CHARACTERIZATION

The technique of characterization can make a person come alive in nonfiction as well as in fiction. Character and description are shown by physical appearance, walk, mannerisms, tastes, choice of friends, choices of work and play, what he thinks and feels, his ambitions, his reaction to situations, how he is affected by his environment and background, his manner of speech and what he says, what motivates him to action.

In straight biographical writing, information and descriptions are gleaned from letters, diaries, comments by observers. James Thomas Flexner adds glimpses of her character to his description of Martha Custis:

Martha decorated her rooms with furnishings from England and her person with imported finery. When she rode out, she had a choice between her chariot and her chair. During the social season at Williamsburg, she glowed with gentle sweetness at the balls.

Although George could not foresee the time when he would have to dance every set so that all the women present "could get a touch of him," even in those days he entered the dancing assemblies as a military hero. It is improbable that he did not bend his great height over the tiny hand of little Mrs. Custis (she was hardly five feet tall). She described herself good-humoredly as "a fine, healthy girl." Her hair was dark, her teeth "beautiful," her eyes hazel, her figure probably already agreeably plump. She wore her elegant clothes with a lack of self-consciousness that seemed to make them an actual part of a pretty, simple soul. In the dance she was quick and affable. Above all, she shed on every occasion she attended an infectious gentleness. She put George in a good humor. However, she was a settled matron, who did not flirt or lead a young hero on.

(George Washington, Little, Brown 1965)

Character is also shown by what others say about a person and so commentary by friends and foes is a valuable tool.

HISTORICAL DIALOGUE RULES

Writers disagree on the amount of dialogue which can be invented for historical fiction and even for some biographies.

Characters should speak in the "flavor" of their times, using some of the words then in current usage. Reading period plays will be helpful. A useful reference book is the *Oxford English Dictionary,* which gives the earliest date when a word was used.

To put words into a real person's mouth or thoughts into his mind, the writer must know that hero very well. He must not speak in a way foreign to his nature. His ideas, his political, religious and social philosophy must be presented authentically.

Noel B. Gerson, author of *T. R.,* a biographical novel of Theodore Roosevelt, and of more than forty nonfiction books, says this about dialogue:

Unless you find actual dialogue you can verify – as in the correspondence of a reliable contemporary, preferably a principal in your book – never invent it. Don't give in, under any circumstances, to the temptation to write this-is-what-they-might-have-said dialogue, or even this-is-what-they-must-have-said. The moment you veer into this type of writing, you are no longer doing nonfiction but fictionalized biography. If you prefer the latter, write accordingly, but be sure you label your work a biographical novel.

In his introduction to *T. R.,* Mr. Gerson explains:

The biographical novel is a sometimes misunderstood medium. It is a form which permits an author to invent dialogue and, to an extent, enter the minds of his characters. But in dealing with Theodore Roosevelt I have followed several strict, self-imposed rules. I have tried to let his actions speak for themselves. And, particularly in all matters relating to his public life, I have tried to fashion the dialogue in accordance with views he expressed.

For example, I have told the Panama Canal story only in terms of what the record can substantiate. The scene between President Roosevelt and the two young intelligence officers must be classified as fiction, in that there is no record of what was said. But the officers were real people, the meeting actually took place, and my invented dialogue conforms to the facts known about their mission and Roosevelt's known reactions after he had seen them.

Here is an example of the way Mr. Gerson in *T. R.* emphasized the problem of poor health which was to plague Theodore Roosevelt for so many years. At the same time the author shows the combined strength and tenderness of the child's father.

The new serving maid appeared in the library doorway. . . . "Excuse me, ma'am, but the baby is whimperin' again."

Martha thanked her, and, although deeply worried, hesitated a moment before interrupting her husband's reading. "Theodore." Her husband continued to read, and her voice became a little strident. "Theodore! The baby is crying again."

Making no attempt to conceal his annoyance, Theodore put down his book. "It seems to me that baby is always wailing," he said. What really outraged him was the thought that a child born to them could be frail; Roosevelts had been healthy, vigorous men and women for generations. ...

He knew if there was a problem she would be incapable of handling it alone. And much as he hated to admit it, he felt a niggling worry about the health of his first-born son. He left the library and bounded up the stairs. Martha, gathering up her rustling bombazine skirts, followed as rapidly as she could.

She found him in the nursery, an expression of pity and alarm on his face as he gazed at the eight-week-old infant in the crib, gasping for breath. "It's the asthma again," he said. ...

"Doctors don't know everything. If they did, they'd have cured Teedee by now." Theodore picked up his son, for whom each breath was a torment. Wrapping the infant in blankets, he held him in the crook of one arm and wrenched open the nursery window with his free hand. ... "What he needs is fresh air." Her husband drew up a rocking chair directly in front of the window and began to rock.

... Martha silently left the chamber and returned with a shawl. Hearing her husband's voice, she stopped short.

"Never you fear, Teedee," he was saying softly. "Maybe some day you'll be as strong as any other boy. If not, you'll be smarter. Papa will help you in every way I can. I promise."

Draping the shawl around Theodore's shoulders, Martha blinked back tears as she crept out into the corridor and closed the nursery door. She wept for her son, her heart heavy at the thought of the crushing burden he would carry with him through life. Only the strong survived.

Using letters, diaries, journals and other personal papers, or published speeches, sermons or oral history transcripts associated with your subject will help you to achieve authenticity in dialogue and give you exact words and phrases. If you don't have access to such material, it is better not to put words you cannot verify into the mouth of a real person. If you do invent dialogue, be sure you tell the reader so.

On the other hand, you can invent dialogue for nonhistorical characters when you place them in historical situations; just be sure the facts are accurate.

Listening is an important step in learning to write dialogue. Most men don't know naturally the style of woman talk, any more than women can readily portray the rougher speech of men. By listening to the speech patterns of the opposite sex, perhaps making a few notes, you can develop a technique which will enable a reader to tell who is speaking. Television watcher-listeners can profit from this activity in the same manner.

Whether it is in fiction or nonfiction, the use of dialogue and conveying a hero's thoughts are methods through which the writer gives insight into his subject's character. Dialogue also helps to forward the action of the story, shows conflict, emotion, hints at the writer's theme, shows motivation — and brings the reader into the story.

Here is an example of the technique used by Mrs. Gaskin in *Fiona* to give the reader both background and theme:

"And will you not, my brothers, set them free? Will you not end this traffic in human misery? Who can expect the blessing of serenity when men and women are still being sold like cattle?"

"You are behind the times, friend. The slave trade was abolished long ago."

A pointing figure from the platform. "*You're* behind the times! Don't you know that a pirate trade still plies from the African shores to the Indies, with conditions worse than ever before? And have you no pity for those already in bondage?"

"And haven't we," he was answered, "taken them from the darkness of their ignorance and shown them the light of the Christian God? And don't the plantations feed and clothe them?"

"Under the lash we have given them the Christian God. Try it, my friend — try just one day working the cane under that sun and under a whip, and you will rise up and demand that Parliament pass the Emancipation Act —"

Dialogue's principal use is to forward the action of the story and to give information in an easy way. Through this bit of conversation, Mrs. Gaskin shows the reader two points of view about slavery, gives a hint about the illicit slave trade, which is important to her story, and shows the plight of the slaves, which is shortly going to bring them to rebellion — and through that rebellion cause tragedy in the lives of Fiona's employers.

ANECDOTES

Without anecdotes, a story is apt to be dull and lifeless. These vignettes, usually only a paragraph or two in length, tell more vividly than the author could describe it what a person is like, how he reacts, what others think of him. An anecdote is similar to setting a scene in a stage play.

Here is a poignant insight into Cole Porter's character, as told by Tom Prideaux in a profile published in *Life,* February 25, 1972:

In 1937, at a Long Island house party, Porter had the riding accident that broke both his legs, led to 35 operations and in 1958 necessitated the amputation of one leg. ... Even after he was crushed by his falling horse and lay in the bridle path waiting for help, Porter busied himself by taking out pad and pencil and writing extra lyrics for *At Long Last Love.*

Victoria Holt in *The Queen's Confession* makes her point about Marie Antoinette's inability to assume the restrictions of her royal life. She had just told her husband about an occasion on which she played the role of Lady Bountiful:

I told my husband of the incident and described the poverty of the cottage.

"I am glad," he said, with rare emotion, "that you think as I do. When I am King I want to do all I can for my people. I want to follow in the footsteps of my ancestor Henri Quatre."

"I wish to help you," I told him earnestly.

"Balls, pageants ... they are an unworthy extravagance."

I was silent. Why could one not be both good and gay?

Most of the time Florence Nightingale was quiet and reserved.

In his biography, *Florence Nightingale,* Cecil Woodham-Smith shows another side:

One afternoon near Christmas they drove up to 120 rue du Bac, and walked into a drawing room crowded with dancing, singing children. ... The children began to play blindman's buff, and without ado, Florence picked up her skirts and joined in. It was the happiest possible introduction. She was never so unself-consciously gay as with children.

In your research, watch for scenes like these, little moments which, more than many words, tell the reader something important about a person.

WRITING AUTOBIOGRAPHY

Shakespeare once wrote "Of all knowledge the wise and good seek most to know themselves." While writing autobiography may teach a person more about himself than he knew before, the writer is subjective about himself or about events he has witnessed. Autobiographies are written as their authors *remember* their lives, which may or may not be the way it really was. As mentioned earlier, autobiography has a limited market with commercial publishers unless the author is already well-known or has had a most unusual and interesting life.

An autobiography can take many forms. For example, *A Traveler's Tale* by Enid Saunders Candlin (Macmillan 1974) is an account of her travels in India during and just after World War II, with her husband and small daughter. Writers who can illuminate a particular time and place for the reader through their personal experience have a better chance with a commercial publisher.

Among the many whose published autobiographies cover a life span there are few women. If you plan to write an autobiography, you may wish to study a variety of ways to handle it in current books.

For example, there is the collaborative autobiography such as *Cavett* by Dick Cavett and Christopher Porterfield, which uses interview and dialogue (Harcourt Brace Jovanovich 1974). In

Mother Goddam, Bette Davis's comments on the work of Whitney Stine are printed in red (Hawthorn 1974).

Those with expert knowledge of another language might uncover an intriguing book to translate for publication, like *Recollections* by Alexis de Tocqueville, an eyewitness account of revolutionary events in Paris in 1848 and 1849, translated several times, the latest by J. P. Mayer and A. P. Kerr (Doubleday 1970). De Tocqueville's *Democracy in America* has also been translated many times and is still read with interest after 135 years.

Some autobiographies are more valuable for their interpretation or expose of events of national or international importance than they are for personal implications. Can you call the experience shared by two people a "duo-autobiography"? One of these, *All the President's Men,* has been called "the detective story of the age" — the narration of how Carl Bernstein and Bob Woodward uncovered the Watergate scandal (Simon & Schuster 1974). Best known in this category is *The Gulag Archipelago 1918-1956* by Aleksandr I. Solzhenitsyn (Harper & Row 1974).

Autobiography using the technique of oral history is increasingly popular. Nikita Krushchev dictated his story into a tape recorder and the results are two books translated by *Time* correspondent Strobe Talbott: *Krushchev Remembers* and *The Last Testament* (Little, Brown 1970 and 1974).

An oral history project like Merle Miller's book *Plain Speaking, An Oral Biography of Harry S. Truman,* can become a cruel caricature when it is unexpurgated of too-salty opinions. This is as much biography as autobiography, for it also includes the comments of those who knew the former President (Putnam 1974).

Another type must be mentioned: the *simulated* autobiography tells a story which is historically accurate through the viewpoint of a real person, but this is an author's device. Usually these are biographical fiction like *I, James McNeill Whistler* by Lawrence Williams, (Simon & Schuster 1972).

PERSONAL PAPERS AND MEMOIRS

There is a current trend to gather the diaries, letters, personal memoirs, and journals of individuals, and through these to write what is really a cross between autobiography and biography.

The Patton Papers combine personal material with brief commentary by Martin Blumenson. Published by Houghton Mifflin, there will be four volumes when completed. Patton was a compulsive letterwriter, keeper of journals and diaries and he saved notes, reports, orders and speeches, enough to fill fifty metal filing cases, which the Patton family turned over to Professor Blumenson, who has arranged his selections so that the General tells the story of himself and the United States Army.

Four volumes of *Collected Letters of Bernard Shaw* are also projected by the editor Dan H. Laurence, who says Shaw wrote at least a quarter million letters and postcards. Dodd, Mead is publisher.

Jonathan D. Spence, professor of Chinese history at Yale, created what he calls an "autobiographical biography" in *Emperor of China*. He has selected from the "Venerable Record" of official documents, letters, memoranda, and verse and private thoughts, the best to tell the history of Emperor K'ang-hsi, who ruled China for sixty-one years in the eighteenth century (Knopf 1974).

Show personalities have joined other public figures in writing their memoirs. Often this is "as told to" or ghost written. A few are "first person," but it is not always easy to be sure. At any rate, they are an important source of information of the past —and prospects for a "collaborative autobiography" written by the freelance writer.

"INTIMATE" BIOGRAPHY

Each life can be revealed in many different methods, and anyone about to write a biography should survey the field, studying what is being published by reading book club notes, bookstore and publishing house publicity, book reviews in magazines and newspapers. Browse in a large public library and study the *Subject Guide to Books in Print.*

In biography, you focus on one person, or perhaps two. Sometimes the emphasis will be on historical events, with the chief character of minor importance. There can also be a biography of a family or dynasty. I have selected a few examples rather arbitrarily.

Biographies are often written by a relative, friend or associate. *To tell all or not to tell* is a question which most face in writing such books. Such a choice is not easy, for those who "know the truth" will be critical if "all" is left untold, while others find it in poor taste. Some readers would rather not know intimate details which sully the memory of a great or well-loved person. Among such books is *An Untold Story: The Roosevelts of Hyde Park* by Elliott Roosevelt with James Brough (Putnam 1973).

Of an alternate opinion is Kathleen Morrison, who for the last twenty-five years of his life was Robert Frost's secretary and protector. In *Robert Frost - A Pictorial Chronicle* (Holt, Rinehart & Winston 1974) Mrs. Morrison remains "protector," not quite "telling all."

Although a biography of a lesser-known personality should bring freshness to the publishing world, a view of the latter shows book after book published about those who are famous: Marie Antoinette, Queen Elizabeth I, Eisenhower, Nixon, Lincoln, George Washington, et cetera. At least seventy books have been written about President John Kennedy and his family, but few have been best sellers.

Biographies are also written about the criminal, the unsavory, the "SOB". So many are being written that it is evident that a writer need not admire his subject, so long as he is one whom the public wants to know about.

Many children's books emphasize only the childhood or another single phase of a person's life. This is one of the "patterns" mentioned earlier in this chapter.

The collective biography idea can be a snare for the would-be-published writer. It sounds easy to get together a number of short biographies, but you must have a good unified idea and not a hodgepodge of materials. The choice must have something in common besides being male or female or black. Moreover, you cannot write a collective biography from an encyclopedia. There must be anecdotes, adventure, vivid prose, a mini-plot, perhaps an all-over look at the times. If you do find a good idea and write a good book, it might sell several hundred copies a year for many years, especially if written for young people.

Women in men's sports, daughters of presidents, women who succeed in industry, women of Texas, Victorian women libbers, great ladies of fashion are a few "collectives" which might be interesting. Publishers are eager for more books about women and girls, particularly those who have equaled men in ability and accomplishment.

Another type is the family-generation biography, which is a chronicle of dynasties abroad and cliques or family sagas. This is wide open for American family subjects. There are many family groups who have made an impact on industry, education and the arts waiting for a biographer.

Stephen Birmingham has written *Real Lace, America's Irish Rich,* which traces the generations of such Irish families as the Murrays, Butlers, Mackays and Kennedys (Harper & Row, 1973), which is another type of collective biography, too.

You can see from these examples that HOW you write a biography requires as much consideration as the choice of subject. A fresh approach, some new material, just the right hero or heroine — and you are on your way.

CHAPTER SIXTEEN

FOUR TYPES OF HISTORY IN FICTION

What is the difference between the biography and the biographical novel? One difference is in the structure: in biography, the writer will probably tell in the third person what his hero said by referring to diaries and other places where his conversations are recorded. In the biographical novel, the writer has more leeway and can bring the reader closer to the hero by writing in the first person or going into his thoughts in greater depth.

Here are two accounts of the same scene. The first is from Catherine Drinker Bowen's biography of John Adams:

It was nearly eight that evening when John got home to Cold Lane. He had been carried triumphantly from town meeting to tavern and the occasion celebrated with toasts, congratulations and one brief but heartfelt speech from Sam Adams. Then he had been hurried across the river to Cambridge, where the Legislature was meeting, and formally inducted. Touched and deeply gratified by these marks of trust and affection, John was nevertheless deeply uneasy. Had he done wrong to let the House proceed so fast? And in God's name how had it happened anyway? He had not lifted a finger to get himself elected. . . .

But would Abigail look on it as a triumph? What would she say, how would she receive this overwhelming sudden change in their life together? Stepping from the Charlestown Ferry, John said farewell to his colleagues and turned alone down Prince Street toward home. . . .

John wished profoundly that he had prepared his wife, talked over with her the possibilities of this election. . . .

John opened his front door, walked in and straight upstairs. The new baby was only eight days old. . . . He crossed the room and without pause for a greeting, stood close before her and began

to speak. "I was elected Boston Representative today," he said.
"The vote was four to one." ... "We shall be poor ... I have
— Abby, can you forgive me? I have deliberately doomed you
and my children ... to a life of poverty and danger."
... She smiled, reached out a hand. "How foolish you are, my
dearest partner! I am very proud of you." ...
Abigail rose, still holding her husband's hand. Her face was grave
and at the same time, tender. "Let me share what comes with
you always, John. I fear nothing but our parting, nothing at all.
I know well the dangers of this position. But you have done right.
And I believe," she finished simply, "that for our future, we must
trust in Providence."

The second is from the Irving Stone biographical novel *Those
Who Love:*

It was the sixth of June, a warm clear day, with a slight tang
of salt breeze in the air. ...
"John, whatever in creation could have happened to you on such
a delightful day?"
"The worst. I was sitting in my office correlating the evidence
of a dozen witnesses when a messenger came in with a paper from
the town meeting. It informed me that I had just been elected
by the Boston freeholders to represent Boston in the House of
Representatives and the General Court."
"But that's wonderful! Grandfather Quincy was a representative
for years, and a member of the General Court, even the Speaker."
John stared at her hollow-eyed.
"I went down to Faneuil Hall immediately, and in as few words
as possible tried to tell them of my insufficiency to fulfill the
expectations of people. They listened to none of it. They thought
it was false modesty. Then I accepted. But it gave me no joy."
"For Heaven's sake why not?"
He cried out in anguish: "When I accepted this seat in the House
of Representatives, my dear partner, I thereby consented to my
own ruin, to your ruin, and to the ruin of our children."
... She realized what was disturbing him. The job of representative paid no salary; it absorbed most of a man's time and

left him free for little other work. John would become occupied by politics almost to the exclusion of a law practice. . . . She burst into tears but stopped almost immediately. It was foolish to decry their fate when it had been leading them upward every step of the way. . . . "I'm willing in this cause to run all the risks with you. We'll place our trust in Providence."

Suddenly she saw the incongruity of the situation.

"It's absolutely impossible. The Bostonians hate you. They couldn't possibly have elected you to represent them."

"The final ballot showed that I had more than four hundred votes out of something over five hundred."

"But how could that be?"

"Samuel Adams . . ."

She sat down in the nearest chair. . . .

"Before I engaged in this Captain Preston case I had more business at the Bar than any man in the province. . . . I'm devoting myself to endless labor and anxiety, and all for nothing except a sense of duty."

Abigail repressed the smile twitching at the corners of her lips.

"To good Puritans like you and me, duty is a short cut to heaven. John, as your partner, I have an offer to make you. My proposal is that you worry about Captain Preston and the trial, the House of Representatives and the General Court. I will take over the worrying about your enfeebled health and the food for our enfeebled family."

If it isn't your forte to be a storyteller, if your imagination works well in research and nonfiction, but not in creating situations and developing character, you may prefer to write biography. Remember, however, that you'll never know unless you attempt it.

When you write historical fiction of any type, you must play fair with your reader, not leading him to believe your situations and characters are true when they are imaginative. This is especially true when you are writing for young people. While a novel is largely based on the author's imagination, he cannot contrive to change actual events and people into something they were not.

What is the difference between the historical novel and the biographical novel? In the biographical novel, all the people in

it have really lived. In the historical novel, many of the characters
may be invented and set in a framework of historical events, in
which some real people may have what in the picture industry
is called "a cameo role." I cannot say too often that you must
never put a real person into a situation in which he could not
have appeared according to the facts known about him.

You will learn as you study the various types of historical fiction
that those who write the historical novel with a main historical
figure as the leading character have been as serious about their
research as the professional historian. Always read the author's
foreword and the bibliography when there is one.

When a skilled writer employs the beauty of language to bring
a scene into the experience of a reader, it may be hard to distinguish
between biography and biographical fiction.

Gore Vidal says that for him the attraction of the writing of
the historical novel rather than a true biography is that one can
be as careful as the historian in research and factual detail, yet
assume the right to rearrange events and even to attribute motive,
which the conscientious biographer could not do.

Sometimes a writer of biographical fiction tells in a foreword
what the scope of the work has been. Rosemary Hawley Jarman
writes in her foreword to *The King's Grey Mare* (Little, Brown 1973):
"All characters with a few minor exceptions really exist." Her
book, *We Speak No Treason* (Little, Brown 1971), tells of the life
of King Richard III through the eyes of a girl, the court jester
and one of his soldiers. Her foreword says:

Although this is a work of fiction, the principal characters therein
actually existed as part of the past and complex fifteenth-century
society and had their recognized roles in history, sparsely docu-
mented though these may be.

I have therefore built around the lives of my narrators. They
were all real people whose destiny was in various ways closely
interwoven with that of the last Plantagenet king. I have endeav-
oured to adhere strictly to the date of actual occurrences, and none
of the events described is beyond the realms of probability. Conversations are of necessity invented, but a proportion of King Richard's
words are his own as recorded by contemporaries.

THE HISTORICAL NOVEL

In the historical novel it is better to recreate a plot around a real situation or event, placing fictional characters in the situation and describing how *they* act, rather than featuring a real historic figure as the main character.

When writing fiction based on history, you must know where history ends and where fiction can legitimately begin. I cannot say too often that you must learn to live in the period, remembering such facts as that for much of the past it took months for news to cross the country or the ocean; you can't have people in a young new country talking about an event that happened only a day or so ago in Paris.

What makes a good novel of any kind makes a good historical novel, too. Plot. Suspense. (Hard to do when the reader may know that later the hero was to be assassinated!) Narrative pace. Romance. Conflict. Believable characters. Historical fiction can also involve readers deeply in problems of another age, and be an easy introduction to history.

But play fair with your reader. Here are ways that writers do this:

Taylor Caldwell, many of whose novels are of key Biblical figures (*Dear and Glorious Physician, Testimony of Two Men, Great Lion of God*), has a quite different type of novel in *Captains and the Kings* (Doubleday 1972) whose foreword says in part: "There is not, to my knowledge, any family like the 'Armagh Family' in America, nor has there ever been, and all characters, except those obviously historical, are my own invention. However, the historical background and the political background of this novel are authentic."

Sometimes in his research, a writer will come upon contradictory eyewitness accounts. An example is the experience of James Sherburne, author of *The Way to Fort Pillow* (Houghton Mifflin 1972) who says:

The reader should know that the account of the events at Fort Pillow represents my own view of what probably happened. The official Northern version and eyewitness reports of Southern officers and men of Forrest's command differ so widely that no one can say with certainty what really happened that bloody day and night. I have tried to reconcile elements from both versions, to form a consistent narrative; I can't swear it *did* happen this way, only that it *could have.*

Mr. Sherburne also lists a bibliography, which combines real and fictional characters in the Civil War period in Kentucky. The book emphasizes the slavery problems and the use of black troops.

THE HISTORICAL ROMANCE

How can one be arbitrary about categories? Theoretically, the historical "romance" is intended to entertain, and requires less research than biographical and historical fiction. A writer can select a congenial period, choose a lively plot (real or imaginary in events), read several books to learn how people dressed and lived, invent characters who could have lived then, invent love interests and conflict, and the historical background can be minimal.

YET you will learn as you study historical fiction that many a writer who creates romance against a historical background has a professional knowledge of her period and does in-depth research to give authenticity to whatever period she writes about. I say "she" purposely, for with the exception of Westerns and stories of adventure, most writers of romance are women, nearly all of them nationally known, and also popular abroad.

Often there are more sex and emotion in the historical romance, and as much daring-do as in the books of adventure.

Many writers in this field are British, and often influenced by the Gothic novel, which in its way is a part of this category.

Catherine Gavin served as a British war correspondent in World War II and out of that experience came the "Great War Series" and these and other historical romances are as popular here as in Europe. Mary Renault has considerable knowledge of ancient Greece in the fourth century B.C. Her novels are based on this period, among them *The Mask of Apollo* (Pantheon-Random 1966). A list of books on the Grecian theatre and author's note indicate this book's authenticity of background.

Among American writers in the field of historical romance is Elswyth Thane, whose seven Williamsburg novels are rather like a saga, carrying the Day family through generations of historical events.

THE FACTUAL NOVEL

Said to be coined by Truman Capote, this term is being assigned to dramatic presentations of true reporting. There are real characters moving as they actually did in the events which actually took place, and with action dramatically presented.

Truman Capote's *In Cold Blood* (Signet 1965) called by reviewer F. W. Dupee "the best documentary of an American crime ever written" may have been the pioneer effort.

Another example is *The Onion Field* by Joseph Wambaugh (Delacorte 1973) which Capote calls "A distinguished contribution toward the gradually enlarging field of the 'factual novel.'"

In the acknowledgment page of *In Cold Blood* is summed up the work to be done for this kind of writing: "All the material in this book not derived from my own observation is either taken from official records or is the result of interviews with the persons directly concerned, more often than not numerous interviews conducted over a considerable period of time. . . ."

People! People make history and that is why the writing of biography can become the most absorbing and satisfying kind of all.

CHAPTER SEVENTEEN

WRITING THE NONFICTION HISTORY BOOK

In this generation facts seem more popular than fiction, and publishers in general are more willing to take a risk with nonfiction titles than with the novel. It is to be expected that history is being emphasized during the bicentennial years. The aims are the same as for the writing of articles: to inform; to entertain and delight; to arouse emotion; to teach and persuade. People are likely to turn to nonfiction to learn more about what is happening in the world than they can learn from newspapers, magazines and television.

A beginning writer has more going for him if he decides to write a nonfiction book. Listen to the conversation in a roomful of people and you will hear discussed such subjects as woman's lib, UFO's, Blacks, Arabs and Israelites, political ideas, conservation, the "Good Old Days," money and other topics rooted in the reality of today's living.

What do you see on television? Documentary after documentary from National Geographic Society and other public-service-minded producers and sponsors, not all on Public Television stations, either: Biography; War adventure and documentary; Reruns of excellent literature of historical content; Tennessee Valley Authority; Civil War; Nostalgia; News documentaries relating past to present.

Good nonfiction today is just as creative as fiction. Note the number of fiction writers who are also writing nonfiction or the nonfiction novel. Note the proportion of fiction to nonfiction books in book review columns: one was twenty nonfiction to six fiction. Note also the large number of regional publishers who publish no fiction at all.

A beginner has just as good a chance to find a salable idea as the professional writer. And don't let anyone discourage you by saying "Oh, that has been done before." Your book will be different or you won't accept the idea in the first place, for the first test of any idea for writing is "Do I have a fresh approach, some new information, something vital to say?"

If you haven't already thought of a book subject, you might proceed to examine ideas as earlier chapters suggest. You are more likely to have the idea come out of your own experience. Perhaps you have specialized in a subject and you have had several articles about it published. Now you realize you have the background and knowledge for writing a book. Stephen Birmingham wrote a number of articles which dealt with "society" which were published in *Holiday* and these, together with much new material, he made into *The Right People,* published in 1968 by Little, Brown.

Is the book you have in mind one which might fill a gap among the titles in print? Just *what* is missing? Talk to book sellers and see what people ask for that they cannot supply. Talk to librarians in public libraries and schools and universities. Talk to teachers. One New Hampshire mother discovered that there were few books on science for readers the age of her young son, so she wrote some and they were published. Her name is Duane Bradley.

Sometimes those involved in newsworthy adventures or situations are approached by a publisher and asked to write a book on their experiences.

Look at the *Subject Guide to Books in Print* in the library reference room. For example, if you have an idea for a book on fashion, look under this subject, and under "Clothing," "Dressmaking," "Costumes" and other similar words to see what has been published lately.

Look in the subject file at several libraries, too. A small library may not stock books on fashion because there would not be many readers interested in the subject. Read several books on whatever subject you select to see what approach the authors have taken.

If you cannot find enough material for a book of at least 60,000 words, your subject is not really sufficient for a book. It might make a good book for children or a regional booklet. Determine the length you think your book will be as soon as you can, so you can plan which publisher to aim for.

Your book must have unity; that is, it should be about one subject or a few related subjects. A book on North American animals has unity; a book on fish and shells does not for the two are too diversified.

Decide how much of your subject you intend to cover. At what point it should begin and where it should end.

After you have studied books on your subject or have learned that there are none, review the previous chapters in this book on research, taking notes, organizing, interviewing, and other writing hints.

Kenneth Roberts used to say that the way to start writing a book was to dream up a good last chapter and write it, or at least to write out the very last paragraph of the book so you'd know where you are going. From that, ideas should come for the first chapter. Write by paragraphs and expand them and it won't frighten you so much, he advised.

I never thought this was a very orderly way to write a book until I read that Marilyn Durham (*The Man Who Loved Cat Dancing*) lived with some characters and didn't know what to do with them. She studied many books to see how writers began their stories, how they set the mood and so on. She decided her book would be set in Wyoming and began to study the geography of the state. Then BANG, it came to her how the story would END, and she sat down and wrote out the last half chapter. And that was how she started to write her book. Who am I to question the writing habits of these two giants?

Joseph Wambaugh, on the other hand, didn't think so much of *how* he was going to write *The Onion Field*: "I just thought about telling *this* story which has been on my mind for years. Actually, this third book made me want to be a writer. When I *thought* about being a writer, it was to write *The Onion Field*." (See interview with him in the December 1973 *Writer's Digest.*)

When you have finished most of your research and have your outline, you are ready to look for a publisher and prepare a query letter.

FINDING A PUBLISHER

Selecting a publisher is a personal thing. You may have acquired a preference for several firms because you like to read the books they publish. Your book may require a regional publisher. What is important: Will the publisher like *your* work? You might not be writing on a subject your favorite publishing firm prints.

You'll want to make a survey of publishing firms. Ask your librarian to lend you recent copies of the *Library Journal* and as many catalogues from publishers as she has, taking a few at a time. The *Journal* not only has thoughtful book reviews but advertising from book publishers, and quarterly most publishing firms announce their forthcoming books. Catalogues give a wide view of what the publishers are planning for the future in more detail than the advertisements can. By the time you have studied a great many of these you will begin to get a feeling for the differences in publishers' tastes.

Which firms like scholarly material or accept material from widely known professionals? Is the material popular in style? Is there a good proportion of historical books in many categories? Which prefer to publish books in the arts, finance, science, biography?

Read the marketing requirements in the latest *Writer's Market* or *Writer's Handbook.* Is any category of history listed? The writers' magazines have specific interviews with publishers and book editors and report on their needs in almost every issue. Check back for six months.

Going to several libraries, look over the books in the cases marked "NEW" and note the publishers. All during this research, keep a selective list of publishers, including regional ones and university presses.

How many publishers who accept material on your subject do NOT have a current book in that category? How many have a book but not one using your particular original approach? List these and select the publishing firm that seems best. Send a specific editor a query letter, accompanied by a complete outline and two sample chapters.

Harry Neal, author of *Nonfiction,* numerous articles and about twenty other books, says that rejection slips are like Boy Scout merit badges; they speak for countless hours of hard work and show your experience. They are what it takes to become a writer. You know of many professional writers who have received many rejection slips, and still get one now and then. Think of this if your query gets a NO the first or second or third time. Meanwhile, keep on writing your book, and improving your query, your outline, your sample chapters each time you put them in the mail to another publisher.

HELPFUL TECHNIQUES

Transition is as important to the writing of history as the narrative style. Readers must be taken from one scene to another, from one thought to a quite different one, from one time period to another. This device is called the *transition.*

As a bridge gets the traveler across the water, a transition moves the reader forward, sometimes with only one sentence, quickening the pace, eliminating the facts which would be dull if just written through exposition. If it is done skillfully, the reader won't realize there has been a purposeful passage of time.

Transitions are made in several ways: *Time* — "Eight months later," "December snows had melted away." Time can also be shown through symbols such as: "There are twenty candles on her cake." *Changing Locations* — "On the interminable ride to Dallas," "The next day they hiked up to the cabin," "From Quincy they drove by coach to Boston, where they boarded the ship." *Description* — "Her brown hair now had threads of silver," "The bus wound up and up, past tiny villages," "At last the gray dawn brightened and sun flooded the valley." *Repeating A Key Word Or Phrase* — "Yesterday had been the best of days. Today was the worst of days." "She sat and watched the apple trees begin to bud. Only a breath of time later, the buds were in full bloom."

Be sure you use active verbs which move the story ahead.

FLASHBACKS

The flashback technique is especially useful in keeping history from being dull. It enables you to begin your story at a time of action, and then — through relating scenes of the past, perhaps in dialogue

— tell enough about events leading to the immediate situation to make the background information clear to the reader.

It eliminates the dry, dull facts which chronology sometimes requires by enabling you to start a chapter at an exciting period and then gradually helping the reader "catch up" by bringing in the facts he needs to know.

It gives an immediacy, a fiction-like quality, to your writing, without destroying the believability of your facts. Flashback often supplies a motive for the conflict in which your story is involved; or explains the reason for a certain character trait or situation which helps the reader to understand why people react as they do.

You must keep the thread of narrative in the present while weaving the necessary details of the past into it through: writer's resume of a past event; recall in thought; through dialogue, action; use of detail, such as a newspaper clipping, a current news story, a photograph, a meeting of two people.

The flashback scene is best when it is dramatized with description, action and dialogue. For example, here's a flashback scene from *The Word* (page 29 of Pocket Book Edition), Pocket Books 1973, by Irving Wallace:

"What are you having?" he asked lightly. "Seven-Up on the rocks?"

"I'm having what you're having," she said.

This was not promising, he decided, as he circled to take the empty chair opposite her. Barbara had not shared liquor with him in years. She would have one or two drinks at parties, but whenever they had been alone, she would refuse to join him in a highball. It had been her way of rebuking him, letting him know that she hated his kind of drinking, the kind of drinking that took you away, put you away, helped you escape any relationship with your wife. Yet here she was with a Scotch.

Look for examples of this technique in your reading and in watching television and copy them into a notebook for further reference.

If you're in the public library when you come across an author's deft handling of a flashback scene, use that nearby photocopying machine to make a copy of those pages for reference.

USING FOOTNOTES

Although with articles footnotes are seldom needed, in books on history there may be times when footnotes are necessary.

If there is any doubt about whether footnotes are required by your publisher, ask him at the beginning of your work, for adding footnotes after the manuscript is completed will take as much effort as doing the original research. This is the reason you must keep your sources in order on the carbon.

All quotations must be identified and a footnote may be the logical solution; however, I prefer to give the source in parentheses or in the text itself, unless my editor says otherwise.

One solution to the footnote problem, may be an appendix and a reference number in the text. In that case, you would put the numbers in order in the text, and explain the reference in the appendix.

It looks like this: "There are only one hundred copies of the book.'" (This is called a *superior number*.) If you do use an appendix for reference notes, be sure you give the chapter headings to make it easier for the reader to follow. You can then start with Number 1 at the beginning of each new chapter.

There is danger in too much footnoting, for it can mean loss of spontaneity and the smooth flow of the narrative. Remember that however you do it, your reader must understand your allusions and know your sources; often items which are clear to an Easterner will not be familiar to a Southerner.

The best way is to be guided by your publisher, but to keep your references in detail on your carbon from the start. I also staple some clippings and source notes to the appropriate carbon page when I need more than a book page reference.

QUOTING AND SECURING PERMISSIONS

It is up to the author to secure permission if he wishes to use quotations in his manuscript.

Unless the book from which quotations come is in public domain — out of copyright — it is imperative that writers who plan to take excerpts from others' published or recorded works receive written permission from the author, composer or publisher. Although (excepting poetry and song lyrics) it is permissible to quote brief passages without asking for an OK, under the "fair use" provision of the copyright law, there are certainly publishers and authors who may disagree with your interpretation of "brief." It is best to be sure.

We all welcome the copyright laws which protect our literary, dramatic, musical and artistic work from bring plagiarized or quoted without our permission. It is right that we make certain our own practices are beyond reproach.

For information on current copyright laws, write to the Register of Copyrights, Library of Congress, Washington, D.C. 20559 and ask for a list of publications. The office will answer questions but will not give legal advice. There are lawyers who specialize in copyright law.

Ideas cannot be copyrighted; nor can works consisting entirely of information that is common property without original ownership. When some unique idea is original with another author, it is ethical to give credit to him rather than to put the material into your own words. Many writers are understandably fearful that they may be using as their own words some phrases which they have read and "adopted" without realizing it — but that possibility of extensive unconscious copying is unlikely. Information in itself can be used, because historical facts belong in public domain; but the original phrasing and conclusions of another author should be acknowledged.

When a work is first published without the proper copyright notice in the book, it falls into the public domain and anyone can use it. This is true of musical arrangements also. It is up to each of us to determine that the market we sell to has a copyright or — if it does not and the material is truly original — to secure a personal copyright so the copyright notice in our name will appear in the publication.

You are free to quote from any United States Government publication without asking permission. But be sure that the booklet is not a reprint of a copyrighted publication. If it is, the Government obtained permission to use it and you must, too.

It is best not to spend the time to secure permissions to quote material for a book until the book has been accepted and the editor has agreed to use the quotations included.

The first step in securing permission to use a quotation is to copy exactly the section you plan to use, with the name of the book or periodical, the author, the publisher, the date of publication and the pages on which the quotation appears.

Write a letter addressed to the Permissions Editor, explaining how you intend to use the quotation in relation to your own words. State the name of your publisher or that you are working on speculation. To the letter you attach the exact quotation, each within the setting in which it is to be used. If you don't do this, you will have to write another letter, for the editor will require this information. Always make a carbon of letter and quotation.

No definite rules for quotation permissions have been established by the publishing industry. Some charge a fee, some allow quotations up to "200 words running consecutively" or "a total of 750 words without fee." You may be referred to the author. Occasionally, an editor will send back a printed form to be filled out.

There is a definite rule for identifying quotations, with or without a fee: They must be acknowledged in the printed form. In a book, the author devotes a page to copyright permissions. In an article or story, a footnote is used or the acknowledgment is a part of the text itself.

Editors and publishers vary in their policies for allowing the use of material. Many will grant limited use free of charge, but set a fee of $10, $25 or $50 for the use of longer material, the price depending on the literary importance of the material or on their contract with the author of the newspaper or magazine article or the book. Permissions for about two-thirds of the material quoted in this book were given free of charge. Several have emphasized that the permission must not exceed what I had typed for the quotation, and three or four stated that only United States publication permission was granted.

Permission must also be requested for the use of photographs, maps and other published or unpublished material as listed in the copyright booklet, following this same procedure. Usually, museums and other sources request a fee for making a copy of the required photo, but do not charge for its use, and some have exactly the opposite rule: They give the photograph free of charge and request a fee for publication use; another new use requires another fee. Acknowledgment must be made in article or book: "Used by permission of the Museum of Fine Arts, Boston."

For this special task of keeping track of all acknowledgments, I go through the complete manuscript and in a "copyright notebook" divided by book chapter, I record the page of my manuscript on which the quotation is to appear (it will have to be checked when the galley proof comes) and add author's name, title of the work, the page of the book where the quotation appeared originally. When each letter of permission comes back, I write OK and the fee beside each quotation. Then I staple the answer to the carbon of my letter and put the chapter number at the top and file it with the book manuscript carbon, ready for the acknowledgment page.

A quotation can be used in the same way as an anecdote and is one way of being specific. A knowledge of when and how to quote can be a valuable tool.

Editors, however, abhor a "scissor and paste" job of writing. Your manuscript should be *your* work. Use quotations only when they give needed emphasis or information or authority or graphic illustration which cannot be given as well in your own words. But they must be used with moderation.

Be sure to check published material which seems beyond copyright limitations. Many, many classics and old-time favorites are being reprinted in paperback, and the copyrights may have been renewed.

You may quote from unpublished manuscripts, diaries, logbooks and similar material by securing the permission of their current owners. The rights in such material remain with the writer rather than with the recipient, and on his death, remain in his descendant's ownership, unless they have been relinquished.

Whenever you can, incorporate the quoted material within the framework of your own writing, so it becomes a part of it, but acknowledged with quotation marks. Sometimes you can give the gist of a necessary reference by using this form: "Dr. Brown, a Houghton scholar, says that —."

Published historical material — which I wrote about my town in publicity on our historic houses for the Chamber of Commerce — has been frequently quoted by other published writers without credit. Take the time to reword such material even though it is "publicity" and so in the public domain. You don't have to give credit or put into quotations this type of publicity material, but neither do you want what you write to have a familiar ring to readers.

When you quote something, be sure you use it exactly as written, unless you are sure there has been a misprint: Use misspelled words, capitalization, punctuation and all. Signify your knowledge of an error by putting *brackets* around the italicized word [*sic*] directly after the mistake. You may often find such errors in diaries, letters and other personal papers. "Wensdy June 5," for example.

Information on the proper use of quotation marks will be found in all style books and grammars. Be sure you know the rules. One important one is that the omission of a word, phrase or sentence in a quotation is indicated by three dots: ...; a fourth dot is used if the ommission is at the end of a sentence. This is to avoid the suggestion that a quotation is consecutive when it is not.

When you quote up to four lines, do so within the paragraph. When you quote longer sections, indent about ten spaces, center it within the text and present it as a continuation of your own work, giving the source.

TITLES

Titles are chosen first of all to attract the eye of readers. Often the one you have given your book will not appeal to your editor. His judgment may be better, but not always. If your title means a lot to you, fight for it, and you just might win.

Unusual and apt titles are not easy to find. Ask yourself: "What words in my central theme could serve as a title? Is there a fresh concept to emphasize?" List the outstanding features of your book and see what that suggests. It should be attractive, accurately describe the book's contents, and be as short as possible. I dislike a title which completely throws off the reader's understanding of what a book is about. You can name several like that and know how irritating it can be.

Here are some suggestions for finding a catchy title:

The title may answer How? Why? What? Who?

It may be a striking statement.

Is there an apt quotation or a paraphrase of a quote to suggest your subject? (Look in *Bartlett's* quotations by subject.)

Sometimes a question gives just the right note.

You may appeal to your reader directly with "You."

Alliteration is often amusing.

Perhaps it could include rhyme. (Anything in Mother Goose?)

What literary allusion from the Bible or other classic might prove interesting?

You might make a pun on a song or play title.

Sometimes the only right title is a label, telling it as it is!

When you open a magazine to the table of contents and glance down the list of titles, which article do you turn to first? THAT will give you a clue for devising a title. You select the title whose subject interests you most? Or intrigues you with its mystery? Perhaps the best title is one which will tell the reader you want to attract, "Come, read me. This is for *you.*"

INDEXING

The effectiveness of a nonfiction book is heightened by the index, and all books which may be used for consultation and study require one.

Although a writer may hire a professional to index his book, it will be accomplished with more sensitivity by the author, who knows what he wants to emphasize.

For you who have completed the research on a book and written it, indexing is relatively easy. You need a card file box, and can often get one free by asking at a stationery store. You will also need an alphabetical card index, and several hundred 3x5 cards. Slips of paper are too flimsy to file well.

Starting on page 1, write a key word on a card, one word to a card. This is called an entry. Put the word at the top left, and below it in the center record the page number. As you progress, add chronologically by page other page numbers that have the same key word. After you have a small pile of cards, alphabetize them, or you may prefer to use a separate card for each reference and put them into chronological page order later.

Sometimes you will find sub-entries, variations of the same topic. With the key word at the top, add a sub-entry just below:

Franklin, Benjamin
In Philadelphia
page 10, 22, 36

Subheads are filed alphabetically under the key word:

In Boston
In Philadelphia
Traveling in Europe

How deeply you go into detail in your index depends on your subject matter. A children's nonfiction book would not require as extensive detail as one for an adult. The test is to be sure the index is complete enough to answer everyone's questions about where a certain topic may be found.

Although you will use the page proofs of your book for the final book indexing, I find it helpful to work on an index long before that time arrives, because it saves time in trying to locate a subject to which I need to refer. Filed alphabetically, the cards can be pulled out and used for the final index, with page numbers changed to those in the printed proofs and, of course, with many additional entries.

Cross references will be needed and you will have to anticipate from your own experience how a researcher will be thinking. We all have times when we have to guess what entry an index maker has listed a subject under when we don't find it where we think it should be.

Illustrations: See under type of,
Cartoons
Photographs
Color photographs: see slides

For further study, you should read *Indexes,* reprinted from *A Manual of Style,* published by the University of Chicago Press, 5750 Ellis Ave., Chicago, Ill. 60637.

CHAPTER EIGHTEEN

WRITING HISTORY FOR YOUNG PEOPLE

"He who brings the romance of America to young America has not lived in vain." These words are attributed to Buffalo Bill Cody, who is himself one of the heroes of youth.

Writers of history have a responsibility to the youth of our country to help them understand how America became great and — in spite of its problems and failures — continues to be great. How better to do this than through stories and books telling how young people and adults of the past have met their problems, surmounted them and made vital contributions to their country?

This means more than the history of battles and generals and presidents. It includes the stories of industry and business, of art and science, of literature and medicine; it includes the record of the country's progress in many fields of technology and social welfare, and the contrast of present social concern with the treatment of minorities in the past.

Whether we Americans can justify the past in relation to the many social problems of the present, whether we can make history relevant to young people today, depends on how well we can help them identify with the heroes of the past, on how we can make the lessons of the past a bridge to a better understanding of today's problems and to finding solutions for them.

Many old values remain the same. Bitter experiences of history and our past mistakes can be used to show young people how to try to make a better world for tomorrow. It is imperative that we keep our writing on the upswing of hope, of caring.

Many young people still search for someone to look up to, an uncommon, courageous person who has done the "impossible." What richness lies in the stories to be told of the real people of the past and the present. The achievements of the great — in every age and of every country — have a universal appeal.

Though we have not yet reached our goal of complete equality for all mankind and for both sexes, we have made progress. We have changed the study of history from emphasis on dates and details of events to an increasing consideration of motives and human relationships and compromises in the "melting pot" of Americanism.

THE "NEW" BOOKS

Current books for young people ten years and older tackle contemporary problems like drug addiction, crime, poverty and sex. Not all writers and publishers agree that we should concentrate on our times as they are rather than as we hope they will become. This must not mean that we omit from our writing emphasis on high standards of morality and social values. "People who don't have the answers shouldn't write children's books," Clifton Fadiman says.

Parents must be alert to the types of history textbooks their children use, to be sure that our American heritage receives its proper emphasis, that our children are taught the positive values of life. Parents must make certain that their children are being taught to accept people at their individual worth regardless of race, religion or sex.

Many recent studies of schoolbooks and readers to determine their treatment of sex roles revealed that adult males were shown in 147 different occupations and females in only 26 and these mostly in home and service type jobs. Boys were lead characters in stories 5 to 2 times and biographies of males lead those of females 6 to 1. In Richard O'Donnell's study of social-studies texts, girls were shown as helpless, incompetent and dependent in nearly all stories. Boys were shown as more ambitious, creative and intelligent than girls. Girls were depicted in housekeeping roles and never as physicians, scientists, musicians, judges and in other responsible, creative positions.

The publishers have eliminated race role stereotyping from their books. Now they are revamping textbooks and other literature to avoid stereotyping the sexes.

This is life as it *is*. We must not, however, allow the new race-sex consciousness to change the facts of the past. We must accept — and tell of — life *as it was,* not change it to what we wish it had been, whether in sex roles or in racism.

A strong example of this is the controversy over children's books like *The Slave Dancer* by Paula Fox, winner of the 1973 Newbery Award, and *The Cay* by Theodore Taylor, winner of the 1970 Jane Addams Children's Book Award, which came under fire in 1974 because diverse groups took issue with the treatment of black characters central to the stories.

The Slave Dancer (Bradbury) drew criticism from black librarians because of what they considered the white boy's apparent callousness toward the cargo of slaves.

The Council on Interracial Books for Children (CIB) later raised objection to *The Cay,* (Doubleday 1969), adapted by Russell Thacher and televised on NBC, starring James Earl Jones. Their criticism was that the author shows blacks (there was only one) "as immature, self-negating, unpredictable and thus, threatening 'creatures' and whites as effectual, commanding and superior beings no matter what their age!" CIB planned to distribute materials to teachers and students to make them aware of what CIB considers harmful connotations in the book.

This tender, true-to-life-as-it-was book and moving picture is the story of an illiterate black sailor and a young English boy brought up with many advantages who are marooned on an island after their ship is wrecked. The story shows their changing relationships and was sensitively accomplished. *This was the way it was* at the period which *The Cay* describes. The fact is that by the end of the story, the black was the effective, influential character.

Any attempt to change or to conceal the facts of history and social action is invalid. It would be a pity not to write about controversial subjects which add to our knowledge of mankind.

While Americans have the inherent right to protest against social injustices, to criticize government, to rebel up to the point of treason, we have read in recent Russian literature that elsewhere rebels or critics may be labeled mentally incompetent and, without a trial, railroaded to an asylum or prison camp. How well do our young people understand the difference?

WRITING CHALLENGES

A beginning writer must not believe that writing for children is an easy way to start a career. Young people have the right to read — and editors demand — a high quality of writing. Librarians are often far from satisfied with the quality and choice of material in books for young people today. Book reviews in *School Library Journal* include comments like these: "too good to be true," "information and theories too complex," "too much background," "limited and somewhat dated bibliography," "realistic but humdrum account," "the serious tone of the story is more likely to appeal to adults than to children," "long, boring and confusing," "ending flat and contrived," "readers may not pick up the references to literary figures," "juvenile demibiography in which the true greatness of the man is slathered over with mediocre fiction," "overlong," "there are historical inaccuracies," "quotations of the character are often too sophisticated for readers who would identify with the boy," "not particularly plausible," "unfamiliar terms not well-defined."

Forget "the right vocabulary" unless you are writing a school reader. Write as you would talk to your children or to your young brother and sister. Most boys and girls from Grade 6 on are capable of understanding an adult vocabulary. For those who cannot, there are the splendid "easy readers" and "I can read" books. Writing for these presents a special challenge.

There is always a question of language suitability in writing for children, especially the middle age group. For example, there were complaints about the large amount of profanity in *A Hero Ain't Nothin' But a Sandwich* by Alice Childress (Coward 1973). The choice of this book as one of "1973 Best Books" was defended by Lillian N. Gerhardt, editor-in-chief of The Book Review *(Library Journal-School Library Journal* December 1974):

... it exemplifies superb characterization and dialogue in fiction of the realistic mode. ...junior high school collection purposes must serve ... in the preparation and development of students toward critical comprehension of the various literary styles employed in both juvenile and adult books published today.

Small children require a simple, uninvolved story, unless it is one of the nonsense yarns they love so much. Listen to their questions, as a clue to what they are thinking, what they are wondering, what they want to know.

Older boys and girls require a brisk pace, brief colorful descriptions, believable characters, an interesting plot told with lots of action and dialogue in an interesting setting. Appealing to the senses, as we have seen, helps to dramatize events, to show setting and character.

There is no substitute for a good story in which "an appealing character strives against great odds to attain a worthwhile goal," as author Lee Wyndham says. When you feel yourself moving silently through a forest watching every shadow for Indians or trembling in fear as you follow a spy through a dark alley, there is a good chance that your reader will feel this way, too.

Don't get bogged down in the details of research. Less research is required for juvenile articles or short stories than for books, because little background material is necessary.

But because children accept what they read as fact, those who write for them have a particular responsibility, and you should not let your reader think events and characters are real if they are not. Think of the number of young people who believe that Ben Franklin's son was a boy when they flew that kite together. In fact, William was twenty-one!

It is usually best to keep a chronological order and to use one point of view when writing for small children. Flashbacks and change of viewpoint can be confusing. Most often, the point of view is that of the main character, but there are exceptions. Go easy on the use of an animal which can think and talk; many editors deplore this. Yet Robert Lawson could write a delightful story told by Paul Revere's horse, and another told by the mouse who lived with Ben Franklin. So you never know!

When you are writing about an adult life for a juvenile audience, one effective technique is to tell the story through the eyes of a child observer. Anne Colver does this in *Yankee Doodle Painter* (Knopf 1955). Through the eyes of her father, Will Colver, who was then a young boy, she tells the story of her great-uncle,

Archibald Willard, and how he came to paint the famous "The Spirit of '76."

It is less difficult to select a story to tell children because to a child, the whole world is a mystery — it is all so new! and questions continuously crowd through his mind.

The Walt Disney staff says that every seven years a new generation of children is ready for Mickey Mouse and the other classic characters they film so well. This is just as true of boy and girl readers, who progress from being-read-to to easy readers to reading alone and, we hope, to reading for fun.

Your first thought should be to choose a topic which can be made exciting; something has to HAPPEN. You must be enthusiastic about it yourself. A nonfiction subject should excite you just as much as one for fiction. If there is no problem to overcome, no conflict in its solving, there is no story. Without a struggle, there can be no suspense.

Television has broadened the interests and knowledge of even the smallest child. Familiarity with the experience is more important than a famous name. That is, a familiarity with the telephone is enough to bring acceptance of its inventor, Alexander Graham Bell. Children know about the exploration of the moon, although they would seldom recognize the names of the astronauts until they read about them.

Older boys and girls will respond to a complete biography about someone whose name is new to them, but he must be someone who has accomplished something in a field which interests them. The lives of presidents and statesmen are not very big with older students who have studied American history. The subject of Sports *is.* YET, new ideas, unusual facts, an imaginative presentation can make even an old subject absorbing.

Local history written especially for children is greatly needed in every state, as you will see if you look for such material in your school and library. Probably every town has a glamorous figure or two whose life would make a good story; and — going beyond biography — town and state history can be exciting even to children.

Spend as much time as you can in the children's room at the library. Read history of all types written for boys and girls of all ages from picture books to full biographies and histories. Adults are missing a lot when they fail to explore the juvenile bookshelves. Ask the librarian to recommend several books about the era or area in which you are most interested.

Another point to consider when selecting a subject is the market for it. Few regional magazines or newspapers accept historical articles or short stories written for children. Among the exceptions are *The Christian Science Monitor* and *Grit*. All juvenile magazines and some family magazines welcome them, as you will note when you study the *Writer's Market*.

A biographical dictionary will disclose a large number of subjects which have not received recognition. Check some of them. You will find the proportion of women in the listings is very small: In the *American Dictionary of Biography*, of 15,000 entries only 706 are about women. This will change in years to come.

KNOW YOUR READER

While you are having fun reading magazines and books written for young people, you will find yourself leaning toward communication with a certain age group. The subjects can be the same for all ages except the pre-school children and perhaps the read-to group. The manner of handling the material is quite different, and this is the chief technique you'll need to learn.

You must be sure that the material you are going to write *about* is suitable for the age group you plan to write *for*.

One way of getting to know your own group of readers is to see what subjects they write about in letters to the magazines they read, what they draw for their own pages. You can get an idea of what older ones are thinking about, what their problems are, by reading their letters in columns like "Buzz Buzz" in *American Girl*.

Children take life for granted at an early age, seldom thinking of themselves, but eager to read about other children and what they do. The childhood of a famous person would interest them. As they grow older, their curiosity about the world and other people intensifies. This happens at an earlier age than it did for their parents and is revealed in subjects shown for them on television, and the material taught in school.

As mentioned earlier, children's books deal with an awareness of current problems, and books formerly read by teenagers are now in the hands of the ten-year-olds. The challenge to meet the sophistication of our readers is a great one, and this does not mean that we forget the sense of fun and imagination which every young person welcomes.

The exception to the change is in the picture books and fantasy written for the very young. The best of the "easy readers" are humorous and beginning nonfiction gives a hint of the world beyond the child's home on popular subjects, the more unusual the better. Sports, a favorite topic from Grade 3, is bypassed at this younger level.

Older boys and girls prefer books with dynamic characters who overcome obstacles through their own resourcefulness; this is a cardinal criterion in juvenile literature. They are occupied with the world around them, wanting no-nonsense books of nonfiction which explain the technology of topics they are learning about. They also want books which tell about the real world and its problems, often reading their parents' books. They are seeking answers to problems they hear about every day.

In fact, young people of today are interested in just what you are, and your job is to give them information in the amounts they can absorb for their own age, told in a lively way, often with lots of dialogue.

There is one category called "young adult" which seems the same as "adult" in most cases. In *Library Journal* and in publishers' catalogues, the YA label sometimes appears in both juvenile and adult lists. While agreeing that for the sake of teachers and librarians and others who buy books there needs to be some classification of books by grade and age, some disagree about this label. If you write a good story, the book will fall into its own classification.

In the YA category, I am more interested in the fact that high school readers are now becoming writers as the vision of *Foxfire* spreads around the world. Hundreds of teenagers will grow into thousands absorbed in working with teachers and historical societies, learning their heritage through personal contact with those who have lived long and useful lives, and communicating all this to others.

You'll have to be very good indeed to write for them!

MARKETS FOR ARTICLES AND SHORT STORIES

No one should write for any group of readers without studying the periodicals and books which they read. This ought to be just plain common sense, but it needs saying over and over.

Writer's Market lists publications for young people under "Juvenile Publications" and "Teen and Young Adult." The former are classified by readership age: Two-to-Five; Six-to-Eight; Nine-to-Twelve, a helpful guide which you can use with a little give-and-take, since age and grade levels overlap. Teenage and young adult is intended as a guide for a readership of 12 to 16, also a very broad spread.

When you go to the library and look at what the children's room has to offer in the magazine field, you will know better what appeals to each age group than you can ever know from a market requirement listing. You will find some magazines for the 12-year-old-and-up there, too. Some magazine editors design their periodical for all ages, such as 2-to-12. Go to the largest periodical shop in your area; browse and then buy a few juvenile magazines not available in the library. A few will be found in your dentist's or doctor's office, too.

Many magazines listed in the market guides are not in either place, because they are published by church groups. Ask local ministers to lend you a few sample copies of each of their Sunday School papers, which are designed by the above age groups as a rule. Those you can't find locally, you can send for. Many are sent free of charge; others ask for a sum ranging from 25¢ to $4.00. At the same time you write, ask for an editorial guideline for writers.

Look under the Religious heading to find periodicals which have junior pages and ask for copies if they sound like possibilities as a market. Among these are *Church Herald, Contact, Insight* and *The New Era.* Under other subjects you may also find other adult magazines which have junior pages or special interest magazines like *Young Crusader* (Junior members of W.C.T.U.) and *Young Musicians* (members of children's choirs).

It is very important indeed that you study the editorial requirements of juvenile magazine editors, looking for these instructions: deadlines for seasonal material (some are a YEAR ahead); payment, which varies from payment on acceptance to payment on publication, and from copies of the magazine to three figure checks; requirements for illustrations (usually VERY definite, and often photos are not returned); publishing rights; taboos; whether query is necessary and conditions; length requirements (some editors demand a definite word count); typing instructions (some require a definite number of type characters to a line); and whether the market is open or requires an assignment (which you might obtain through your query). Don't underestimate the importance of these requirements.

In the short space of 300 to 3,000 words allowed in most juvenile magazines, there is little room to write a short story or article of any great depth. Here are some of the historical subjects published as articles or short stories in children's magazines:

A boy involved in the Black Hawk War; a girl who guided General George Washington to Princeton after the Battle of Trenton; growing up with Abe Lincoln; a boy's life in a fourteenth-century castle; the story of the American eagle; how "Old Glory" got its name; the night Booker T. Washington was lost in a coal mine; how cheese was first made and how two children fooled the British Navy in the War of 1812. Poetry, puzzles and quizzes based on history are also frequently used.

Each of these, you see, evolves around an incident, a short space of time, one subject. Your short story or article will be more effective if you select one phase of a subject and write in depth on that, and leave the longer period of time for book-length material.

Writing an article or a short story for a young person involves the same techniques as those required for adult material, as explained earlier. What is different is the *pace* of the material. In fact, it is this difference which may determine whether your make-up is better geared for writing short stories or a novel, articles or a book.

THE BOOK MARKET

Study the book market as suggested earlier, for there's not much difference in the subjects for adults and young people. You will note that publishers usually have a special section in a general catalogue or separate catalogue for the books they publish for youngsters. *School Library Journal,* found in school libraries, will be useful to you for reviews of juvenile books.

Look especially for, and make a list of, the continuing series, profiles or special categories which some publishers have. Here are only a few of many, to give you an idea what to look for:

Putnam: Building America Books for Grades 3 to 5

Let's Go Exploring with Magellan (W. U. Granberg)

Coward: Life Long Ago Books for Grades 3 to 5

The First Farmers: In the Stone Age (Leonard Weisgard)

Watts: Minorities in American History Series for Grades 7 to 9

From the Progressive Era to the Great Depression (William Loren Katz)

Westminster: High Interest - Low Reading Level (Content geared to teenagers)

Marian Anderson: Lady from Philadelphia (Shirlee P. Newman)

Nothing you write will be suitable for every publisher in this field, for there are many differences in age level, goals of the publishers, content, space limitations and what the publishers like and do not like. Unless you learn your market, you may never sell a book!

Watch for special and new series and without doubt there will be more like the Crowell series on Women of America.

Whatever you are writing for children — short story, article, book — ask yourself these questions:

Do I have a story to tell?

Do I have a hero or heroine with whom my reader can identify?

Does he have a problem a child will care about?

Does my main character solve the problem himself?

How can I begin to capture the reader's attention at once?

How can I plan to keep the reader involved to the end? How can I arouse suspense, curiosity, imagination, perception?

Have I answered all the questions a reader might ask?

Can my story or article or book or play compete with television?

The world of children's literature is a large and exciting one, sure to bring great rewards to those who venture into it. Those who do are in splendid company. Elizabeth Yates, commenting on writing for children, once said, "When one's pen is dipped in enthusiasm, one's words will live." And John Masefield encouraged writers with these words: "Venture on. Next to enlighten all men may be you."

CHAPTER NINETEEN

WRITING AND PUBLISHING LOCAL AND REGIONAL HISTORY

Every town has dozens of dramatic stories of events and people of the past waiting to be discovered. Many legends and reminiscences of past history are being lost because no one is recording them. The information waiting to be discovered in your town and state will furnish you with material to be used in a variety of forms, all the way from short fact articles to published books.

Sometimes I have walked past a potential story day after day without seeing it. Then some "outsider" will find it, write it and sell an article or even a book. Again, facts of local history can become so familiar that it seems boring to write about them — or you may think everyone already knows about them. I've been "scooped" with familiar material, too.

A new generation comes along every few years: Children become aware of their heritage; newcomers move into town, eager to know more about their adopted home; residents either never heard, or have forgotten, local history.

I remember going to Leominster, Massachusetts, to find the birthplace of John Chapman, better known as Johnny Appleseed. Of the four or five people I queried, not one had even heard of him. The librarian knew — and there's a good lesson in that. Since then, books and articles have been written about Johnny Appleseed, and Walt Disney produced a motion picture. Young in historical research, I was discouraged and put the story aside. No one in his town wrote it, either. In FACT, he is better known in Ohio and Indiana, where he distributed many of his apple seeds, than he is in Massachusetts. Perhaps he will receive his due now that Leominster has established an annual Johnny Appleseed Festival!

Local history is a gold mine for the beginning writer and a continual source of information for the experienced one. You may be more interested in writing fiction or book-length material, but you will learn your craft more quickly, and with less discouragement, if you first do research and write articles about the people and places and events of your community and region. Divide your time: Work on that book or short story a measure of time, but give an hour or two each day to writing short articles which have a chance of being sold to regional markets. I promise that this will give you just the lift you need to keep on with the long-term projects. Your local research sources include librarians, of course; but also town and county records, oldtimers' scrapbooks and photographs, family diaries, letters, etc.

Begin with submissions to local newspapers or regional magazines or Sunday newspapers, and when you find you have a story of national interest, reach out for slick magazine publication.

A good way to begin is to offer to handle the publicity for the town historical society. Becoming a member will give you entre' to the library and archives. Writing about the buildings a society or town maintains, when they open for the season or when a special event is held, will give you confidence to write articles on your own. Be sure to file for future reference all the information you gather while doing this volunteer work.

Sometimes the local chamber of commerce hires a writer to do its publicity, to prepare news articles intended to attract visitors. If the town has several attractions of a historical nature, it might provide you with an opportunity to prepare brochures and booklets for public distribution.

For five years — first as a volunteer publicity chairman and then as a paid executive director — I wrote numerous articles describing the beauty of the York, Maine seacoast and its historic buildings for publication across the country. A result of this — coming out of the recognized need — was the *York Historical Booklet,* which I wrote, designed and edited. This has been a popular souvenir for York tourists and residents for many years. Now and then I recognize my wording in the work of others writing about York.

Out of this experience have come other opportunities to write historical material, not only about York, but about other communities. In each town, I have found a library, a historical society and individuals experienced in local history who could help me secure source material.

HOW TO WRITE PUBLICITY

An important part of local historical writing is the publicity which is sometimes necessary to attract tourists, to secure new members and to encourage financial support for both historical society and chamber of commerce. If you come to a community with the intention of singing its praises through your articles, you'll be warmly welcomed. Often photographs and descriptive pamphlets and other material will be given to you free of charge.

Occasionally you will receive enough information to write a booklet like those published by the Government to describe historic sites and battlefields. Across the country are hundreds of other subjects waiting to be written about in this way. Sometimes historical societies are willing to finance the printing of this type of publicity, but have not found anyone to do the writing. Here is your chance.

The person who does publicity for the historical society or chamber of commerce needs to know a few techniques to do a good job. Sometimes this work is given to a professional writer, or to a public relations firm, which also prepares an advertising schedule and copy for it. The organization might be very willing to let a freelance writer try his hand at it, expecially if he has had a few articles on local history published.

Here is one way to go about handling the publicity for an organization or a historic house:

First, make a list of the news media to which articles will be sent, and the deadline each newspaper requires. In our area, two weekly newpapers published on the same day of the week have different deadlines. (The *deadline* means the last hour at which your copy will be accepted for the next issue.) Your list should include every newspaper, radio and television station and regional magazine in the area. It would also include newspapers in areas of the country where readers might be persuaded to visit the town and its historic attractions.

Articles would be sent to the travel editor, the woman's page editor or to the feature editor, depending on the type of material, and the way you handle the story. A quilt exhibit, for example, would be of interest to women, while a display of antique guns would arouse the curiosity of men.

For one summer I did all the publicity for a historic house in Portsmouth, New Hampshire, and the records there showed a doubling of attendance for the season in comparison with the previous one. Perhaps you can use statistics like these to help you get publicity assignments in your area.

I worked to make each lead paragraph one which would appeal to people in the area where the newspaper was published. For an inland paper, I would stress the York coastline and beaches, for example. With each article went one or two 7x9 or 8x10 photographs with captions. Although the basic story might be the same, the approach and photographs would be different for that week. Perhaps during the whole season each newspaper would receive the same five or six photographs but not in the same week.

Each editor likes to receive material tailored to his readers, and although it took longer to type the material and to find an individual approach, it was worth it. Articles going to local newspapers were usually exactly the same, but the city editors are used to this type of publicity and those who cared changed it around to make it different.

The publicity director also needs to prepare a list of the town's future events and anniversaries, and those which various organizations are planning. I kept a calendar of events, and we mimeographed this each week for the week ahead for the convenience of our visitors.

Basing a story on a current topic is called a "news peg" and gives the writer a legitimate reason for sending out a story. You can write such articles ahead of time, marking at the top of the first page "Release on ..." and giving the date it is to be published. Be accurate, be brief, be original. Learn to discriminate between routine and newsworthy events. The former are simple news stories; the latter can be true feature material, with a historical background woven in and a livelier style than an ordinary news items requires.

Here are samples of an ordinary news story (1) and the lead for a feature article which gives the historical background of the historic building and a description of the many artifacts of the period (2):

1. The John Hancock Warehouse, Lindsay Road, York, Maine,

will be open for the summer season on June 28. Maintained by Historic Landmarks, Inc., this historic building was once owned by the Boston merchant of American Revolutionary fame. Hours are 11 a.m. to 5 p.m. weekdays, and 1:30 to 5 p.m. Sundays. A small admission fee is charged all but York residents.

2. Few Maine people realize that John Hancock, whose famous signature leads the names on the Declaration of Independence, owned property in York and in 1791 while Governor of Massachusetts made a visit filled with pomp and ceremony to see his old friend Judge Jonathan Sayward, York's leading citizen.

From 1787 to 1794 the Boston merchant and one Joseph Tucker jointly owned the John Hancock Warehouse, on the bank of the tidal York River. It was used to store items bought and sold in his merchant marine trading up and down the New England coast: furs, lumber, wine, molasses, rum, salt fish.

Once much larger, the warehouse was saved from complete destruction by Historic Landmarks Inc. and opened as a museum during the summer months.

On local history articles, keep these suggestions in mind:

Always keep carbons of your material, noting on each which photo accompanies it and what the caption says. I used to put "Special to the ....." and name the newspaper, so that was on the carbon already. The carbons help you to know which photographs and stories went where, so you won't repeat yourself. File carbons and news clippings for ready reference. Unless you read the newspapers to which you send material, you'll seldom know whether the material was used until a visitor comes in and says she read your story in Montreal.

RADIO AND TELEVISION

Radio publicity material should be much shorter than that provided a newspaper. It would be a good idea to visit a nearby station, introduce yourself in your official capacity, and ask how the station prefers its copy to be prepared. Sometimes it will use spot announcements, which you can send on a postcard. Once in awhile, it will agree to use a short feature. To merit a share of time on the air, news must appeal to a wide audience and have a quick-paced style.

I once wrote and delivered a weekly radio series about local history for the D. A. R. This was fun to do and well received. It was necessary to remember that this was for listeners rather than for readers or watchers; to avoid prominent "s" and harsh repetitive sounds, to use short sentences, so that breathing between thoughts was natural, to speak more slowly than usual, to strive consciously for natural change in tone.

The radio program director helped me to time my speaking and to write a script the correct length for the period of delivery. This differs with each person's speech pattern and adjustments may have to be made.

Most radio copy, of course, will be delivered by the station's own personnel.

Occasionally, it is possible to secure free time on television for a program about a special event like the historical militia festival coming next week. Programming is always tight on television, but most stations do offer free time for community programs now and then. It is worth asking for an opportunity when what you offer is newsworthy and entertaining. To prepare such a program, you would need to talk first with the television station's program director, tell him what you have in mind, and get his approval. Then together you would arrange for the interview or presentation of historical information. Go to visit the director thoroughly prepared, with your ideas written in a small notebook.

HISTORICAL BOOKLETS

If your chamber of commerce does not publish a booklet giving the history of the town and a description of its historical attractions, its industries and so on, why not suggest such an enterprise and apply for the job as editor. You would write a short essay about each point of interest and secure an illustration for at least the most important. You would also write a brief history of the town and its current appeal. An attractive booklet with an imaginative cover will be in great demand as a souvenir. It may be sold for a small sum to help pay the printing bill or given away. Our booklet had a map drawn by a famous local artist, and a tour map numbered with the location of historic spots which were described according to the numbers in the accompanying text.

Sometimes you can make a booklet like this pay for itself by securing advertisements. If you get the ads, you will make more money for yourself, too. I have worked under several financial arrangements: paid by the hour; paid a percentage of the advertising; paid a sum for the complete job. Preparing the booklet itself was a part of my work for the chamber of commerce. The advertising was done on my own time and I received twenty percent of the total receipts. For a freelancer to do the booklet alone, the return would be from $200 to $500, depending on the size of the organization and its financial status.

The cost of advertisements is determined by asking the printer for an estimate of the complete printing job and dividing this sum by the number of pages. Estimate what your profit should be. Then divide the total for each page by 1/2, 1/4, 1/8 to find the price for each advertisement. A whole page costs less than two half pages; figure out the other sizes accordingly. For example, if a full page is estimated at $100 ($50 per page for printing 5,000 copies, $50 for profit, which goes to you, or is shared with the chamber of commerce, depending on your arrangement), half a page would be $60. The printer's price is determined by the number of pages plus the number of copies, and the more copies printed, the less each book costs. You have to include the cost for getting photographs and having cuts made for illustrations, and some pages will have no advertisements.

You may want to engage a freelance artist to design the map, the cover, the arrangement of the editorial content, but you can do this yourself, learning by studying the sample booklets your printer will give you. Usually, the advertisers pay for their own cuts.

I devote one page to each attraction (park, beaches, historic site, church) with a short text accompanying the photo. Below each attraction there may be room for a quarter-page ad. On the opposite page place advertisements, preferably those which are associated with the attraction; that is — a historic site in the center of town would have advertising of merchants in that area.

Put the map in the center fold with a tour guide, if you have one, printed on the front and back.

Of course, it is more attractive to have a booklet without ads, but if financing is needed, or you want to make a good fee, this is an excellent way to get that historical booklet printed — and that is what is important.

FAMILY HISTORY & GENEALOGY

Probably more local history buffs are interested in family history than in any other one topic. It is a field which requires a long apprenticeship, and it can become fascinating and time-consuming. Those who devote much of their time to the study of genealogy of a single family or of the people of a community can be of great help to the rest of us. I have used family histories and unpublished genealogies, prepared by our town expert, with great satisfaction.

Don't get "hooked" on the study of genealogy unless you have many free hours to spend on it. This is what is called "the bare bones" of biography, a small but important part of the whole person.

Sources for family history are biographical and historical as well as genealogical, and have been mentioned several times in this book.

Local genealogical research for someone else should pay between $3 to $10 an hour. Some searching projects are paid by the project instead of by the hour, but that is rather foolhardy for anyone less than a professional genealogist to determine.

Sometimes one must be truly a detective to find family names and dates and other data. Once I looked for several months for the family of a woman and quite by chance discovered that her mother had been married three times since the daughter was born. Another time, I went to the county court house as a last resort in an effort to find information about a subject's mother. Looking at the father's will, I saw that the mother was not mentioned, and so knew she had died before that date of the will's probate.

When you go seriously into the study of genealogy, you must have charts to carry the lines along, and learn how to record your findings. You will find books to help you in the bibliography. Be sure you note the source of all material, for you may never be able to find it again unless you do.

Genealogists will welcome a feature in *Prologue,* the quarterly journal of the National Archives. James D. Walker, genealogy and local history specialist, is editor of a section of information and advice on genealogical research in the federal records. Address him at the National Archives, Washington, D. C. 20408.

One of the finest research centers in the country is the New England Historic Genealogical Society in Boston, Massachusetts. Fast becoming the most complete genealogical authority in the United States is the Genealogical Society of the Church of Jesus Christ of Latter Day Saints, Inc., Salt Lake City, Utah. Many families, not just church members, are recorded here. Teams from the society have been touring the country, microfilming vital records of historical societies and other holdings at no cost.

REGIONAL HISTORIES

Regional presses are located in all parts of the country. *The Literary Market Place,* an annual to be found in your library, lists publishers by geographical location, just as N. W. Ayer's *Directory of Newspapers and Periodicals* locates these items for you. When you have the list of regional magazines, use the *Writer's Market* to learn their editorial requirements. When you have located regional publishers, study their catalogues in the *Publisher's Trade List Annual* in your local library, their published catalogues, also in most libraries, and their requirements in *Writer's Market.*

When you know your market, then you will be able to decide how much you intend to write on the subjects you've selected. Will it be a full-length book? A booklet which a historical society or business firm might commission you to write? A mini-book which you could publish yourself? An article of local or regional scope?

Besides those just mentioned, there are other possibilities for writing regional or local history: a play, filmstrip with text or a motion picture documentary; a family history commissioned by an individual or family group; a pageant for a town celebration; picture books or coloring books or short history books or fiction for children; the text to accompany a brochure for an advertising firm, a chamber of commerce, or a tour map for visitors to a city or town; material for guide books like *New England Guide;* your own guide book if your town or county doesn't have one. Advertising agencies hire freelancers to create booklets and brochures and for some of the other activities listed here, paying an average of $20 per hour or a flat fee for the complete job.

Some of these may seem small writing opportunities, but if you are using material already gathered for another project, it is an "extra," and doing some of these jobs for partial support will give you some free time to write that book you have in your head.

For example, the Clay County Historical Society, Vermillion, South Dakota, published two guides for visitors. One is a "ninety mile historic venture" around the county, with a map and photos on one side of the four-fold sheet (17 inches by 20 inches) and county history and site descriptions on the other. The other one is a walking tour of the city, using a similar format.

Many historic sites are using cassettes which give a site-by-site description for walkers or automobilists to follow, either renting or selling them. Someone has to prepare these, why not you, for the sites near you?

Do you have a collection of old postcards of your region? The Cumberland County Historical Society of Pennsylvania has published an album of early postcards called *Wish You Were Here* (35 pages, $2, sold by the Society, located in Carlisle). If you don't have postcards, visit local antiques shops and flea markets or collaborate with others who do have collections. Each card in the album was identified and the present status of the pictured site was given whenever possible. A picture album of an old-time postcard side by side with photos of the site as it is now is another thought.

Unless you sell your material to a top magazine or publishing house, regional or national, there's not much money to be made out of regional history. It is, however, the very best way to break into the publishing field, and it is a step up on the way to selling a book to a publisher. The climb up can be satisfying and bring a lot of pleasure to many people who care about local history.

To me, the difference between regional and local history is that the former is of an area larger than a community or county. Regional can mean part of a state, a group of states, an area along a river or canal. The geographical size of the readership may be a criterion, although some of those listed below indicate that the subject *can* be of wide enough appeal to capture the attention of a national publisher.

Here are some examples of commercially published books on regional history: *The Pictorial History of the Royal Canadian Mounted Police* by S. W. Horrall (McGraw-Hill Ryerson, Ltd., Toronto 1973); *Mark Twain's Mississippi* by T. H. Watkins (American West Publishing Company 1974); and *Americans and the California Dream* by Kevin Starr (Oxford 1973).

What ideas do you have for a regional history that might interest a national or regional publisher? Even some local history has been published commercially.

For example, *Freedom by the Bay* by William G. Schofield, the originator of the idea of Boston's Freedom Trail, was published by Rand McNally, and *The Appletons of Beacon Hill* by Louise Hall Tharp by Little, Brown. Many books on local history are published by university presses and some regional books of scenic areas become picture books, lavishly illustrated.

REGIONAL AND LOCAL FREELANCE MARKETS

Perhaps you will be especially interested in one phase of town history, preferring to concentrate on military history or regional crafts or biography. It is better to study a phase of history rather than to try to become an expert in the whole area. At least begin this way and add to your knowledge gradually.

My first published article in the field of history was a very short biography of Celia Thaxter, who lived a long time ago in neighboring Kittery and whose poetry I enjoyed. It was published in the *Lewiston Journal Magazine,* which paid space rates (by the inch) but this is a prestige publication in the state.

While I was a correspondent and reporter for the *Portsmouth Herald,* I wrote several articles about John Paul Jones, who lived in that city in 1777 when he was supervising the building of his famous ship, *The Ranger.* At the time of York's Tercentenary I wrote articles about town history almost daily and these were published in a variety of media.

Locally, regionally, nationally and in anthologies my articles have been published about school and church history, Indians, volunteer firemen, much-loved doctors, Maine islands, literary associations, colonial crafts, area history, historic buildings and sites, and countless people of past and present from York, surrounding towns, and throughout New England.

After you have studied general background history about your town, you'll find numerous ideas coming to mind, some of local or state interest, a few of national importance.

TOWN AND REGIONAL BOOKS

Town histories are often written by older people who have gathered material over many years. This is a labor of love and personal satisfaction, for in comparison to the years of research required, the financial returns are small.

There are, however, other uses for the material found in this type of research. There are numerous books of fiction written against a town's background or based on historical events within a state. Some like *The Waltons* and *The Little House on the Prairie* become movies. In addition to the thousands of Westerns (romantic, adventurous and historical) you will remember *Gone with the Wind* by Margaret Mitchell; *Giant* by Edna Ferber; *The Grapes of Wrath* by John Steinbeck; and the midwest pioneer stories of Loula Grace Erdman. All of these began with a study of local history.

For those who prefer this area of historical writing, the research is joyous and the rewards exciting.

In a survey of methods adopted in writing and publishing a local or regional book I have found a variety: 1. An individual citizen who spent years preparing a book, who financed and sold it himself, with moderate success. (Before taking this step yourself, make every effort to find a publisher, for such a venture costs at least $5,000, for a hard-cover.) 2. An individual commissioned by a town, who was paid a flat sum by the town ($500 up) or who had an agreement to share in the profits. 3. A committee of citizens, or perhaps members of a historical society, who prepared the material, either securing patrons to finance its publication or a regional publisher willing to take a chance on making a profit. 4. A historical society or other group which prepared and financed the publication of a new history or paid for the reprinting of a fine old history out of print.

An excellent source of help is your local university press which may sponsor a worthy manuscript.

Some publishers prefer the specialized book like Americana or railroad history or crafts. Others make room for one or two regional books a year to diversify their listings. There are regional publishers who make a specialty of town histories, sometimes acting only as printers and assisting the historian with many details of publishing for which he or she pays, and sometimes subsidizing the book if the publisher thinks he can make a profit.

AUDIOVISUAL OPPORTUNITIES

Closely related to written regional and local history, and requiring as much research, are the audiovisual arts of presenting information about your region. Photographers and artists who are historically-minded can profit by working in this field.

Across America young people are following the *Foxfire* tradition begun about ten years ago by Eliot Wigginton in Rabun Gap, Georgia. His work with his English classes has served as an example for similar projects as they continue to preserve the traditions and culture of their region by taping the reminiscences of older people and filming the demonstration of fast-disappearing skills and crafts. Students in the high school tape interviews, write articles, edit and publish *Foxfire,* a school magazine, some of them going into related fields as careers.

IDEAS Inc., 1785 Massachusetts Avenue, N.W., Washington, D. C. 20036, has been established to help initiate similar programs all over the United States, including *Salt* of Kennebunk, Maine, the pilot project for New England. The students' teacher-advisor, Mrs. Pamela Wood, has traveled widely to assist other schools in the development of programs.

Some ideas for writing in this field may be obtained by writing for a catalogue of the material produced by the Society for Visual Education Inc., 1345 Diversey Parkway, Chicago, Illinois 60614. Charles J. Hagan, vice president in charge of production for this firm, says that he would welcome a proposal from a freelance writer, and that fees are established on the basis of amount of work to be done. Study the catalogue *first.* This firm is the largest producer of educational filmstrips for elementary schools. Other audiovisual firms are listed in *Writer's Market.*

"Stories of Maryland" — a film series dealing with historic incidents and individuals from Maryland's past — is being distributed state wide by the Maryland Center for Public Broadcasting. The series was produced by the company with the cooperation of local and state historical societies, whose help included research, loan of costumes and study materials, and the use of historic sites and buildings. The films are available to every public school in the state. Other states are developing similar programs to tell the story of regional history, some through the efforts of organizations or television studios, others through the work of individuals.

What can you create to make regional and local history more attractive to young people of your area?

WRITING "MINI-BOOKS"

You have seen the small paperback booklets which many historic houses, villages, museums and historic sites have for sale for about $1.50 or $2. The Government, particularly the National Park Service, engages writers to prepare the booklets distributed at the historic places it maintains.

Some of the village restorations carry a line of paperback booklets in their gift shops. Among these is Old Sturbridge Village in Massachusetts. Booklets in the OSV series are varied in subject but all deal in some manner with history, crafts, customs of early

New England. Booklets are written by staff members or by outside
writers. A professional writer might be assigned a subject in which
he is an expert. A writer is welcome to come up with an idea
and be given an opportunity to write a booklet if it is suitable
for the village's areas of interest. A flat fee is paid, currently $100.
The same fee is paid for each reprinting or revision.

Subjects would vary with the history of the region and arrangements might differ, too. If the village has a catalogue, you could
ask for a copy. Otherwise, a visit or query by letter would help
you to determine the needs or whether your idea would be
acceptable.

Another type of book is the commemorative booklet. Business
firms have centennials or move into new quarters. A church, town,
civic group, university, might be celebrating an anniversary or other
important event which could be publicized in a booklet.

Don't wait for news of such events to appear in a newspaper;
that is too late. Go through old newspapers, read the columns
of calendar events of "fifty" or "twenty-five" years in local papers,
find out when business firms were established, when towns in your
area were founded, or churches or other groups are celebrating
important anniversaries.

The earlier you can find out about a celebration date the better,
for you need plenty of time to see the person in charge and suggest
that you write a booklet. Go to the president of a corporation,
to the chairman of a church board, to the mayor, the head of
a family group, with your ideas. Write a few pages to suggest the
contents and outline the rest, have a sample booklet (a printer
will help you there) and a dummy made up, and take along
something you have published.

A *dummy* is composed of pages which form the size of the
proposed booklet. I take 8½x11" sheets of unlined paper and fold
them in half, a good size for a booklet. Then I find an attractive
picture in a magazine or sketch an idea for the cover. Inside I
put tentative headings with suggestions for photographs and text,
which would be different for each subject, of course. This same
form is used to prepare copy for the printer and to secure advertising. The dummy would have the same number of pages as you
plan for the completed booklet. During the six years I was editor

of the *Maine Federation News* I used the same system, although the page size was larger.

State your terms at your first visit and by the second meeting have a simple contract ready for signing. Your fee will be determined by the amount of work you will have to do, and may include expenses or not, according to the agreement. The amount will vary from $3 an hour to $25 an hour or may go as high as $1,000 for the completion of the booklet.

The contract should spell out in detail such things as: deadline, size of booklet, number of photos and where they are to be obtained, how many copies are to be printed, who pays expenses of travel, telephone and so on, who will select the printing company and who will negotiate with the printer, who will pay him, what typing help you can expect, copyright ownership, what other use will be made of the booklet and its contents, and your fee.

Sometimes printing costs, and perhaps the writing costs, are made by advertisements sold to local merchants and business firms. If you secure the ads, you should get a percentage of this in addition to the writing fee, or the latter should be higher. If you don't like to solicit advertising, you must make it clear that someone else will have to be hired to do it. If you have a friend who likes to deal with the public in this way, you might cooperate on booklets and do the whole job for your clients.

Be sure to figure in the cost of securing photographs and reproducing them in the booklet when you estimate the cost of the reproduction of the brochure.

You must keep your research and everything to do with the booklet in good order, according to instructions given several times in this book. You may be doing several types of projects at the same time, and unless you have a separate portafile or drawer in a steel file or a box for each project, you will soon be in trouble.

It is important to keep in touch with whoever is doing publicity for the event, for the work you are doing should be included in reports of progress. If the publication of the booklet is announced far ahead, you may get some valuable information from people reading about it. Many have personal papers and scrapbooks hidden away in attics and a news story might remind them that this would be a good time to share them.

If the booklet is to be sold, all publicity will be welcome and needed.

Writing experience of this kind is a good foundation for other opportunities in the field of writing and in the interpretation and writing of history in particular.

PUBLISHING YOUR OWN MINI-BOOK

Printing prices vary by the community, and the times, but by investing about $600, you can write and sell booklets of many kinds as a personal venture, if you have the proper background of writing skills. Writing for one's self is a particularly vulnerable thing, for we writers love our own words, and if you are your own editor, you must exercise considerable self-discipline and discrimination in what is to be published. No faults of writing, no inaccuracies, can be hidden when they show up on the printed page. Find a reliable person to edit the material for you, and accept his advice.

Prices given in 1975 by a Maine publishing firm for printing a booklet were these: $9.30 per page for 300 copies of a booklet 8½x5½"; $9.90 per page for 500 copies; $11.55 per page for 1,000 copies. This newspaper printing firm publishes a great many books of this type for young poets and for those who write about geology, nature and local history. A 52-page booklet (it must be divisible by 4) of a 500-copy run would cost $514.80, plus about $2 for each black and white print of an illustration. Color runs much higher and is not practical for a first venture.

The booklet should sell for at least one-half more than its cost, and double is better if the readership you have in mind is not a large one. If you distribute it yourself, you would offer sets of 10 or 12 copies, either on consignment (you get paid when they are sold) or bought outright by gift shops, stores and shops at historic sites. Arrangements for commission have to be made on the first visit, so have this clearly in mind. One shop I know takes 25¢ on a $1.25 book, but it usually averages out to thirty or forty percent of the selling price.

While you might not make a great deal of money on your first publishing venture, your name will become known to many readers and editors. Rose Labrie, a noted primitive artist in New England, told me that if it had not been for the amateur painting which she prepared for the cover of her *Nubble Light* booklet, with its resulting publicity, she could not have established a reputation which led her into the primitive art field.

If you do a good job with your first one, your next booklet will be easier to write and to sell.

I'd like to share with you the experience of several writers who have published their own books. First of all, doing this the way I am outlining is not "vanity publishing." It is a business venture in which you sell your own product, confident of the quality of your work.

Mrs. Nellie M. Carver of North Conway, New Hampshire, for many years gathered old photographs and stories of the early days of her village, while she taught school in South Conway. She found many examples of country life in numerous sources — old histories, documents and, most of all, talking with old folks. Several urged her to write a town history and in March 1971 *Goshen, South Conway, New Hampshire,* was published by a Portland, Maine, firm.

She paid the printer $3,450 for 1,000 copies, only 500 of which were bound. She sold the book for $7.50, making $3.50 on each one. She spent $250 for mailing bags, advertising folders, advertisements and postage, and distributed the books herself to book stores and gift shops. Many friends and descendants of Goshen people bought the book. She had news stories in local newspapers and was given an autograph party. Using a list she found in a big library index, she sent out many folders and learned that libraries buy books like hers, and so do historical society libraries and genealogical societies. She also got good results by advertising in regional publications.

Did she make any money? No. Would she recommend such a venture to other writers if they can afford it? *Yes.* "I had a very special reason for doing my book. The satisfaction in the pleasure I gave to people, and the fact that it is still selling at Goodspeed's (a Boston bookstore which specializes in history) and our local bookstore and gift shops make it worthwhile for me."

She continued, "Unlike other books that have a short life, local histories are good for many years and increase in value as time goes on. So, I hope to, at least, come out even on my venture sometime. I believe that 300 books are considered enough to start with. Local printers are perhaps better than the big houses to handle such books. They are a lot of fun to do, and I would not have missed the experience for anything."

Mrs. Labrie, who lives in Portsmouth, New Hampshire, has published two lighthouse histories, with the cooperation of the Coast Guard, who obtained many of the photographs for her. The first, *Nubble Light,* published in 1958, and now going into its fifth printing, has sold more than 10,000 copies at $1 each The next edition will be sold at a higher price. She had color plates made for the third edition, at considerable cost, which has now been absorbed in sales. She figures she made about thirty percent profit.

The second booklet, *Pemaquid Light,* would have been more successful except for distribution problems, since Mrs. Labrie lives too far from Pemaquid to do a good distribution program.

She places the booklets in New Hampshire and Maine department stores, supermarkets, gift shops, drug stores, a camera shop, hotels. The *Nubble Light* cover is also printed on a postcard, which is not only sent through the mail but *collected* by those who buy them as souvenirs, according to storekeepers. Having a second item to sell gives her a better percentage in travel expense. After trying a gift shop distributor for a year, Mrs. Labrie found she could do better on her own, since she still had to visit other types of stores.

More than 2,000 of the *Nubble* booklets have been sold by mail, the result of word-of-mouth recommendations and resales to the tourist trade, through her own mail campaign. She sent advertising leaflets to all the schools in seven states, obtaining the lists from the state departments of education, and received orders from nearly all of them, and from libraries and universities. In Maine schools the booklet is used as a social studies text in Grades 5 and 6, as a history reference in Grades 7 and 8, and as a library reference in all grades.

Elaine Peverly of Kittery, Maine, has published two soft-cover books on her own. *The Dummy,* the history of a small railroad which once ran in the Old Orchard section of Maine, was written in cooperation with a railroad buff, William H. McLin, formerly of Old Orchard, now of South Harpswell. Photographs are abundant and came from friends, associations of railroad buffs, family albums and collections. Mrs. Peverly and Mr. McLin were given an autograph party.

Bridge Over The Piscataqua came out of Mrs. Peverly's work as a newspaper reporter, during which time she covered all the action involved in building the bridge which spans the river between Maine and New Hampshire. The book was written chronologically and the photographs were her own. Both books have been well advertised and are selling well enough to return a profit. "The Bridge" is also on a postcard which Mrs. Peverly distributes along with her books to a wide variety of stores.

Both these young women have received great satisfaction from their publishing ventures and have earned considerable prestige in the seacoast area of Maine and New Hampshire from their writing. Both began their writing careers by selling feature articles.

Here is a different situation and approach: Mrs. Virginia R. Nordhaus, now of Westerly, Rhode Island, lived in New Mexico, where she had a financial interest in tram and ski companies at Sandia Peak, Albuquerque, and she had written advertising brochures for them. Then she decided to write and publish *The Sandia Mountains* (1966). She spent a year in research, checking everything with experts in the various fields (flowers, birds, animals, trees, climate, history and so on) and with university professors. Some photographs were bought from professionals, others were donated.

She ordered 35,000 booklets at a cost of $6,000 including photographs, services of layout man and printing. The sale price was 75¢ and the booklet was sold in bookstores, banks, real estate offices, gift shop and museum at Sandia Peak, and large companies in the area. She distributed the booklets until she came East, after which the Tram Company took over. The original investment was repaid by sales within a year, and since then her profit has been more than $7,000.

The booklet was widely quoted by travel writers and by major magazines, and she gave permission to quote information to all who asked. Not many were sold by mail, but the book was mentioned in many local news stories, *New Mexico Magazine,* and by word of mouth.

Mrs. Nordhaus says, "It was very rewarding in every respect. I don't think it is typical of most self-publishing ventures, as I had a built-in market with the Tram Company, and many personal contacts that I was able to pursue."

Very few ski or vacation spots have a book like *The Sandia Mountains.* Such books will sell year after year.

One woman I know bought an offset press and began to design, write, illustrate and print books for children, first as money makers for church fairs, and then, when they sold well, for a Portland bookstore. After that, she placed the books she created in gift shops and craft shops in several towns near her home. She made a profit and had a good time doing it. A poet I know also prints his own books of poems, not a vanity venture, for his poetry appears regularly in regional publications. He has been invited to read his poetry on local television several times.

You might write a series of articles for a newspaper and then put them into a book; the publisher and you would share the profit. One problem: You couldn't copyright the book if material was previously published in an uncopyrighted newspaper. You could *rewrite* the material and then secure a copyright. A Maine newspaper has sponsored several books on Maine waterfront history, using articles first published in the state-wide newspaper.

Your first step is to see if there would be a market for the booklet you are thinking about. For example, I have learned from visits to historic spots that no brochure is available to acquaint tourists with several of them. There's need for short biographies about famous writers whose homes are open to the public. The selling market for each of these would extend over at least two states, with a likely market for all schools and libraries.

The director of a museum in our town looked in vain for someone to plan a coloring book. Finally, the museum committee paid a local artist to draw the pictures and the director wrote the text herself. The profits go to the committee, but they could have been shared by a local writer and artist working as a team.

Pictures for coloring books must be simple in line, for if they are too "busy" in detail, they will not be attractive to children.

Since children comprise a large proportion of the visitors at museums and historic places, those which do not provide books for them are missing a good opportunity. Possibilities range from story-coloring books, picture books and the mini-history book for young readers to historical novels, biographies and short histories for teenagers. If you know a region which has not seen these possibilities, prepare to cash in on a brand new market.

PROCEDURE FOR PUBLISHING THE MINI-BOOK

1. Do the research and writing as outlined in this book.
2. Plan the photographs. Ask the printer for advice on the correct size for the process he is to use. If you can take expert pictures, do so, but don't sacrifice quality when an expert can do a better job. Be sure to keep a file of picture credits to put in the book.
3. Order a few booklets from the Government Printing Office; a list of booklets on historical subjects will be sent to you on request. Explore the gift shops and nearby historic places, buying several booklets. Talk with someone who has published such a booklet and listen to his suggestions. Your printer can give you names. Compare your material and writing with these and be sure you have done your work well.
4. Be sure your title is eye-catching and yet easy to understand. Sometimes a title will sell a book. An attractive cover will, too.
5. Consult several printers, asking for samples of their work, prices and procedures. Use the booklet you consider most attractively printed to guide you and to show the printers what you are expecting. Remember that the least expensive job may not be the best one for you.
6. While you are visiting the shops to see what booklets they carry, ask what people are inquiring for that they do not have. This will give you ideas for the future.
7. Make up a dummy of your book, arranging it just as you want it to look when it is printed. Select an eye-catching color and good stock for the covers. Be sure you have a title page, table of contents, list of illustrations with credits, an acknowledgment page, and perhaps a preface. Be sure the booklet is arranged in

a logical order. Mark the space for copyright claim on the inside front cover.

8. Write to the Library of Congress copyright office for information on this important subject. You must fill out a form and send a fee, together with the printed book, to secure your copyright. Be very sure your printer includes the copyright in the front of your book. Your material will be in the public domain if you forget this.

9. Determine with the printer the number of words he will print per page and add or eliminate material until it conforms with the size you have planned. Get a firm publishing date from him.

10. Long before your booklet is finished and goes to the printer, start planning your publicity campaign; very necessary if you are going to sell your book.

PLANNING PUBLICITY AND SELLING

When you go into business for yourself, you must assume the responsibility of promoting your own book. Here are some methods for doing this. You may think of more.

1. Make a list of places which might sell your booklet and visit each one when the book is published; take a box of books with you so you can leave some if they agree to sell them. You would include bookstores and gift shops and book sections of department stores in every town in the region covered by the subjects in your book. Adjoining towns will be interested in subjects in your town.

One friend sells more booklets in a gift shop in a summer hotel than in any other one place. Camera shops may have a book and magazine section; some drug stores will, too. List every store which sells magazines, and visit each, even if they don't presently sell books like yours.

Remember, however, that you will have to keep up the service at all the shops you place books in. You will have to decide if you wish to share your profits with a distributor, if you can find one.

While I was doing research for this chapter, Mrs. Dorothy Slavin of the Ogunquit Camera Shop told me that she feels she is helping writers who are known to her personally when she sells their books. That seems to be an important part of self-distribution.

Mrs. Slavin told me that she could use many more paperback books about local history and that she herself had written short material to meet the demand for specific subjects. She agreed that each booklet is easier to sell if it covers only one subject, is small size and does not cost too much. Her arrangement on commission varies with the individual writer and the cost of the book and she sells hundreds of booklets each summer, nearly all regional in scope.

2. Send copies of the booklet to the book editors of all regional magazines and nearby city newspapers. Often your book will be reviewed or at least mentioned. Send copies to your state historical society and the state library, and perhaps to these places in neighboring states.

3. Write newspaper articles announcing the book's publication date. Perhaps local reporters will give you even more publicity by asking for an interview. Send an article back to your home-town newspaper.

4. Call or write the program directors of radio and television stations covering your area. Tell them of your project and ask for an opportunity to talk about your book. If you are a woman, call the radio's and TV's women's affairs editor, who sometimes does interviews.

5. One of the periodical stores in a nearby city arranges a window display when a local author has a book published. Be sure those near you know about your book.

6. Another approach is to send an announcement by mail to prospective buyers. Have a folder mimeographed or printed and send it to friends, teachers, libraries, historical societies, and others who you think might be interested in your subject. Include an order form at the bottom of your notice, with your own address. Depending on the quantity, the cost of mailing the letter may be offset by the resulting orders and cost less than a shop's commission.

Look ahead several years to important anniversary dates which might be celebrated or noted in your region. Start at once and you may have more than a mini-book ready for that significant period of publication.

CHAPTER TWENTY

MORE JOB OPPORTUNITIES FOR WRITERS OF HISTORY

Some of those reading this book will care only about writing for the sake of writing. Others will be interested in history in itself, and those with good command of language and a share of imagination, initiative and factual knowledge of history will also find a challenge in work which can be an offshoot from writing.

Among positions which still involve writing are public relations and representative of a historical society, museum, restoration village or historic building committee; editor of a magazine or newsletter published by any of these; ghost writing for a celebrity or non-celebrity who wants to write an autobiography, which may be on a salary basis while you are following the personality around and taping reminiscences or paid for as a complete job (you are paid a sum and the subject gets the glory and the money from publication); as a staff member of a museum or other historical complex, writing brochures required to fill special needs; as staff member of a magazine devoted to history, writing a column or fill-in articles; with expertise in an important period of history, a chance to be a consultant to another writer or to a film studio; research assistant to magazine editor or publisher; freelance research consultant; photographing and captioning historic collections; editing historical material as a freelancer.

Other positions associated with an interest in history include teaching special groups in research techniques and the writing of history; planning and conducting workshops for children at museums; conducting tours at historic sites; acting as docents in museums; cataloguing museum collections; creating a new art as Mrs. I. Roberta Bell of Chicago has. She makes educational dolls representing aspects of Black History, including authentic facial and costume portrayals of the personalities and she lectures with the dolls as visual aids.

State and national governments offer opportunity to combine writing skills and a knowledge of history in a variety of jobs. Each state has a department of tourism or information, which goes under varying names. Each year new booklets are written to extol the history and beauties of the state and its regions. State historic sites sometimes offer opportunities as curators or guides. These and the opportunities for employment under the federal government require a college degree and often a master's degree in history or related field.

There are hundreds of jobs for writers and editors in the departments of the United States Government, most of them under Civil Service, with a written examination required. Allowing for periodical salary increases for cost of living, the pay goes from GS-9 through GS-12 with salaries ranging from about $13,000 to $23,000. Information about current job opportunities and tests may be obtained from the Interagency Board of U. S. Civil Service Examiners, 1900 E Street, N.W., Washington, D.C. 204155.

Positions include those of writer, editor, radio and television script writer, motion picture script writer, technical writer, copy editor and others. The work is done for press, radio, television, magazines and other public information media; and also writers create pamphlets, including those offered for sale by the Government Printing Office.

Agency publications which might interest those considering a writing job for Uncle Sam are *A Time for Decision* — Choose a Career with a Future — Publications and Printing Management (write to Director, Navy Publications and Printing Service Bldg., 157-3, Washington Navy Yard, Washington, D. C. 20390); and *Careers in the National Park Service* (write to NPS, Department of Interior, Washington, D. C. 20240). Educational requirements are a major in the sciences, engineering, history, archaeology or architecture. Among the positions covered by the Federal Service Entrance Examination are geographer, historian, museum curator, writer and editor, librarian, and public information officer.

Heath Pemberton, Branch of Special Projects, Division of Publications, National Park Service, sent me the following:

We do occasionally commission manuscripts, almost always on

the basis of a demonstrated mastery of the subject and the ability to write interestingly. Our fees will probably disappoint the Author's League. Nevertheless, prospective writers whose interests parallel ours are welcome to discuss projects and proposals with us.

As for fledgling writers, they should seek jobs through the Civil Service Commission, but it wouldn't hurt to visit offices whose work interests them and see what specific opportunities are available. My guess is that the National Archives, the Smithsonian, the Library of Congress, the National Gallery, and the various branches of the Department of Defense just about exhaust the historical writing possibilities in government. Most often, writing in government is a byproduct of an activity, and so a prospective writer might better begin by becoming versed in a subject.

Are there job opportunities in the National Park Service for history-oriented people? Yes! For those interested in seeing and working with history on the job, activities of the Historic American Engineering Record will be exciting. Other government programs reached through the National Park Service, Washington, D.C. 20240, are the Historic American Building Survey, the National Register of Historic Places, and the National Historic Landmarks Program (Historic Sites Survey).

Donald E. Sackheim, Historian of the HAER above, sent me the following information:

We do indeed hire people every year, primarily for the summer survey teams which we send out to document historic engineering and industrial works in various parts of the country. A typical team consists of a college professor acting as supervisor, a graduate student in history, and several student architects and engineers. They work for twelve or thirteen weeks to produce original measured drawings, professional photographs, and written historical and technical reports for selected sites. . . .

Our main objective is to produce archival records of important engineering and industrial structures in order to guarantee that in case these structures are destroyed, at least some evidence of their existence will remain. We call this historic preservation through documentation.

The function of historians in all this is to complete historical monographs on the sites which are recorded.... We have only occasionally used freelance writers in the past, but there is no reason we could not use more in the future if the need arose.

Among the 1974 activities included in this program are the site of Eli Whitney's gun factory in New Haven, Connecticut, where several archaeologists worked on excavating the factory itself, under two feet of fill; historic structures in the Boston Naval Shipyard; shops and terminal facilities of the Central of Georgia Railroad in Savannah, perhaps the best preserved antebellum railroad complex in the South.

Here is further evidence that history is concerned not only with the written word but with everything associated with people and their activities at work and at home.

There are still other positions in the field of history, including one type which is increasing in number: that of work in a museum or historical society.

Here are some of the positions and the qualifications required: assistant director of interpretation and education, to assist director in administration, general programming, school workshops and so forth, and the qualifications are graduate work in education, history or museum-related field; visitor services supervisor for a historic preservation, and qualifications are experience at historic sites, BA plus three years of related experience or MA and two years; author-editor for an industrial society to compile a handbook for industrial archaeology, fulltime for a year; museum director with knowledge of the French language and provincial history; museum curator of a Victorian mansion operated by a state park district, with BA with experience or MA with museum training.

New England and the Pacific West pay the highest salaries for administrators in historical agencies: for 1975 monthly salaries for agency heads range from $1,578 to $1,177; for assistant head, $1,355 to $850; division head, $1,139 to $809; advanced professional, $1,133 to $820; and beginning professional, $916 to $603.

You can see that your study of local history can lead to many other avenues of activity in the field of writing history. The opportunities are there to use your knowledge and experience. Are you preparing yourself for them?

MARKETING YOUR HISTORY MSS

Poring over the thousands of entries sent by editors to *Writer's Market* can set your thoughts astir like the wide road calls to an adventurer. Those tantalizing little notes seem like invitations through a magical door into a place where you can easily become a published author.

The invitations are there all right. Many writers have accepted them and gone on to fame and fortune.

But it's not that easy. There are techniques to learn, experience to gain. In this book techniques have been touched on, methods for gaining experience discussed. There are numerous other books devoted exclusively to in-depth treatment of techniques in each category of the writing craft. But all that is not enough.

To go with confidence and knowledge traveling on that wide road, you study a map and read a traveler's guide. To get published, you must first of all know your market.

Not only do you save a great deal of time and postage, but it is professional to see that your manuscript goes to the *right Market,* the term given by writers to newspapers, magazines and book publishers.

While you are studying the requirements given by editors in the writer's magazines, make careful note of the following: Is a query demanded? What are the photographic requirements? Word length? What type of historical material will be accepted? Watch for hints of editorial preferences, especially in magazine articles written by editors or given in magazine interviews.

Send for editorial guidelines for writers and for copies of magazines you can't buy on newsstands. Many are offered free in the market listings.

Watch for trends in subjects. In 1965 you read little about drug abuse or the generation gap or conservation. There's a new trend in the writing of history, too, with more emphasis on social concerns. The observation of the years centered around the American Revolution Bicentennial is bringing out material stressing both patriotism and rebellion; and the Tory viewpoint is getting a hearing.

HOW TO EVALUATE PUBLICATIONS

Sit down with your group of periodicals and check these points:

1. What does the cover tell you about editorial preference?

2. Study the headings in the Table of Contents. Note the proportion of fiction to nonfiction. Note the choice of titles.

3. What is the length of each article and short story?

4. What is the subject matter of each? How has the editor selected subjects to emphasize his particular type of periodical? Is the material diversified or focused on one field of interest? Is *one* article a little different from that focus? How are the stories handled by their writers? Studying beginnings, endings, transitions, flashbacks and so on will be helpful.

5. Advertising: Does it appeal to the low-income, middle-income or high-income family? To men or women only? Children? What is advertised? This reveals what the reader's interests are, what he will buy, what he wants in his home, what appeals to him. If there are no ads for liquor or tobacco, you'd better watch for these taboos in the editorial content.

6. Study the editorial policy. Is there an editorial or editorial comment? Does it help you to learn how the magazine is focused? Do the articles give readers food for thought, appeal to reason or to emotion? Do they inspire, urge action, give guidance, entertain? What is stressed in editorial content? What material is staff-written?

7. Are photographs used with articles those of the writer or by a featured photographer, or are they by a staff photographer? Are other types of illustrations used and what was the source? (Make notes for your illustration file.) Some editors require photographs and will not accept material without them. Others have access to illustrative material and prefer to provide it. Some editors send a photographer to work with a writer.

8. Does your manuscript compare favorably with what is published? (Be objective!) Is it suitable for this market? Are some of these periodicals good markets for other ideas you have?

9. Style may be harder to analyze, since the same publication uses the work of different writers; but studying other writers' ways of putting words and ideas together can be useful. Does the material lean toward the scholarly or the informal? What is the *tone* of the magazine's contents? Is there humor, or a sense of urgency or a tongue-in-cheek presentation? *(Saturday Review,* for example, has all of these in one issue.) Is the material always in a serious vein or does most of it seem lively and exciting? When you find that a periodical buys material which treats a serious theme with humor or offers an expose or tells a tale in a spicy way, you know what type of manuscript that editor prefers.

Note the variations in content and style of magazines which publish similar material. You might see the same subject in several history magazines, but the presentation would usually be different.

For example, let's look at three magazines which have published articles about George Washington at Mount Vernon. *Smithsonian,* using the more scholarly treatment (but writing in popular style), has an article on the first president's variety of swords, with color photos, and describing those to be seen at Mount Vernon, among other places. *American History Illustrated's* article is featured on the cover with an N. C. Wyeth painting of "Washington the Farmer," and goes into details of his life at home after his retirement from the presidency. There are numerous sepia and black and white illustrations. An article in *Early American Life* about Mount Vernon has a modern point of view, introducing the visitor to the historic estate, merely touching on the past and, through illustrations, showing what he will see there.

10. It is important to know *market deadlines.* Features for newspapers should go to the proper editor any time from a week to six weeks before the date of publication of your feature. Editors of magazines and Sunday newspaper magazine sections may work a year ahead on special issues, and look for holiday material or an anniversary tie-in at least six months in advance. Ask editors what their deadlines are if this is not given in the market list or in the magazine. (Send a stamped, self-addressed envelope.)

Editors for juvenile magazines work far ahead of other publications, expecially with holiday material. Be alert to this.

With some special holiday material in mind, you might find a weekly, or even a monthly magazine, open to a filler even after the deadline. I sold a quiz on Father's Day to a national weekly just about two weeks before publication date, because it filled a special niche.

You may think of other ways to compare the periodicals you are studying. While you read, keep in mind the manuscripts you have ready to send out, those you are writing now, and ideas for the future.

CHECKING ON MANUSCRIPTS

How long should you wait to hear from an editor? A magazine editor will take from six weeks to three months. A newspaper editor may not answer at all; it might be better to telephone him. A book publisher may take from three to four months to send a reply.

You might enclose a postcard, self-addressed, with your book manuscript, to be returned by the editor upon its receipt. A book should be insured with return receipt requested.

After the maximum time limit, it is all right to send a brief note in inquiry, asking if your manuscript or your query has been received and is still under consideration. Enclose a self-addressed, stamped envelope for a reply. On magazines, if no answer is forthcoming within two weeks, you may send a registered letter to the editor saying that you are withdrawing your article or short story. Then if you still get no reply within a month, you are free to retype the manuscript and submit it elsewhere.

I know of one eager writer whose article had been held for several months by a very good, well-paying magazine. It was being considered for publication when the writer telephoned the editor for the second or third time and was so rude the editor not only returned the manuscript, but told the writer never to submit anything there again.

Get busy on other work and wait!

THE BOOK MARKET

Writing and publishing hundreds of articles, even in top magazines, will not have the impact on a writer's life which writing a successful book can have, even though a writer may become extremely well-known and popular in his own region.

A book is usually the foundation of a writer's career, and many writers achieve success, even in a heart-breaking, unpredictable and precarious business like book publishing.

Unless a book is a hit, it has a life expectancy of about three months on book stands. As soon as it is issued in paperback, if it is, the hardcover copies go back to the publisher and are often remaindered, or sold to job distributors for sale in chain stores. Very few novels last more than six months unless they are best sellers and go into paperback editions. Of course, in the public library readers will continue to borrow these books for months or even years, but we are talking here about SALES.

Publishers look for book manuscripts which will be good enough for subsidiary rights: paperback, magazine series publication, movie or drama rights, television rights or chosen by a book club. There are more than 500 of the latter.

Because publishers' advertisements seldom reach newspapers beyond the Eastern border, the book reviews in the *New York Times Book Review,* a few important weekly or monthly magazines with review columns, and television interviews have the most influence on book buyers. The amount of space given to book reviews in newspapers depends on the amount of space for advertising bought by book publishers. More than 40,000 books are published each year, but only about 2,500 are reviewed.

About ninety percent of all children's books are bought by schools, libraries and other institutions. This includes paperback sales through children's book clubs.

SUBSIDIARY RIGHTS

Here are reasons why you must make sure your book contract covers all subsidiary rights.

When a publisher realizes that his popular authors will make many subsidiary sales for his firm, he cannot be blamed too much for his lack of enthusiasm for a new author, whom he must build up. He has to think of the ways in which he can profit from sales to book clubs and paperback publishers and other subsidiaries. Sometimes a publisher starts his own paperback firm. Readers buy books at a bookstore, but many more buy books from a book club and thousands more buy paperbacks. These are different markets and seldom compete.

A book sold to a book club will net publisher and writer an excellent additional sum, but not many writers will receive as much as the $250,000 which the Book-of-the Month Club paid William Manchester for *Death of a President.* Some publishers must bid with agents, in an auction, for the work of writers who have potential best selling books.

A writer whose book is selected as an alternate and his publisher would share equally between $5,000 and $25,000 at current rates. (The Authors Guild maintains that there should be a two-third, one-third split between author and publisher as a fairer deal.) Smaller book clubs give guarantees of $1,500 to $5,000 and up. The amount of the guarantee against royalties is based on projected sales.

Selections for first place and alternate are made by judges or by editors from about 2,500 books submitted by publishers. Some are monthly, some quarterly. It is interesting to note that a great many club nominations continue to sell for many years on the publishers' backlist.

There are many types of book clubs founded to meet particular interests: mystery, nature, history and nostalgia among them. There are thirty or more clubs for children's book sales, basing them on age and reading level, rather than on subject matter. The variety of these clubs opens up new markets and opportunities for little-known writers whose books fit into the category. Many small specialized clubs are eager to find new books in their area of interest.

Scholastic, which has the largest book club for children, will develop its own original books when unable to find the type of book needed for its lists. Although fiction is still ahead with younger children, older ones are leaning toward biography, science, history and historical fiction, and editors cannot always find enough to meet the demand.

Club sales make the difference between profit and loss for some publishers, and subsidiary rights are important to all publishers. Selection of his book for a book club can help to build up a writer's literary reputation and the prestige increases trade sales and influences a higher price for the paperback edition, if there is one.

At one publishing house, where 400 books were published, the subsidiaries included 75 sold to book clubs; 150 reprinted as paperbacks; 24 first serial rights for magazines; 12 movie options, 3 movie sales; 6 dramatic rights; and 75-100 foreign rights. These are important to the writer, of course, as well.

Once in a while, a book which fits into a special category like those mentioned will make more than one book club list, for publishers often send a book to several clubs.

The sale of a book is influenced not only by its selection by a book club, but by book reviews, newspaper, television and radio interviews with the writer, talk show appearances of the author, especially if he or she has charm and the ability to communicate ideas. The sale of a book is sure to go up sharply if it is made into a movie or a television special.

MAILING MANUSCRIPTS

When mailing book manuscripts, after an editor has asked to see the complete book, put the pages loose in a box without stapling or binding the pages in any way. The box which contained your bond paper on which you typed the manuscript will be right. Reinforce the corners of the box with tape to prevent their breaking. Wrap the whole in brown mailing paper.

An explanatory letter in an envelope addressed to the editor can be taped to the package or placed inside with a notation that a first class letter is enclosed. Insure the manuscript and ask for a return receipt. Send the box special fourth class mail or parcel post. For an additional sum, you can buy "special handling" which will get the package to the editor more quickly. Be sure your return address is on the package and it's marked "Return Postage Guaranteed"!

Send your work out with the knowledge that not all good work can make the grade against super competition. You would not have reached this stage without encouragement from an editor and that means the manuscript has something in its favor. If it does come back, have confidence in it and send it out again, each time with a green light from an editor as a result of your query.

Knowing your market well does not always mean successful publication. It does mean, however, that you are working in a professional manner, and knowing your market well puts you one step nearer to the day when you will see your name in print.

I wish you good fortune!

CHAPTER TWENTY-TWO

THAT PROFESSIONAL TOUCH

There is a one-word answer to the question "How can I learn to write well?" It is WORK. Poet John Ciardi once said that those who have moments of magic are those who have worked hardest in between.

This story is included in an article Jack Valenti of the film industry wrote for the *Washington Post*. He has this to say about the trained professional:

One evening last spring, after a question-and-answer period with college students interested in motion-picture work, a 21-year-old film major told me of his intense desire to direct a feature movie. He then angrily denounced the Hollywood "establishment" for shutting him out.

What, I asked, was his experience in film making? He had shot a ten-minute 8-mm documentary about his college basketball team. Did he have a script prepared and ready to shoot for someone in Hollywood? No, but he had seen a lot of movies, and had some ideas about what he wanted to film. He didn't believe in scripts; he believed in improvising as he moved along. Nobody, he said sourly, would give him a chance to produce the movie he knew he was capable of creating. . . .

A widely prevalent notion today seems to demand instant achievement of goals, without any of the wearying, frustrating preparation that is indispensable to any task. As the exemplar of a way of life, the professional — that man or woman who invests every new task or duty, no matter how small, with discipline of mind and spirit — is a vanishing American, particularly among those who too often believe that dreams come true because they ought to and not because they are *caused* to materialize.

All writers whose names and works you know began the same

way: Writers become writers by writing, trying to improve each day the work of the day before.

The chief danger to the tender bloom of creativity is the lack of discipline which even the most professional writer is sometimes subject to. It is necessary for continuous progress that you write regularly, setting a realistic goal of 200 or 500 or 1,000 words every day, or 3,000 words a week.

Try every kind of writing while you are a beginner. Venture into new fields if your writing has settled into a rut. Put your manuscripts aside and in a month or two take them out and compare them with your latest work. You'll be surprised to see the progress which you cannot see day by day.

EDUCATION AND STUDY

Writers who get to the top are those who never end their search for knowledge and perfection of craft, whose minds range beyond their own special field of work.

Returning to school may bring a new dimension to one's life. I was a grandmother when I returned to college and earned a master of art degree in history. My intention was to take one course dealing with the period of the American Revolution because I needed more background for a book. I became so enthralled with the new ideas I was learning at the university that I took more courses, did well enough to receive a full scholarship to complete the degree.

While every college and university has courses and graduate degree programs in the field of history, most of the emphasis has been on training students to teach social studies. Now history departments are beginning to train their students for other careers than teaching. These will lead into the establishment of new courses in phases like work with historical societies, museums and other similar agencies.

Most of these programs are very new and not yet well-known. Those eager to take such courses will have to inquire at nearby schools to see what is offered. Many will be following in the footsteps of Texas Tech University at Lubbock, which cooperates with the

Texas Historical Commission to provide students with opportunities to explore phases of state and local history. The B.A. and M.A. degree programs offered by the university's department of park administration include eight courses which focus on historic interpretation. A master's degree program in museum science was initiated by Texas State in the fall of 1974 and is designed to train students for a wide variety of postions in museums and related organizations. Among the options are art, historic restoration, history, anthropology and natural science. A number of university departments are cooperating.

Boston University offers a graduate course for students interested in historical society and museum careers. Students design their own course of study, working closely with faculty members from historical societies in the program, which emphasizes the inter-relationship of the arts and social history.

Since 1971 students in the historiography classes at Armstrong State College, Savannah, Georgia, have been working as volunteers with the Historic Savannah Foundation and the Georgia Historical Society in an experimental research program. They are helping to provide historical data for more than 1,100 buildings and becoming familiar with research techniques ordinarily not experienced until graduate study. Several have continued research at the conclusion of a yearly couse through independent study.

Students who attend the course Introduction to Modern Archives Administration, sponsored by the American University, Washington, D. C., will receive a three semester credit from its department of history. It is held each spring in cooperation with the Library of Congress and the Maryland Hall of Records.

Restoration villages and other institutions are performing a splendid service by offering courses in history and museum interpretation, some in summer and others during the winter. Graduate and research fellowships are given by several historical societies, among them the Illinois State Historical Society, American Antiquarian Society, Civil War Roundtable, and the New Jersey Historical Commission.

College students are gaining experience at the headquarters of the National Trust for Historic Preservation, Washington, and it has been so successful a program that the National Trust is expanding it to provide on-the-job training at other museums and restorations. Students will work for ten weeks during the summer.

Old Sturbridge Village offers a number of training programs, among them museum training internships. The New York Historical Association, Cooperstown, New York, has a three-year program in Conservation of Historic and Artistic Works, and summer seminars which offer a variety of courses in the study of crafts and historic interpretation for amateurs and professionals.

Young people of high school and college age, as well as adults, are offered many opportunities to learn more about historical research in summer courses provided by museums, national park and institutional services. The Maine State Museum has a summer museum apprenticeship program open to teenagers entering their senior year of high school.

Living History programs administered by the Student Conservation Association bring girls and boys to national historic sites across the country. Among these are Hopewell Village, one of the oldest ironworks standing in the country, where, dressed in nineteenth century costumes, students cook over open fires, care for a large house, garden, spin and weave; Fredericksburg and Spotsylvania National Military Park where students give living history demonstrations, assist in the library and work as curators; at Challis National Forest, Idaho, they help renovate historic sites relating to 1870 gold-rush mining, greet visitors and backpack into back country sites to clear trails and clean campsites; at Pea Ridge National Military Park, Arkansas, volunteers do Civil War research and park maintenance projects.

Complete information on these summer opportunities and many others is available from the Student Conservation Association, Inc., Olympic View Drive, Route 1, Box 573A, Vashon, Washington 98070.

Volunteers in Parks and Volunteers in Forests also enable people of all ages to work without pay on a part-time basis in areas maintained by these two national services, where they give demonstrations of local or historical arts and crafts, take part in living history programs; a heartening movement toward raising future generations of Americans who will be aware of their heritage and eager to share their knowledge.

Going back to school may not be for you. You can learn a great deal by reading at least one hour a day. We writers of history need to read not only to know better how to write, as we all must, but to refresh the spirit.

A home correspondence course can be valuable for those who need to know more about writing techniques. However, there is no sense in spending money on this unless you intend to follow through.

Another type of adult education is the writers' conference. You will find much inspiration meeting and listening to topnotch writers.

Enrolling in a writing class is helpful for a beginning writer. The Y.W.C.A. may have such a course. Several classes in writing may be offered at a nearby university. Only those who are willing to accept criticism and direction with humility will profit from a writers' conference or a writing class. Don't expect miracles or an easy way to fame and fortune from such participation, but there are other benefits.

Sometimes a writer needs to talk shop and the answer may be a writers' club. Just to meet with other writers and share experiences will be helpful. While you grow professionally, however, your need for honest criticism will grow. The writers' club most helpful to members is that which fosters the professional attitude, when members desire to learn from their mistakes and to help each other.

THE BUSINESS END OF WRITING

Those who wish to acquire the professional touch will give attention to the business details demanded in a writing career. Here are some of the "musts."

1. Develop your own library. Put back into your profession some of the money you receive from your writing.

2. Keep good records. Beginning writers sometimes are amused at the thought of keeping records for income tax purposes. The fact is that as soon as you seriously begin to send out manuscripts, you can claim deductions from your income tax. You must keep accurate records of the cost of postage, supplies like paper, envelopes, carbon paper, typewriter ribbons, cost of photographs, file

folders, magazines you buy to study, tape cassettes, and any other expenditures directly related to your writing, either for work or for study.

Whenever you buy supplies, jot down the items and cost on cards, with the date, and put them in a special folder. Keep cancelled checks for magazine subscriptions and writing classes. You may claim depreciation of your typewriter and recorder.

You may also claim deductions for membership in professional groups, tuition at writers' conferences, professional books, all history books and others related to your work. Keep a record of mileage for all trips connected with research; keep a diary with total expenditures listed, dates and places and so on. This will help you to remember necessary facts and exact names of the towns and places visited and give you statistics from which to estimate the expenses for the articles you write about your travels.

Admissions to museums and historic sites should also be recorded, and whatever booklets and illustrative material you may buy there. If you order photostat copies of material you find in a library, that too should be noted. When you are working on a story which takes you to a museum or historic site, you should not have to pay admission. Ask to see the curator or director, establish your credentials and there will seldom be a charge.

Even when you show a loss, Uncle Sam will allow these expenses, plus one more: If you use one room *exclusively* for writing, you are allowed to deduct the maintenance cost from income tax. You estimate the total cost of housing for the year, divide this by the number of rooms in your home, and take this percentage as your deduction. (If you have five rooms and use one as your study — not a spare bedroom — and the upkeep for the year was $4,500 including mortgage, taxes, utilities and so on, you may take $900 as a deduction.)

For income tax purposes, you must fill out a self-employment form. I know of some senior citizens who are building social security on their writing checks.

3. Market records are absolutely necessary to a writer. Select your own method of gathering your personal file of market require-ments. With the annual market guide for reference, you may find that you need only go through the appropriate listing and mark

the margin "History" or "Biography" alongside the entry in *Writer's Market.* Check the monthly writers' magazines for changes in editors or addresses and requirements.

And, of course, make notations of any shifts in editorial emphasis you note in examining actual publications.

4. Your files are important and it is the rare professional who does not have at least one steel cabinet full of material in his particular field of interest. Here you file research material as you complete your manuscript, your carbons, ideas for future work, folders on individuals, events and places. I am such a newspaper and magazine clipper, I can't keep up with the filing, but the most important items are put in their proper places promptly.

My writing file has proved of great value through the years. This includes a folder on each kind of writing technique, plus tear sheets of sample articles, pages cut from paperbacks with descriptive passages marked. I have folders for directions on writing dialogue, background, character delineation and so on.

5. Remember my advice about keeping several kinds of notebooks to make it easier to do research. Robert Louis Stevenson kept a notebook in which he recorded unfamiliar words, choice paragraphs, ideas for plots, and notes from his reading.

6. You will get at your writing more quickly if you have a place to store your paper, carbon and other supplies. If you cannot have a room in which to write, at least keep your supplies in a shoe box, ready to go with you to the kitchen table or a corner of the bedroom. A roll of stamps and a small postal scale save much time. Never let yourself get out of two sizes of envelopes in which to mail out manuscripts, and you will be less apt to toss your writings in a drawer.

While my children were growing up, my refuge was a corner of the bedroom, with a table, typewriter and small bookcase for reference books. Now I have a small study, but I often write at the kitchen table and think of other authors who did the same.

If you like to write your first draft with a pen, buy a clip board and sit in an easy chair. I often use the legal size pads of yellow lined paper in this way.

The secret is to have all your writing tools close at hand, for you will find many bypaths when you have to go looking for them.

REJECTIONS

When you receive a rejection slip, don't take it personally. Everyone who sends out manuscripts gets a rejection now and then, sometimes even after an editor has expressed an interest in an idea. The professional has several manuscripts in the mail at once and is too busy writing to take affront when an editor rejects his work. It hurts, of course — but forget it.

Read May Sarton's *Journal of a Solitude* and Kenneth Roberts' *I Wanted to Write* to understand what real discipline and devotion to one's craft can mean.

THAT PROFESSIONAL TOUCH

1. Get to writing every day until it is a habit you would be lost without. Don't wait until you complete your research.

2. Master the basic principles of good writing. Only by constant practice can you learn your craft.

3. Cultivate self-discipline but don't neglect your family and friends altogether.

4. Do some reading every day for both knowledge and inspiration (and relaxation, too).

5. Stretch your powers of curiosity and look constantly for original ideas.

6. Master the basic principles of historical research and make accuracy your taskmaster, but remember it is the story that counts.

7. Work constantly to improve your writing. Revise and rewrite. Emulate not imitate. Strive for the winged word.

8. Prepare every manuscript with care. Remember the stamped, self-addressed envelope.

9. Keep up with current trends in publishing. Know your markets.

10. Don't try to reach the top by skipping the preliminary steps.

11. Finish what you start.

12. Deepen your sense of values every day. Take time out for meditation and prayer and self-searching.

It doesn't matter what methods you use to write. It has to be right for you. Suddenly, if you are really trying and not just playing at writing, the whole idea will come into focus and you will be on your way.

On the wall before me are the words "God is the source of all right activity," words which I believe with all my heart.

No writer can tell another many of the things he needs to know. I have written this book to tell you what I longed desperately to know when I was a beginning writer, and I did not learn most of it until many years later. Now I know that it is best when you learn the answers for yourself, with a boost now and then from those with more experience. We writers will continue to learn more about the craft of language and communication as long as we live.

The heights by great men reached and kept
Were not attained by sudden flight,
But they, while their companions slept,
Were toiling upward in the night.

Henry W. Longfellow
Ladder of St. Augustine

BIBLIOGRAPHY

Bibliographies are arranged by chapter to make it easier for the reader to find books by subject matter.

The books listed are suggested as a start for your own exploration of the subject. In the library you will find many books with the same subject call number and by browsing among them, you will find other volumes which may interest you.

If your library doesn't allow you to browse in the stacks where books are stored, look under the general subject headings in the card catalogue and jot down the titles that sound useful, and order them for desk study. Since most books dealing with history have a bibliography, examining these will guide you to other references.

Look under specific subjects that interest you in *Books in Print* and *Subject Guide to Books in Print* (reprinted annually by R.R. Bowker, New York) and the *Cumulative Book Index* (annual, H.W. Wilson Co., New York).

To find inexpensive copies of books you would like to own, look at *Paperbound Books in Print* (monthly announcements, with cumulative index, Bowker). You will find this in bookstores, in most public libraries and in all university bookshops. Do examine this before trying to find what you want in the paperback stacks, which are usually arranged by publisher. Some university shops arrange them by subject.

Each region of the United States, and each country, has its own flavor, its own bibliographical material, which is unfamiliar to the average historian in other regions, so your territory is a resource unique to you.

D.R.M.

CHAPTER ONE: A Pathway to Adventure and Understanding

Becker, Carl, *Detachment and the Writing of History,* Edited by Phil L. Snyder, Cornell University Press, 1958.

Ceram, C.W.. *The First American, A Story of North American Archaeology,* Harcourt Brace Jovanovich, Inc., 1971.

Commager, Henry Steele and Allan Nevins, editors, *The Heritage of America,* Little, Brown & Co., 1951.

Durant, Will and Ariel, *The Lessons of History,* Simon & Schuster, 1968. All of their books.

Garraty, John and Peter Gay, editors, *Columbia History of the World,* Harper & Row, 1972.

Hamilton, Edith, *Mythology,* Little, Brown & Co., 1942.

Morison, Samuel Eliot, *The European Discovery of America* (Series) Oxford University Press, 1971 and 1974, vol. 2. *The Oxford History of the American People,* Oxford University Press, 1965.

National Geographic Society, *America's Beginnings, The Vikings, We Americans, World of the American Indian.*

Nevins, Allan, *The Gateway to History,* Anchor Books, 1962.

Nevins, Allan, "The Old History and the New" in *The Art of History,* Library of Congress, 1967.

Prescott, Orville, *History as Literature,* Harper & Row, 1970.

Schuster, M. Lincoln, editor, *A Treasury of the World's Great Letters,* Simon & Schuster, 1940, (334 B.C.-A.D. 1675; 1747-1896).

Smith, Page, *The Historian and History,* Vintage Books, 1964.

Solway, Clifford, "Turning History Upside Down," *Saturday Review,* June 20, 1970.

Toynbee, Arnold, *Experiences,* Oxford University Press, 1969.

Webster's *Dictionaries,* (Geographical, etc.), G.&C. Merriam.

CHAPTER TWO: How to Find the Right Ideas

American Heritage Guides and Histories

Associated Publishers of American Records, *The Journal of American History,* New Haven, Conn., 1907.

Beginning Writer's Answer Book, Writer's Digest.

Books in Print and *Subject Guide to Books in Print* (annual), R.R. Bowker.

Brande, Dorothea, *Wake Up and Live,* several editions, Cornerstone Library.

S.G.F. Brandon et al, editors, *Milestones of History,* Norton, 1971. 100 decisive events in the history of mankind.

Cather, Willa, *On Writing,* Alfred Knopf, 1949.

Collingwood, R.I., *The Idea of History,* Oxford University Press, 1946.

Cumulative Book Index, H.W. Wilson Co., annual.

Irwin, L.B., *A Guide to Historical Reading,* McKinley, Revised, 1970.

Mathews, William, *American Diaries:* An Annotated Bibliography of American Diaries prior to 1861, Berkeley, 1945.

Schapper, Beatrice, editor, *Writing the Magazine Article, From Idea to Printed Page,* Writer's Digest, 1970.

State and Local Histories

United States Government (A sampling)
   American Military History, 1973. *The American Revolution 1775-1781,* (An atlas of 18th century maps and charts: Theatres of operations), 1972.

CHAPTER THREE: The Historian as Detective and Scholar
CHAPTER FOUR: Library Research

Altick, Richard C., *The Art of Literary Research,* Norton, 1964. *The Scholar Adventurers,* Macmillan, 1951.

American Historical Ass'n., *Writings on American History,* Indexed annually.

America: History and Life, abstracts of historical articles, C.L.I.O. Press, Santa Barbara, Calif. 1964, 1974.

American Periodical Series (1741-1850) Microfilm, 481 reels, Ann Arbor, Mich. 1942-1957. (Include all known and located periodicals published in U.S. prior to 1800)

Book Review Digest, H.W. Wilson, Revised annually.

Encyclopedia of Associations, Gale Research Co., 9th ed. 1975.

Freidel, Frank and Richard K. Showman, editors, *The Harvard Guide to American History,* Harvard University Press, 2 vol., revised 1974.

Gregory, Winifred, editor, *American Newspapers* (1821-1936), Union List of Files

Available in U.S. and Canada, 1937.

Guide to Historical Literature, various editors, American Historical Ass'n., Macmillan, 1961.

Hale, Richard W. Jr., *Guide to Photocopied Historical Materials in the United States and Canada,* Cornell Press, 1961. *Methods of Research for the Amateur Historian,* Technical Leaflet #21, American Ass'n. for State and Local History.

Hamer, Philip M., editor, *A Guide to Depositories of Archives and Manuscripts in the United States,* Yale University Press, 1961.

Library of Congress *Catalog,* lists all books available in government institutions. *National Union Catalog of Manuscript Collections.*

Poole's Index to Periodical Literature (1802-1907), Houghton, 1882-1908, 7 vol. Subject index only.

Reader's Guide to Periodical Literature (1900 to date), Wilson, 1905 to date.

Rundell, Walter, *In Pursuit of American History: Research and Training in the United States,* 1970, Norman, Okla. sponsored by National Historical Publications Commission.

Winchell, Constance, *Guide to Reference Books,* American Library Ass'n.

World Almanac and Book of Facts, World Telegram, 1868 to present.

CHAPTER FIVE: The Historian as Explorer: Museums and Places

Columbia Lippincott Gazeteer of the World, Columbia University.

Harvard Guide, "Historical Sources for Maps of the United States."

Konikow, Robert B., *Discover Historic America,* Rand McNally, 1973.

Mountains of the United States, Board of Survey and Maps.

United States Government (Government Printing Office)
Federal Government, A Directory of Information Resources in the United States. Geography and Map Division, Library of Congress, 845 S. Pickett St., Alexandria, Va., *Living Historical Farms Handbook, Living History in the National Park System, National Parks and Landmarks, National Parks of the United States, The National Register of Historic Places.*

CHAPTER SIX: Exploring Through Personal Involvement

Erdman, Loula Grace, *A Time to Write,* Dodd, Mead, 1969.

Jameson, J. Franklin, editor, *Original Narratives of Early American History,* 19 volumes 1906-1917, Rev. 1952.

Maritime Historical Association (Mystic Seaport, Conn.), *American Maritime Library* series, Wesleyan University Press, Middletown, Conn.

U.S. Government offers many opportunities to become personally involved in "live-in" and "living history" experiences. "Volunteers in Parks" program - National Park Service. Among the numerous booklets published to guide you to interesting experiences are: American Revolution Bicentennial Administration, *Above Ground Archaeology,* Government Printing Office, 60c. National Endowment for the Arts, *Museums USA,* Government Printing Office, $4.40. National Park Service, *Living History in the National Park System,*

CHAPTER SEVEN: The Interview: Oral History

Baum, Willa K., *Oral History for the Local Historical Society,* American Ass'n. for State and Local History, Revised, 1974.

Bowker, R.R., *Oral History Collections,* 1974.

Brady, John, *The Craft of Interviewing,* Writer's Digest, 1976.

Columbia University, Oral History Research Office, *Oral History Collection* 1973, ed. by Elizabeth B. Mason and Louis M. Starr.

Dorson, Richard M., editor, *Folklore and Folklife,* University of Chicago Press, 1972, (Includes variety of techniques on oral history, including how to record traditional music, tips for beginners, etc.).

Shumway, Gary L., *Oral History in the United States,* a Directory, The Oral History Association, 1971.

Starr, Louis M., *Oral History: Problems and Prospects,* Reprinted from *Advances in Librarianship,* Vol. 2, Seminar Press Inc., 1971. Louis M. Starr, editor, with Elizabeth B. Mason, *Oral History Collection* Columbia University, 1973.

Terkel, Studs (Louis), *Hard Times: An Oral History of the Great Depression,* Pantheon 1970.

Tyrrell, William G., *Tape-Recording Local History,* Technical Leaflet #35, American Ass'n. for State and Local History, 1966.

Wasserman, Manfred, *Bibliography of Oral History,* Oral History Association, 1971.

CHAPTER EIGHT: Exploring Through Audiovisuals

Academy of Motion Picture Arts and Sciences, Beverly Hills, Calif. Library of more than 9,000 books, pamphlets and periodicals about the movie industry.

Brewer's *Dictionary of Phrase and Fable,* revised by Ivor H. Evans, Harper & Row, 1974.

Sears, Minnie E. and Phyllis Crawford, compilers *Song Index.* An index of more than 12,000 songs, reprint of 1934 edition. Shoe String Press.

Wasserman, Paul, editor, *A Biennial Directory and Index of Publications and Audiovisuals Available from United States and Canadian Institutions,* Gale Research Co., Detroit, 1973.

CHAPTER NINE: Writing Features and Short Articles
CHAPTER TEN: Those Opening Paragraphs
CHAPTER ELEVEN: Types of Articles and Markets for Them

Bain, Robert and Dennis G. Donovan, *Writer and the World of Words,* Prentice Hall, 1975.

Boggess, Louise, *Writing Articles That Sell.* B&B Press.

Burack, A.S., editor, *Writing and Selling Fillers and Short Humor,* The Writer.

Editor & Publisher Syndicate Directory, Editor & Publisher.

Giles, Carl H., *Writing Right— to Sell,* Barnes, 1970.

Greer, Rebecca E., "How to Query An Editor," *Writer's Digest,* October, 1973.

Gunther, Max, *Writing the Modern Magazine Article,* The Writer, 1968.

Holmes, Marjorie, *Writing the Creative Article*, The Writer, 1969.
Jacobs, Hayes B., *Writing and Selling Non-Fiction*, Writer's Digest, 1968.
Levin, Marj Jackson, "The Making of a Salable Article" (TAPE), Writer's Digest.
Newcomb, Duane, *A Complete Guide To Marketing Magazine Articles*, Writer's Digest, 1976.
Neal, Berniece Roer, "Writing the Basic Article" (TAPE), Writer's Digest.
Neal, Harry Edward, *Nonfiction*, Funk & Wagnall, Paperback, 1967.
New York Times Index, New York Times, current information.
Newspapers and Periodicals, Directory of, N.W. Ayer & Sons, 1880 to date.
Nichols, William, *Writing From Experience*, Harcourt Brace Jovanovich 1975.
Writer's Digest, *A Treasury Of Tips For Writers.*

CHAPTER TWELVE: Historical Poetry and Short Fiction

Anderson, Margaret J., *The Christian Writer's Handbook* Harper & Row.
Boggess, Louise, *Fiction Techniques That Sell*, B&B Press.
Burnett, Hallie and Whit, *Fiction Writer's Handbook* Harper & Row, 1975.
Cassill, R.V., *Writing Fiction*, Prentice-Hall, 1975.
Curry, Peggy Simson, *Creating Fiction From Experience*, The Writer.
Elwood, Maren, *Characters Make Your Story*, The Writer.
Emrich, Duncan, *American Folk Poetry*, Little, Brown, 1974.
Engle, Paul, "Writing the Poem," Workshop discussion on TAPE Writer's Digest.
Fugate, Francis L., *Viewpoint: Key to Fiction Writing*, The Writer.
Hillyer, Robert, *First Principles of Verse*, The Writer.
Holmes, John, *Writing Poetry*, The Writer.
Jensen, Eileen, "Writing Popular Fiction," (TAPE), Writer's Digest.
Jerome, Judson, *The Poet and The Poem*, Writer's Digest, 1974.
Koch, Kenneth, "Teaching and Writing of Poetry" (TAPE), Writer's Digest.
Koontz, Dean R., *Writing Popular Fiction*, Writer's Digest, 1972.
McWhirter, Millie, "Characters in Your Short Story" Workshop discussion on TAPE, Writer's Digest.
Neal, Harry Edward, "Writing the Basic Short Story" (TAPE) Writer's Digest.
Rockwell, F.A., *Modern Fiction Techniques*, The Writer.
Untermeyer, Louis, editor, *Story Poems*, Washington Square Press 1969 (Paperback).
Wood, Clement, editor, *Complete Rhyming Dictionary*, Doubleday.
Writer's Digest Handbook of Short Story Writing, 1971.

CHAPTER THIRTEEN: Illustrating Your Work

Artist's Market, Writer's Digest, published annually.
Cirker, Hayward and Blanche, editors, *Dictionary of American Portraits*, Dover Publications, 1967.
Collins, Alan C., editor, *The Story of America in Pictures*, Doubleday.
Davidson, Abraham A., *The Story of American Painting*, Abrams, 1975.
Dreppard, C.V., *Early American Prints*, from Colonial Times to the Civil War, Published in 1930.

Evans, Hilary and Mary, *Sources of Illustration 1500-1900,* Hastings House.

Lipman, Jean and Alice Winchester, *Flowering of American Folk Art 1776-1876,* Viking, 1974.

Mayor, A. Hyatt, *Prints and People* (Social History of Printed Pictures), Metropolitan Museum of Art, 1974.

Museum of Cartoon Art, Greenwich, Conn. More than 20,000 original cartoons and comic strips, etc.

Nevins, Allan and Frank Weitenkampf, editors, *A Century of Political Cartoons 1800-1900,* Scribner's, 1944; Scholarly Press reprint available.

Peters, H.T.. *Currier & Ives, Printmakers to the American People,* 2 vol. 1925-1931.

Putnam Pictorial Sources, G.P. Putnam's Sons, numerous subjects

Time/Life Editorial Staff, *American Painting 1900-1970* and other books about art and illustration.

U.S. Government, Numerous books and pamphlets. Ask for lists in specific subjects from Supt. of Documents. Inventory of American Paintings, Smithsonian, will be ready for researchers in late 1976 (National Collection of Fine Arts, Washington, D.C. 20560). The Smithsonian has thirteen museums and galleries of art. The Archives of American Art (with branches in several cities) has more than 70,000 photographs and other information on artists and related subjects. Ask for brochures from The Smithsonian Institution, Washington, D.C. 20560.

CHAPTER FOURTEEN: The Writer as Photographer

Berner, Jeff, *Photographic Experience,* Doubleday, 1975.

Gilbert, Karen Diane, *Picture Indexing for Local History Materials,* Library Research Ass'n., Monroe, N.Y. 1973.

Jonas, Paul, *Photographic Composition Simplified,* American Photographic Book Publishing Co. (Amphoto).

Logan, Richard H. III, *Elements of Photo Reporting,* Amphoto, 1971.

McDarrah, Fred, editor, *Photography Market Place,* R.R. Bowker, 1975.

Milton, John, *The Writer-Photographer,* Chilton.

Smith, Arthur L., *Producing the Slide Show,* American Assn. for State and Local History (AASLH), #42, 1967.

Sussman, Aaron, *The Amateur Photographer's Handbook,* Crowell, 1973.

Vanderbilt, Paul, *Filing Your Photographs,* Leaflet #36, AASLH.

Weinstein, Robert A.. *Collecting, Care and Use of Historical Photographs,* AASLH.

Where and How to Sell Your Photographs, Amphoto Books, 1975.

CHAPTER FIFTEEN: Writing the Biography

Adams, John, Letters of. Several editions. Considered one of the best letter writers in American history.

Associated Press, *The Danger of Libel,* (Paperback).

Bowen, Catherine D.. *Adventures of a Biographer,* Little, Brown, 1959. *Biography, The Craft and the Calling,* Little, Brown, 1969. "Biography, History and the

Writing of Books" in *The Art of History,* Library of Congress, 1967.

Bowker, R.R., *Subject Guide to Books in Print* (in your library).

Chamber's *Biographical Dictionary.*

Cripe, Helen, *Index to the Manuscripts of Prominent Americans* 1763-1815. Project housed at the American Antiquarian Society, Worcester, Mass.

Garraty, John A., *The Nature of Biography,* Knopf, 1957.

Garraty, John A. and Jerome L. Sternstein, editors, *Encyclopedia of American Biography,* Harper & Row, 1974.

James, Edward T. et al, editors, *Notable American Women* (1607-1950), Harvard University Press, 1972.

Kendall, Paul Murray, *The Art of Biography,* Norton, 1965.

New York Times Index.

New York Times Obituaries.

Rowbotham, Sheila, *Hidden From History,* Pantheon, 1973.

Scribner's *Dictionary of American Biography.*

U.S. Government, Numerous titles on biographical subjects.

Webster's American Biographies, Biographical Dictionary, Dictionary of Proper Names.

Who Was Who in America.

Who's Who in America.

Who's Who of American Women.

See also *Who's Who* on special subjects (art, science, etc.)

Wilson, H.W. Co., *Biography Index* (1947 to date, published quarterly). *Current Biography* (1940 to date).

Zolotow, Maurice, *Writing Biography,* (TAPE), Writer's Digest.

CHAPTER SIXTEEN: Four Types of History in Fiction

Braine, John, *Writing a Novel,* Coward, 1974.

Burack, A.S. editor, *Techniques of Novel Writing,* Writer, 1973. *Television Plays for Writers,* Writer.

Dickinson, A.T. Jr., *American Historical Fiction* (listed chronologically) Scarecrow Press, 1963.

Fugate, Francis L., *Viewpoint: Key to Fiction Writing,* Writer.

Highsmith, Patricia, *Plotting and Writing Suspense Fiction,* The Writer, 1972.

Lawson, John Howard, *Theory and Technique of Playwriting,* Hill and Wang.

Logasa, Hannah, *Historical Fiction,* (arranged geographically), McKinley, 1964.

Meredith, Richard C. and John D. Fitzgerald, *Structuring Your Novel,* Barnes and Noble.

Michener, James - An Interview on TAPE, Researching and Writing a "Best Seller," Writer's Digest.

Perry, Richard, *One Way to Write Your Novel,* Writer's Digest.

CHAPTER SEVENTEEN: Writing the Nonfiction Book Involving History

Adams, Ramon F., *Six Guns and Saddle Leather,* University of Oklahoma Press, 2,491 Western characters.

Cooper, John Charles - "Writing the Nonfiction Book," (TAPE) Writer's Digest.
Groner, Alex et al, *History of American Business and Industry,* American Heritage
Publishing Co., 1972.
Gunther, Max, *Writing and Selling a Nonfiction Book,* Writer, 1973.
McCormick, Ken - "Book Publisher and the Writer" (TAPE), Writer's Digest.
Meredith, Scott, *Writing to Sell,* Harper & Row, 1974.
Morris, Dan and Inez, *Who Was Who in American Politics,* Hawthorn, 1974.
Wilson, H.H. Co., *Business Periodicals Index,* monthly except August; *Humanities
Index;* Index to *Book Review Digest* from 1949; *Play Index* from 1949. Includes
directory of publishers.

CHAPTER EIGHTEEN: Writing History for Young People

Adams, Bess Porter, *About Children's Books,* Holt, Rinehart & Winston 1972
Bowker, R.R., *Literary Market Place,* Annual.
Brownrigg, Ronald, *Who's Who in the New Testament,* Holt, 1971.
Carson, Rachel, *The Sense of Wonder,* Harper & Row, 1965.
Children's Book Council, *Calendar,* published twice a year. Historical events,
book listings, author interviews, publishing notes, etc. Available for one-time
handling charge of $5, no subscription fee, from Children's Book Council,
Inc., 67 Irving Place, New York, N.Y. 10003.
Christian Writers Institute, *Christian Writer's Handbook,* Harper & Row.
Colby, Jean P., *Writing, Illustrating and Editing Children's Books,* Hastings.
Comay, Joan, *Who's Who in the Old Testament,* Holt, 1971.
Commire, Anne, Editor, *Something About the Author:* Facts and Pictures About
Contemporary Authors and Illustrators of Books for Young People, Volumes
1-3 1972, Gale Research Co., Detroit.
Elwood, Maren, *Writing the Short Short,* The Writer.
Fisher, Margery, *Matter of Fact: Aspects of Non-Fiction for Children,* Crowell,
1972.
Fitz-Randolph, Jane, *Writing for the Juvenile and Teenage Market,* Funk & Wag-
nalls.
Horn Book Magazine, The Horn Book, Inc., Boston, Mass., published six times a
year, devoted to commentary and information about books for children, with
book reviews.
Whitney, Phyllis, *Writing Juvenile Fiction,* The Writer, 1966.
Wyndham, Lee, *Writing for Children and Teen-Agers,* Writer's Digest, 1972.
Yolen, Jane, *Writing Books for Children,* The Writer, 1973.

CHAPTER NINETEEN: Writing and Publishing Local and Regional History

American Ancestry: Giving the Name and Descent in the Male Line of Americans
Whose Ancestors Settled in the United States Prior to the Declaration of Inde-
pendence, 1776. 12 volumes 1887-1899, Joel Munsell's Sons, reprinted 1968.
American Antiquarian Society. One of the nation's best sources of genealogy records.
Worcester, Mass. 01609.

American Association for State and Local History, *Directory of Historical Societies and Agencies in the United States and Canada,* biennial, 1400 Eighth Ave., South, Nashville, Tenn. 37203.

Ash, Lee and Denis Lorenz, *Subject Collections,* R.R. Bowker, 1967.

Brigham, Clarence S., *History and Bibliography of American Newspapers 1690-1820,* 2 vol., American Antiquarian Society, 1947.

City Directories, Telephone Books and Guide Books.

Doane, Gilbert Harry, *Searching for Your Ancestors,* University of Minnesota Press, Revised, 1960.

Everton, George B. Sr., *The How Book for Genealogists,* Everton, 1965.

Finberg, H.P. and V.H. Skipp, *Local History: Ojective and Pursuit,* David & Charles, North Pomfret, Vt. 1973.

Goodspeed's *Catalogue of Family and Local History,* Goodspeed's Book Shop, Boston, Mass. 02108. Family and Local Histories.

Greenwood, Val D., *The Researcher's Guide to American Genealogy,* Genealogy Publishing Co., 521-523 St. Paul Place, Baltimore, Md. 21202.

Gregory, Winifred, *American Newspapers, 1821-1936,* a Union List of Files Available in the United States and Canada, H.W. Wilson, 1937.

Hale, Richard W., *Methods of Research for the Amateur Historian* AASLH Leaflet #21.

IDEAS Inc., (Information about the Foxfire program), 1785 Massachusetts Ave. N.W., Washington, D.C. 20036.

Jones, Vincent L. et al, *Genealogical Research: A Jurisdictional Approach,* Woods Cross, Utah, Revised, 1972.

Kirkham, E. Kay, *The Land Records of America and Their Genealogical Value,* The Deseret Book Co., Salt Lake City, 1959. *Research in American Genealogy,* (tells where to write in each state), Deseret, 1956.

Lancour, Harold, editor, *A Bibliography of Ship Passenger Lists, 1538-1825,* revised and enlarged by Richard J. Wolf, New York Public Library, 1963.

Miller, Carolynne L., *Genealogical Research,* Tech. Leaflet #14 American Ass'n. for State and Local History (AASLH).

Munsell, Joel, Publisher, *List of Titles of Genealogy Articles in American Periodicals and Kindred Works,* 1899.

National Genealogical Society, 1921 Sunderland Place, Washington, D.C. 20036.

National Society, Daughters of the American Revolution, 1776 D Street N.W., Washington, D.C. 20006.

National Society, Sons of the American Revolution, 2412 Massachusetts Ave., Washington, D.C. 20008.

New England Historic Genealogical Society, 101 Newbury St., Boston, Mass. 02116. Publishes a Register and Index.

Pine, L.G., *American Origins,* Doubleday 1960, Reprinted, 1967. A Handbook of Genealogical Sources showing how Americans may trace their European family backgrounds and family histories, not only in the British Isles but also in the countries on the continent.

Proctor, Samuel, "Research in State and Local History" (TAPE) AASLH.

Rubicam, Milton, editor, *Genealogical Research Methods and Sources,* American Society of Genealogists, 1966.

Russo, David J., *Families and Communities: A New View of American History,* AASLH, 1974.

Stevenson, Noel C., *Search and Research,* addresses of libraries and societies having genealogical collections, Deseret, 1959.

Tuttle, Charles E. Co., *Catalogue 379, Genealogy and Local History.* Lists over 3,000 genealogies, 2,400 town and county histories, plus books on heraldry, etc. Rutland, Vt.

U.S. Goverment: Library of Congress: *American and English Genealogy* 1919; 1967. Free leaflets from the General Reference Disision; Guide to Genealogical Research; Reference Services and Facilities of the Local History and Genealogy Room. *Surnames:* A Selected List of Books. National Archives: General Information Leaflets, free Guide to Genealogical Records in the Archives. Superintendent of Documents: Birth and Death Records; Marriage Records; Divorce Records.

University Presses - Explore the publications of the university presses for regional material. A list of university presses is listed in the *Writer's Market.* All will send catalogues. Many publish inexpensive paperbacks.

Warner, Sam B., *Writing Local History: The Use of Social Statistics,* Tech. Leaflet #7, AASLH.

Williams, Ethel W., *Know Your Ancestors,* Tuttle, 1963.

CHAPTER TWENTY: More Job Opportunities for Writers of History

Adams, Alexander B., *Handbook of Practical Public Relations,* Crowell.

Alderton, William T., *Marking and Correcting Copy for Your Printer* AASLH Leaflet #51.

Barzun, Jacques, *Writing, Editing and Publishing* University of Chicago Press, 1971.

Hill, Donald E., *Techniques of Magazine Layout and Design,* Graphic Arts and Journalism Publishing Co., 1972.

History News, official publication of American Ass'n. for State and Local History. Every issue has information on job opportunities, bibliography in the history field, etc.

National Trust for Historic Preservation, 740 Jackson Place N.W., Washington, D.C. 20006. Write for on-the-job-training program for students. *Work,* a bulletin giving news of positions open in historical agencies and preservation groups, $3 year.

Nicholson, Margaret, *A Practical Style Guide for Authors and Editors,* Holt, Rinehart & Winston, 1967.

Polking, Kirk, *How to make money in your spare time by writing,* Writer's Digest Guide, Cornerstone Library, 1971.

Wittenberg, Philip, *The Protection of Literary Property,* The Writer.

CHAPTER TWENTY-ONE: Marketing Your History Manuscripts

Ayer, N.W. & Son, *Directory of Newspapers and Periodicals.*

Christian Writers Institute, *Handbook for Christian Writers,* Creation House.

Gebbie Press, *All-in-One Directory,* addresses of 22,100 newspapers, radio and television stations and magazines.

Gunther, Max, "Queries That Sell" in *Writing the Modern Magazine Article,* The Writer, 1968.

Polking, Kirk, "Where and How to Market What You Write" (TAPE), Writer's Digest.

The Writer Inc., *The Writer's Handbook,* published annually.

Writer's Digest, *Writer's Market,* published annually. *The Writer's Yearbook,* published annually.

CHAPTER TWENTY-TWO: That Professional Touch

Asimov, Isaac, An Interview on TAPE, about writing, discipline and literary responsibilities, Writer's Digest.

Hailey, Arthur, An Interview on TAPE (personal writing habits and tips for new writers) Writer's Digest

Mathieu, Aron, *The Creative Writer,* Writer's Digest, 1972.

Roberts, Kenneth, *I Wanted to Write,* Doubleday, 1949, (your library).

U.S. Government, *A Guide to the Study of the United States of America* 1960, Reprinted 1971.

Writer's Digest, *The Beginning Writer's Answer Book.*

Yates, Elizabeth, *Someday You'll Write,* Dutton, 1962, (for teenagers).

INDEX

required for writers, 49; expense
records for, 225; foreign, articles
on, 94; importance to historian, 4,
48; local history, 203-204; *Travel*
magazine, 95; plans for, 49; tax
records for, 49
Trends, market, 212, 226
Trenton, Battle of, 45
Tucson, Old, 57
Tuition, tax deduction for, 225
Tulane University, New Orleans, La.,
70
Twain, Mark, *see also* Sam Clemens,
53, 194
Tumacacori National Monument, 58

"Uncle Sam," 91
*Union List of Serials in Libraries of the
U.S.,* 34
U.S. Army Medical Library, 40; Coast
Guard, 40, 202; Forest Service, *see
also* National Forests, 223; Govern-
ment, *see* Government, National,
departments; *Organizational
Manual,* 40; Printing Office, 41;
Publications, 16; Naval Library,
110; Office of Education,
Catalogue, 72; film strips, motion
pictures, slides, 116; Weather
Bureau, 45
University of Texas Museum, 15
University Press, regional material,
194, 196
"Unto These Hills," Cherokee, N.C.,
57
Utah, Pipe Springs National Monu-
ment, 53; Salt Lake City, 37;
Genealogical Society, 192
Utopia, dreams of, 97

Valenti, Jack, 220
V.F.W. Magazine, 87
Vidal, Gore, 137-138; on writing, 155
Viewpoint, *see also* Point of view; in
fiction, 103; narrator's, 155

Village restorations, courses offered,
222-223; job opportunities at, 208;
photograph source, 113; research
sources, 56; selling booklets to, 197
Virginia, City, Nevada, 57; Fredericksburg and Spotsylvania National Military Park, 223; George
Washington birthplace, 53; History
Trail, 53; Jamestown (glass blowing), 56; Mount Vernon, 214;
Williamsburg, "The Common Glory," 57; Yorktown, 52
Visual education as a writing field, 197
Vocabulary, 175, *see also* Dialogue,
Speech; of the period, 103; sources
for research, 42
Volunteers in Forests, demonstrations,
223
Volunteers in Parks, demonstrations,
223

Wallace, Irving, 164
Wambaugh, Joseph, 158; on writing,
161
Washington, George, 53, 142, 214;
Martha (Custis), 141-142
Washington Post, 220
Washington's Crossing, Penna., 51
Watergate, 94, 148
Weather resources, 45
West, Bancroft's History of the, 64
West Point Museum, 51
Western films history, 64, 195; collec-
tion of (Huntington Library), 36
Westville Village, Ga., 56
Whaling, 51
Who's Who, 33
Williamsburg, 57
Woodbury, David Oakes, 24
Woodham-Smith, Cecil, 146-147
Word usage, examples of, 137-138
World libraries, 37
Writer(s), advice for, 226-228; check-
ing copyrights, 166-168; checking
on manuscript, 215; fellowships,

Books of Interest From Writer's Digest

Art & Crafts Market, edited by Lynne Lapin and Betsy Wones. Lists 4,498 places where you can show and sell your crafts and artwork. Galleries, competitions and exhibitions, craft dealers, record companies, fashion-related firms, magazines that buy illustrations and cartoons, book publishers and advertising agencies — they're all there, complete with names, addresses, submission requirements, phone numbers and payment rates. 672 pp. $10.95.

The Beginning Writer's Answer Book, edited by Kirk Polking, Jean Chimsky, and Rose Adkins. "What is a query letter?" "If I use a pen name, how can I cash the check?" These are among 567 questions most frequently asked by beginning writers — and expertly answered in this down-to-earth handbook. Cross-indexed. 270 pp. $7.95.

The Cartoonist's and Gag Writer's Handbook, by Jack Markow. Longtime cartoonist with thousands of sales reveals the secrets of successful cartooning — step by step. Richly illustrated. 157 pp. $7.95.

A Complete Guide to Marketing Magazine Articles, by Duane Newcomb. "Anyone who can write a clear sentence can learn to write and sell articles on a consistent basis," says Newcomb (who has published well over 3,000 articles). Here's how. 248 pp. $6.95.

The Confession Writer's Handbook, by Florence K. Palmer. A stylish and informative guide to getting started and getting ahead in the confessions. How to start a confession and carry it through. How to take an insignificant event and make it significant. 171 pp. $6.95.

The Craft of Interviewing, by John Brady. Everything you always wanted to know about asking questions, but were afraid to ask — from an experienced interviewer and editor of *Writer's Digest*. The most comprehensive guide to interviewing on the market. 256 pp. $9.95.

The Creative Writer, edited by Aron Mathieu. This book opens the door to the real world of publishing. Inspiration, techniques, and ideas, plus inside tips from Maugham, Caldwell, Purdy, others. 416 pp. $6.95.

The Greeting Card Writer's Handbook, by H. Joseph Chadwick. A former greeting card editor tells you what editors look for in inspirational verse . . . how to write humor . . . what to write about for conventional, studio and juvenile cards. Extra: a renewable list of greeting card markets. Will be greeted by any freelancer. 268 pp. $6.95.

A Guide to Writing History, by Doris Ricker Marston. How to track down Big Foot — or your family Civil War letters, or your hometown's last century — for publication and profit. A timely handbook for history buffs and writers. 258 pp. $8.50.

Handbook of Short Story Writing, edited by Frank A. Dickson and Sandra Smythe. You provide the pencil, paper, and sweat — and this book will provide the expert guidance. Features include James Hilton on creating a lovable character; R.V. Cassill on plotting a short story. 238 pp. $6.95.

Law and The Writer, edited by Kirk Polking and Attorney Leonard S. Meranus. Don't let legal hassles slow down your progress as a writer. Now you can find good counsel on libel, invasion of privacy, fair use, plagiarism, taxes, contracts, social security, and more — all in one volume. 265 pp. $9.95.

Magazine Writing Today, by Jerome E. Kelley. If you sometimes feel like a mouse in a maze of magazines, with a fat manuscript check at the end of the line, don't fret. Kelley tells you how to get a piece of the action. Covers ideas, research, interviewing, organization, the writing process, and ways to get photos. Plus advice on getting started. 300 pp. $9.95.

The Mystery Writer's Handbook, by the Mystery Writers of America. A howtheydunit to the whodunit, newly written and revised by members of the Mystery Writers of America. Includes the four elements essential to the classic mystery. A clear and comprehensive handbook that takes the mystery out of mystery writing. 275 pp. $8.95.

One Way to Write Your Novel, by Dick Perry. For Perry, a novel is 200 pages. Or, two pages a day for 100 days. You can start — and finish — your novel, with the help of this step-by-step guide taking you from the blank sheet to the polished page. 138 pp. $6.95.

Photographer's Market, edited by Melissa Milar and Bill Brohaugh. Contains what you need to know to be a successful freelance photographer. Names, addresses, photo requirements, and payment rates for 1,616 markets. Plus, information on preparing a portfolio, basic equipment needed, the business side of photography, and packaging and shipping your work. 408 pp. $9.95.

The Poet and the Poem, by Judson Jerome. A rare journey into the night of the poem — the mechanics, the mystery, the craft and sullen art. Written by the most widely read authority on poetry in America, and a major contemporary poet in his own right. 482 pp. $7.95 ($4.95 paperback).

Stalking the Feature Story, by William Ruehlmann. Besides a nose for news, the newspaper feature writer needs an ear for dialog and an eye for detail. He must also be adept at handling off-the-record remarks, organization, grammar, and the investigative story. Here's the "scoop" on newspaper feature writing. 314 pp. $9.95.

A Treasury of Tips for Writers, edited by Marvin Weisbord. Everything from Vance Packard's system of organizing notes to tips on how to get research done free, by 86 magazine writers. 174 pp. $5.95.

Writer's Digest. The world's leading magazine for writers. Monthly issues include timely articles, interviews, columns, tips to keep writers informed on where and how to sell their work. One year subscription, $12.

Writer's Market, edited by Jane Koester and Bruce Joel Hillman. The freelancer's Bible, containing 4,454 places to sell what you write. Includes the name, address and phone number of the buyer, a description of material wanted and how much the payment is. 912 pp. $13.95.

Writer's Yearbook, edited by John Brady. This large annual magazine contains how-to articles, interviews and special features, along with analysis of 500 major markets for writers. $2.75 (includes 80¢ for postage and handling).

Writing and Selling Non-Fiction, by Hayes B. Jacobs. Explores with style and know-how the book market, organization and research, finding new markets, interviewing, humor, agents, writer's fatigue and more. 317 pp. $7.95.

Writing and Selling Science Fiction, compiled by the Science Fiction Writers of America. A comprehensive handbook to an exciting but oft-misunderstood genre. Eleven articles by top-flight sf writers on markets, characters, dialog, "crazy" ideas, world-building, alien-building, money and more. 191 pp. $7.95.

Writing for Children and Teen-agers, by Lee Wyndham. Author of over 50 children's books shares her secrets for selling to this large, lucrative market. Features: the 12-point recipe for plotting, and the Ten Commandments for writers. 253 pp. $8.95.

Writing Popular Fiction, by Dean R. Koontz. How to write mysteries, suspense thrillers, science fiction. Gothic romances, adult fantasy, Westerns and erotica. Here's an inside guide to lively fiction, by a lively novelist. 232 pp. $7.95.

(Add 50¢ for postage and handling.
Prices subject to change without notice.)
Writer's Digest Books, Dept. B, 9933 Alliance Road, Cincinnati, Ohio 45242

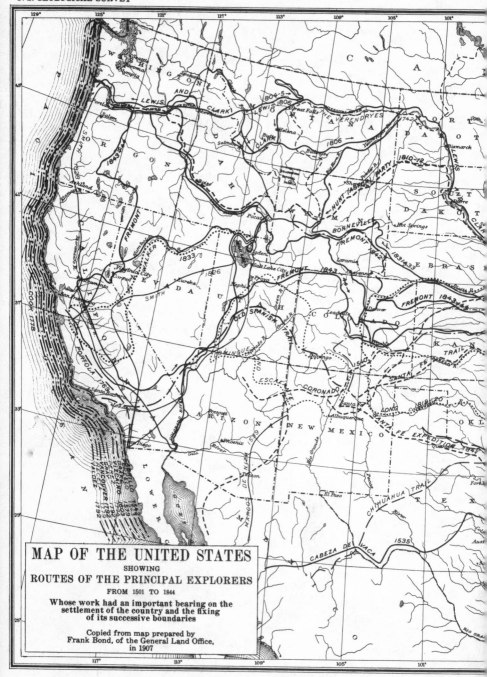

MAP OF THE UNITED STATES

SHOWING

ROUTES OF THE PRINCIPAL EXPLORERS

FROM 1501 TO 1844

Whose work had an important bearing on the
settlement of the country and the fixing
of its successive boundaries

Copied from map prepared by
Frank Bond, of the General Land Office,
in 1907